BIRDSONG, SPEECH AND POETRY

In the long nineteenth century, scientists discovered striking similarities between how birds learn to sing and how children learn to speak. Tracing the 'science of birdsong' as it developed from the 'ingenious' experiments of Daines Barrington to the evolutionary arguments of Charles Darwin, Francesca Mackenney reveals a legacy of thought which informs, and consequently affords fresh insights into, a canonical group of poems about birdsong in the Romantic and Victorian periods. With a particular focus on the writings of Samuel Taylor Coleridge, the Wordsworth siblings, John Clare and Thomas Hardy, her book explores how poets responded to an analogy which challenged definitions of language and therefore of what it means to be human. Drawing together responses to birdsong in science, music and poetry, her distinctive interdisciplinary approach challenges many of the long-standing cultural assumptions which have shaped (and continue to shape) how we respond to other creatures in the Anthropocene.

FRANCESCA MACKENNEY is Research and Teaching Fellow in Romanticism at the University of Leeds. Her research and related work in environmental education has been funded by an AHRC Doctoral Award, a BARS/Wordsworth Trust Early Career Fellowship, an award from Creative Scotland and an AHRC International Placement at the Library of Congress.

CAMBRIDGE STUDIES IN NINETEENTH-CENTURY LITERATURE AND CULTURE

FOUNDING EDITORS
Gillian Beer, *University of Cambridge*
Catherine Gallagher, *University of California, Berkeley*

GENERAL EDITORS
Kate Flint, *University of Southern California*
Clare Pettitt, *King's College London*

EDITORIAL BOARD
Isobel Armstrong, *Birkbeck, University of London*
Ali Behdad *University of California, Los Angeles*
Alison Chapman, *University of Victoria*
Hilary Fraser, *Birkbeck, University of London*
Josephine McDonagh, *University of Chicago*
Elizabeth Miller, *University of California, Davis*
Hillis Miller, *University of California, Irvine*
Cannon Schmitt, *University of Toronto*
Sujit Sivasundaram, *University of Cambridge*
Herbert Tucker, *University of Virginia*
Mark Turner, *King's College London*

Nineteenth-century literature and culture have proved a rich field for interdisciplinary studies. Since 1994, books in this series have tracked the intersections and tensions between Victorian literature and the visual arts, politics, gender and sexuality, race, social organisation, economic life, technical innovations, scientific thought – in short, culture in its broadest sense. Many of our books are now classics in a field which since the series' inception has seen powerful engagements with Marxism, feminism, visual studies, post-colonialism, critical race studies, new historicism, new formalism, transnationalism, queer studies, human rights and liberalism, disability studies and global studies. Theoretical challenges and historiographical shifts continue to unsettle scholarship on the nineteenth century in productive ways. New work on the body and the senses, the environment and climate, race and the decolonisation of literary studies, biopolitics and materiality, the animal and the human, the local and the global, politics and form, queerness and gender identities, and intersectional theory is re-animating the field. This series aims to accommodate and promote the most interesting work being undertaken on the frontiers of nineteenth-century literary studies, connecting the field with the urgent critical questions that are being asked today. We seek to publish work from a diverse range of authors, and stand for antiracism, anti-colonialism and against discrimination in all forms.

A complete list of titles published will be found at the end of the book.

BIRDSONG, SPEECH AND POETRY

The Art of Composition in the Long Nineteenth Century

FRANCESCA MACKENNEY

University of Leeds

Shaftesbury Road, Cambridge CB2 8EA, United Kingdom

One Liberty Plaza, 20th Floor, New York, NY 10006, USA

477 Williamstown Road, Port Melbourne, VIC 3207, Australia

314–321, 3rd Floor, Plot 3, Splendor Forum, Jasola District Centre, New Delhi – 110025, India

103 Penang Road, #05–06/07, Visioncrest Commercial, Singapore 238467

Cambridge University Press is part of Cambridge University Press & Assessment, a department of the University of Cambridge.

We share the University's mission to contribute to society through the pursuit of education, learning and research at the highest international levels of excellence.

www.cambridge.org
Information on this title: www.cambridge.org/9781009074681

DOI: 10.1017/9781009075909

© Francesca Mackenney 2023

This publication is in copyright. Subject to statutory exception and to the provisions of relevant collective licensing agreements, no reproduction of any part may take place without the written permission of Cambridge University Press & Assessment.

First published 2023
First paperback edition 2025

A catalogue record for this publication is available from the British Library

Library of Congress Cataloging-in-Publication data
NAMES: Mackenney, Francesca, author.
TITLE: Birdsong, speech and poetry : the art of composition in the long nineteenth century / Francesca Mackenney, University of Leeds.
DESCRIPTION: Cambridge ; New York, NY : Cambridge University Press, 2023. | Series: Cambridge studies in nineteenth-century literature and culture | Includes bibliographical references and index.
IDENTIFIERS: LCCN 2022012583 (print) | LCCN 2022012584 (ebook) | ISBN 9781316513712 (hardback) | ISBN 9781009074681 (paperback) | ISBN 9781009075909 (ebook)
SUBJECTS: LCSH: English poetry – 19th century – History and criticism. | Language and languages in literature. | Birdsongs. | Literature and science – Great Britain – History – 19th century. | BISAC: LITERARY CRITICISM / European / English, Irish, Scottish, Welsh | LCGFT: Literary criticism.
CLASSIFICATION: LCC PR585.L3 M33 2023 (print) | LCC PR585.L3 (ebook) | ddc 821/.80934–dc23/eng/20220516
LC record available at https://lccn.loc.gov/2022012583
LC ebook record available at https://lccn.loc.gov/2022012584

ISBN   978-1-316-51371-2   Hardback
ISBN   978-1-009-07468-1   Paperback

Cambridge University Press & Assessment has no responsibility for the persistence or accuracy of URLs for external or third-party internet websites referred to in this publication and does not guarantee that any content on such websites is, or will remain, accurate or appropriate.

For my mother, Linda

Contents

List of Figures	*page* viii
Acknowledgements	ix
Introduction	1
1 The Science of Birdsong: 1773–1871	20
2 The Science of Language: 1755–1873	38
3 'Prelusive Notes': Coleridge and the Wordsworths	60
4 'Undersong': John Clare	101
5 'We Teach 'Em Airs That Way': Thomas Hardy	137
Conclusion	180
Notes	185
Bibliography	217
Index	233

Figures

1 Athanasius Kircher, from *Musurgia Universalis* (1650). *page* 5
2 William Thorpe, from 'The Process of Song-Learning in the Chaffinch as Studied by Means of the Sound Spectrograph', in *Nature* (1954). 7
3 Papageno: 'I am the bird-catcher, yes! Always cheerful, fiddle-di-i, fiddle di-da!' Act I of *The Magic Flute* by Wolfgang Amadeus Mozart (1756–91), engraved by Friedrich Wilhelm Meyer Senior (b.c. 1770). 22

Acknowledgements

This book developed out of many years of thinking and writing about birdsong in poems. The work began as a PhD thesis submitted to the University of Bristol in 2016. I am grateful to my supervisors Ralph Pite and Daniel Karlin; in their different ways, these two men set me thinking, and I would not have written the same book without them. For their insight and sound practical advice on turning the thesis into a book, I would also like to thank my examiners Hugh Haughton and Stephen James. Bethany Thomas at Cambridge University Press guided me through the review process and secured two readers who offered both encouragement and critical scrutiny; their comments led me to revise and dramatically improve the manuscript in places, in a process that has, I hope, made me a better writer. Various others have been kind enough to read parts of the book at different stages of its development: I would especially like to thank Heather Glen, Jeremy Mynott and David Rothenberg for their kind words of encouragement, which buoyed my spirits at times of doubt, blockage and frustration.

I am grateful to the Arts and Humanities Research Council (AHRC) for funding my doctorate. I would also like to thank the Wordsworth Trust and the British Association for Romantic Studies, which awarded me an Early Career Fellowship that enabled me to further my research on birdsong in the writings of the Wordsworth siblings. Many of the ideas explored in this book have been developed through my related work in environmental education and various endeavours to engage young people in ongoing debates about how and why birds sing. I would especially like to thank Sophie Thomas and Mandy Leivers for participating in these activities, as well as Creative Scotland, which provided me with funding to develop an educational podcast about birdsong (waysoflistening.net). To all the young people who took part, thank you.

Some of the ideas for this book were developed through a series of conference papers and articles about birdsong in the poetry of John

Clare (*Romanticism*, 2019) and William Wordsworth (*The Eighteenth-Century Bird*, 2020). I would also like to thank the Northamptonshire Public Library, which allowed me to pore over many beautiful books of natural history from Clare's library, and to Nicholas Freville and others at the Kettering and District Naturalist's Society, who kindly forwarded me James Fisher's essay on 'John Clare's Birds' from their society's record of proceedings. My thanks also to the Wein Museum for providing the cover image. Springer Nature provided permission to use William Thorpe's sonogram recording of the male chaffinch's song ©1954.

They say it takes a village to raise a child, and books are a little like children. I could not have written this book without the love, support and endless patience of my friend and partner Alastair, my brother George, my uncle Mark and my grandmother Joyce. Lastly, the book is dedicated to my mother Linda. My love of literature began with many punishingly long car journeys across the Scottish border, in which she talked in her dreamy way about Shakespeare, theatre and socialism. These conversations were 'my nurse's song', and I am forever grateful.

Introduction

> And that no man should make a doubt that there is great Art and cunning herein, doe but marke, how there is not one Nightingale but hath many notes and tunes. Againe, all of them have not the same, but every one a speciall kind of musick by her selfe: nay, they strive who can do best, and one laboureth to excel another in varietie of song and long continuance: yea and evident it is, that they contend in good earnest with all their will and power: for oftentimes she that hath the worse and is not able to hold out with another, dieth for it, and sooner giveth she up her vitall breath, than giveth over her song. Ye shall have the young Nightingales studie and meditate how to sing, by themselves: yee shall have them listen attentively to the old birds when they sing, and to take out lessons as it were from them, whom they would seem to imitate staffe by staffe. The scholler, when shee hath given good eare unto her mistresse, presently rehearseth what she hath heard; and both of them keep silence for a time in their turnes. A man shall evidently perceive when the young bird hath learned well, and when againe it must be taught how to correct and amend wherein it did amisse: yea and how the teacher will seeme to reproove and find a fault.
>
> – Pliny the Elder, *Naturalis Historia* (77AD)

Recent studies have emphasised the dangers of anthropomorphism in the interpretation and representation of other species.[1] In particular, scholars from across the arts and sciences have drawn attention to what Daniel Karlin describes as the 'irresistible' pressure of the figurative in poetic renderings of birdsong: the tendency not only to impose human motives and values upon an animal mind that exists properly outside the poet's own frame of reference, but also, on a deeper and more fundamental level, to inevitably '(mis-)translate' a non-human sound into human forms of signification – words, music, poetry.[2] While Karlin and others have observed the apparent and irreconcilable differences between the bird's own voice and the human forms that attempt to, in John Clare's phrase, 'syllable the sounds', this book outlines an alternative approach to the 'Art' of birdsong.³ Whatever the formal differences between birdsong and human speech, between what is sung and what is said, writers from Pliny the Elder to Charles Darwin recognised underlying similarities between how the nestling bird learns to sing and how the human child learns to speak.

The following pages trace the development of a scientific analogy which challenged definitions of language and, consequently, of what it means to be human. In the late eighteenth century, the ornithologist and friend of Gilbert White, Daines Barrington, conducted a series of experiments on three nestling linnets from which he concluded that 'notes in birds are no more innate, than language is in man'.⁴ In a passage strongly reminiscent of Pliny, Barrington delineated the process by which the nestling listens to, recites and eventually perfects the song of its parents:

> Whilst the scholar is thus endeavouring to form his song, when he is once sure of a passage, he commonly raises his tone, which he drops again when he is not equal to what he is attempting; just as a singer raises his voice, when he not only recollects certain parts of a tune with precision, but knows that he can execute them.
>
> What the nestling is not thus thoroughly master of, he hurries over, lowering his tone, as if he did not wish to be heard, and could not yet satisfy himself. (p. 251)

This book explores the 'science of birdsong' as it developed from Barrington's innovative analyses to Darwin's use of such findings in increasingly controversial, evolutionary arguments in *The Descent of Man* (1871). It traces the development of this line of scientific thought, the threat it posed to the perceived uniqueness of human language and the heated arguments that consequently arose between evolutionary scientists, notably Darwin, and established philologists, such as Max Müller. My research in this area seeks to reveal a legacy of thought which informs, and consequently affords fresh insights into, a canonical group of poems about birdsong in the Romantic and Victorian periods. Focusing especially on the writings of Samuel Taylor Coleridge, William and Dorothy Wordsworth, John Clare and Thomas Hardy, I elucidate how these writers used birdsong as an analogy through which to explore the faculty of language: how language is learned and how it may have evolved, and what this may further tell us about how poets compose.

Birdsong, which Darwin termed the 'nearest analogy' to human speech, raises a set of questions about how language works: how it is acquired, how it is transmitted across generations and how it may have evolved.[5] In exploring the deep connections between how birds learn to sing and how infants learn to speak, this book seeks to redirect attention away from the form to the *faculty* of language in literature. Throughout the long nineteenth century, poets like Clare drew parallels between the 'muttering' of the bird while learning to sing and the poet's own processes of composition:

> When first we hear the shy come nightingales
> They seem to mutter oer their songs in fear
> & climbing e'er so soft the spinney rails
> All stops as if no bird was any where
> The kindled bushes with the young leaves thin
> Lets curious eyes to search a long way in
> Untill impatience cannot see or hear
> The hidden music—gets but little way
> Upon the path—when up the songs begin
> Full loud a moment & then low again
> But when a day or two confirms her stay
> Boldly she sings & loud for half the day
> & soon the village brings the woodmans tale
> Of having heard the new come nightingale.[6]

As they observed the young nightingale in its first, faltering attempts at song, poets like Clare were, throughout this period, led to reflect on the creative processes at work in the making of poetry. In tracing this analogy, this book seeks to analyse, test and break down some of the binary distinctions which continue to structure responses to Romantic and Victorian poetry: 'natural' and 'artificial', 'instinctive' and 'learned', 'spontaneous' and 'premeditated' art. As this book will seek to show, birdsong provided poets in this period with a crucial analogy for exploring some of the most vexing questions surrounding the art of composition in the long nineteenth century.

I

In his highly influential book *Why Birds Sing* (2005), the musician and philosopher David Rothenberg draws together the different ways through which human beings have interpreted, and sought to understand, the song of birds. Rothenberg traces our engagement with birdsong all the way back to our first and most rudimentary attempts to 'translate' these sounds into human words and phrases:[7]

Eastern towhee:	Drink your tea!
White-throated sparrow:	Old Sam Peabody, Peabody, Peabody.
Yellowhammer:	A little bit of bread and no cheese.

These traditional birdsong mnemonics have throughout the centuries proved useful in enabling ornithologists and amateur birders to remember and distinguish between the notes of different species. But it is not difficult to see the problem here. Some of the rhythms of the white-throated sparrow may be captured in that repetition of 'Peabody, Peabody, Peabody'. And the yellowhammer's patter of notes with its prolonged closing wheeze may also be detectable in 'a little bit of bread and no cheese'. But is the eastern towhee really telling us to drink our tea? Of course, the birds are not really speaking, not to us anyway. Whenever human beings attempt to 'translate' the sounds of birds into our own words and phrases, we are always thus in danger of descending into anthropomorphism and absurdity – of making the birds sound ludicrously like ourselves. In many ways, the transcription of the yellowhammer's call tells us less about the bird itself than it does about the very thin and very hungry ploughboy whom the writer and naturalist Richard Jefferies heard repeating its phrases over and over to himself in the late nineteenth century: 'for', as Jefferies dryly noted, 'to have only a hunch of bread and little or no cheese' was all too frequently this poor boy's 'own case'.[8]

In one respect, musicians may appear free from this problem of having to 'translate' a bird's song into words. In the seventeenth century, the Jesuit scholar and polymath Athanasius Kircher attempted to transcribe the notes of birds in musical notation (see Figure 1). Kircher's transcriptions are part of a work in which the composer seeks to reveal a universal harmony uniting all creatures of the earth: *Musurgia Universalis* (1650). In this rather literal attempt to *fit* the notes of birds to human music, however, Kircher betrays an inability to fathom any alternative sense of harmony from his own. Where composers have experimented with those more irregular, alien rhythms of birdsong, the result has sounded distinctly unmusical to human ears. In tribute to a much-beloved pet starling, Wolfgang Amadeus Mozart composed 'A Musical Joke', which all too successfully emulated the disjointed songs of its subject: 'in the first movement', observed one commentator, 'we hear the awkward, unproportioned, illogical piecing together of uninspired material'.[9] Whether or not the 'joke' was intended, Mozart's cadenza points to an essential irony in musical renderings of birdsong: the more closely the composer attempts to emulate those alien, inhuman rhythms, the further they stray from our own sense of harmony

Figure 1 Athanasius Kircher, from *Musurgia Universalis* (1650).

and music. In their attempt to make the birds keep time with them, musicians are ever thus at risk of imposing their own order upon avian voices that sing, as the composer Olivier Messiaen observed, 'in extremely quick tempi' and 'excessively high registers' which are 'absolutely impossible for our instruments'.[10] Throughout the centuries, composers like Messiaen have been drawn to the 'strange, iambic rhythm' of the corncrake precisely because those rhythms at once tantalise and elude every attempt to 'translate' them into our own human music.[11]

In the 1950s, the scientist William Thorpe was able to obtain a far more precise *picture* of birdsong following the advent of a new piece of technology: the sonogram. Figure 2 shows Thorpe's sonogram recording of the male chaffinch's song. The sonogram enabled scientists like Thorpe to slow down and visually analyse the complex patterning of a bird's voice: here we have a precise visual *picture* of the sounds the bird is making. Notice the timescale at the bottom of the diagram. These are sounds and structures which escape the human ear, which we cannot hear in the bird's own time, never mind translate into our music or, least of all, our language.

So where does this leave poetry? In comparing different interpretations of birdsong in science, music and poetry, Rothenberg's interdisciplinary approach raises certain questions about poetic form. His book invites its readers to compare, for example, the precision of the sonogram with some rather less precise, though in many ways more evocative, renderings of the nightingale's 'fast thick warble' in poetry.[12] Consequently, Rothenberg's study has inspired scholars in my field of literary criticism to reflect on the *difficulties* of representing birdsong in poems, and what poetic attempts to 'translate' this sound into written words may tell us about the medium of poetry – what poetry can and cannot do, and how it differs from, for example, a piece of music. Rothenberg's analysis is central to Karlin's careful scrutiny of birdsong as a figure for poetry in *The Figure of the Singer* (2013).[13] Set within a work which outlines 'the long quarrel (which is also a love-affair) between poetic language and song', Karlin's chapter on birdsong questions its status as an inimitable ideal in nineteenth-century poetry; in the various efforts of Romantic and Victorian poets to emulate the songs of birds, Karlin detects an underlying and 'subversive tendency to affirm the primacy of human language, with all its failures and defects, over the ineffable idea of song to which it claims to aspire'.[14] Rothenberg's particular praise of Clare has also inspired Stephanie Kuduk Weiner's detailed analysis of this poet's renderings of birdsong and other natural sounds in *Clare's Lyric: John Clare and Three Modern Poets* (2014).[15] For Weiner, Clare's attempt to 'syllable the sounds' of the nightingale is part of a sustained and 'humbling struggle with the inspiration provided by nature's music and the difficulty of rendering his experience of it in poetic language'.[16] Both of these works, to which I am deeply indebted, are centrally concerned with the question of mimesis and poetic form. In testing the limits of language, birdsong has inspired generations of poets to experiment with as well as to profoundly reflect upon the nature of the medium in which they work.

Introduction 7

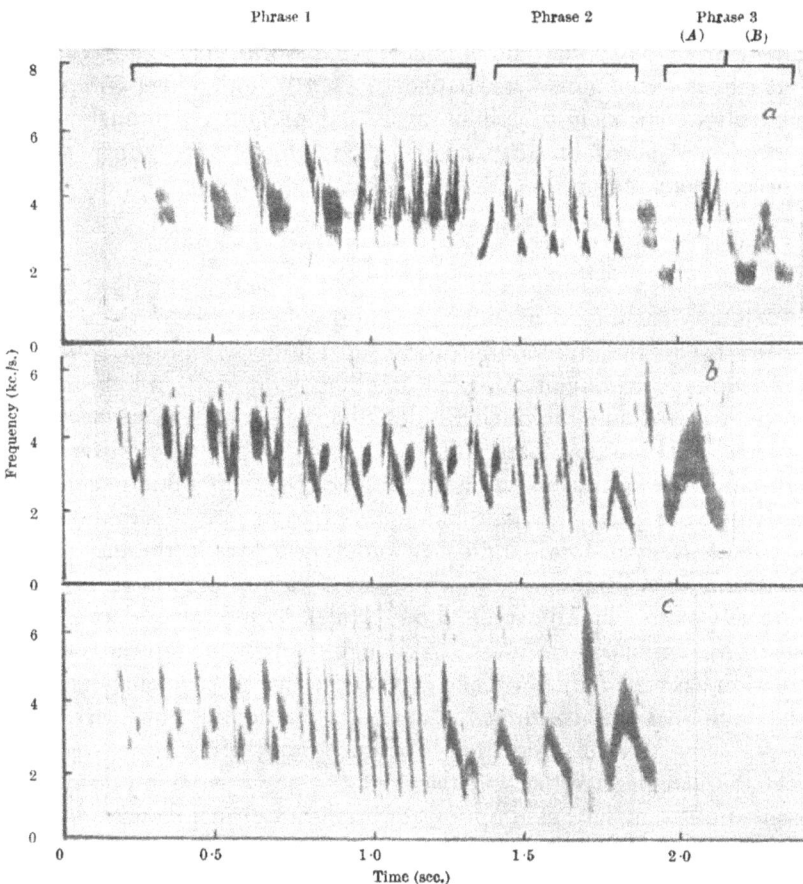

Figure 2 William Thorpe, from 'The Process of Song-Learning in the Chaffinch as Studied by Means of the Sound Spectrograph', in *Nature* (1954).

Unquestionably, the song of birds is central to a wider exploration in the Romantic period of the relationship between word and world, between poetic form and the natural sights and sounds it seeks to portray. Although poetry may never be able to disclose the secret of why birds sing, it can, as these interpretations show, tell us something about itself – about language and how it shapes our world. While Karlin and Weiner have emphasised the formal differences between birdsong and poetic language, my own approach in this book has been to draw attention to the deep and underlying affinities which have historically disturbed and unsettled our sense of being different, and in doing so have exposed a human desire and need to be different, to be special and unique in the world. This book explores birdsong not as a figure or a metaphor or a poetic trope, but as an 'analogy' through which scientists, philosophers and poets have, throughout the centuries, explored the nature and origins of our own human arts of music, speech and poetry (Darwin, *Descent*, p. 108).

II

Recent approaches are informed by a more general attempt to cure what scientists have described as the 'disease' of anthropomorphism, which has been thought to impair our understanding of animals and chronically infect the language in which we describe them.[17] In the sciences, this 'disease' has been diagnosed and treated as a threat to objectivity; in the arts and humanities, it has been seen to result in innumerable and unscrupulous acts of cultural appropriation. As Harriet Ritvo, Christine Kenyon-Jones and other founding figures in the burgeoning field of animal studies have shown, representations of animals in literature very often tell us more about our own views and values than they do about the animals themselves.[18] Although the tendency towards appropriation has been duly noted and exposed, researchers and analysts across the disciplines have continued to question whether it is possible, or even desirable, to cure ourselves entirely of anthropomorphism or to cleanse it from our language. While scientists 'rightly want to avoid importing into their studies any false assumptions or implications that could vitiate the results', the writer and naturalist Jeremy Mynott puts his finger on the certain point at which language, when reduced to 'a system of symbols capable of describing a bird in terms only applicable to a bird', becomes 'almost by definition' a language we 'no longer understand'.[19] Writing from a literary critical perspective, Karlin not only questions the attainability of phonetic 'accuracy' in poetic representations of birdsong but also remains unconvinced that such accuracy in any case 'matters': 'if all you are trying to do is sing *like* a nightingale, why not listen to the original?'[20] For Karlin, anthropomorphism is to some extent unavoidable, and in another sense positively desirable, provided that its proper limitations are recognised and acknowledged with intellectual honesty.[21]

Others have more fundamentally questioned received definitions of 'anthropomorphism'. The philosopher Mary Midgely, for example, observes a discrepancy between the definition of the word and the examples cited in the *Oxford English Dictionary*. Words such as '*alarm, hunger, surprise* and *pain*' have, Midgley argues, 'no bearing on personality', but are 'common aspects of animal life'.²² In his study of Richard Garner's attempts in the late nineteenth century to compose a 'vocabulary' of primate calls in *The Simian Tongue: The Long Debate about Animal Language* (2007), the cultural historian Gregory Radick has traced this scholarly concern with anthropomorphism back to the 'extreme skepticism' of Victorian science.²³ Throughout the nineteenth century, Darwin's opponents inveighed against what they categorically dismissed as 'figurative', 'personifying' and 'anthropomorphic' interpretations of the lives of other species. Georges Cuvier, for example, criticised the 'puerility of those philosophers who have conferred on Nature a kind of individual existence, distinct from the Creator', and praised those in the 'advanced' sciences who had 'renounced the paralogisms which resulted from the application of figurative language to real phenomena'.²⁴ In a review of Darwin's *Origin of Species* (1859), Cuvier's protégé and successor at the Collège de France, Marie-Jean Pierre Flourens, similarly noted that 'the author throughout uses figurative language without being aware of it' and this language 'deceives him as it has deceived all others who have used it'.²⁵ One of Darwin's most outspoken adversaries, the first professor of philology at the University of Oxford, Max Müller, attributed the 'reopening' of 'the floodgates of animal anthropomorphism' to the 'rise of Mr Darwin's theories'.²⁶ As John Holmes broadly summarises, Darwin's attempt to demonstrate 'a continuity between the behaviour and emotions of human beings and those of other animals' was 'dismissed as naïvely anthropomorphic for much of the twentieth century'.²⁷

'We are incessantly at fault in our tendency to anthropomorphise, a tendency which causes us to interpret the actions of animals according to the analogies of human nature', concluded George Henry Lewes in *Sea-Side Studies* (1858); human observers must resolutely remain, Lewes insisted, 'on our guard against the tendency to attribute psychological motives to the actions of animals'.²⁸ In an article on 'the anthropomorphic fallacy', Alexis Harley has identified the 'intractable methodological problem' faced by Lewes and others.²⁹ Confronted with the question of 'what it feels like' to be another species, philosophers such as Lewes were rightly nervous of speculating about how other species experience emotions such as pain or pleasure. As the American philosopher Thomas Nagel would later reformulate the problem in his classic essay 'What Is It Like to Be a Bat?' (1974), human beings can never know what it is like to be another organism because we can never enter another creature's mindset and share in their experience of the world.³⁰ Or, as Ludwig Wittgenstein famously put it in the 1950s, 'if a lion could talk, we could not understand him'.³¹ In showing respect for the differences between human beings and other animals, however, philosophers such as Lewes, as Harley points out, 'risked falling into another methodological error': namely, that of 'construing more *difference* between species' phenomenological experience than he could possibly verify'.³² In what one commentator has identified as 'possibly the most important single sentence in the history of animal behaviour', the ethologist Conwy Lloyd Morgan concluded in the 1890s that 'in no case' should any 'animal activity' be 'interpreted as the outcome of the exercise of a higher psychical faculty, if it can be fairly interpreted as the outcome of one which stands lower in the psychological scale'.³³ Ironically, such 'objectivism', which insists that an animal must be presumed without reason until it can be proved otherwise, may be seen to base itself on a no less subjective *a priori* mode of reasoning. As the primatologist Frans de Waal has argued, the scholarly obsession with anthropomorphism all too easily slides into a form of what he terms 'anthropodenial': 'the *a priori* rejection of shared characteristics between humans and animals' which 'denotes willful blindness to the human-like characteristics of animals or the animal-like characteristics of ourselves' and 'reflects a pre-Darwinian antipathy to the profound similarities between human and animal behaviour (e.g. maternal care, sexual behaviour, power seeking) noticed by anyone with an open mind'.³⁴ Whereas de Waal and others have called for a more open-minded approach to the behavioural parallels which connect human beings with our nearest relatives, the primates, I have in this book sought to sketch out a long history of 'willful blindness' towards the special affinities between birdsong and human speech.

'I am a firm believer, that without speculation there is no good & original observation', wrote Darwin in 1857.³⁵ For Darwin, speculation about the lives of other species was crucial to scientific thought and progress; without some degree of speculation, for all its attendant dangers and risks, the scientist risks becoming beholden to the accepted views and theoretical assumptions of his or her predecessors. Such conformity inhibits intellectual progress, as it prevents scientists from making the kind of 'good or original observation' that derives from their own independent analysis of the flora and fauna that surrounds them. When he was presented with a copy of Müller's *Lectures on the Science of Language* (1861) by the author himself, Darwin scribbled on the back leaf:

> When it is objected that we can know nothing of what is in mind of an animal, so it may be said of any savage, whose language we do not understand. – we can judge only by action & have our doubts.[36]

With characteristic swiftness, Darwin touches on the politics of difference explored throughout this book: the tendency, that is, to assume *a priori* the intellectual inferiority of all those whose language we cannot, or will not, understand. Acknowledging the wider cultural and political sensitivities surrounding his own theories, Darwin insists that both his own and Müller's approaches were subject to the same methodological problem: if it is true that 'we can know nothing' of what passes in the mind of another animal, then we can surely neither rule in nor rule out the existence of cognitive faculties comparable with our own. 'We can', Darwin concludes, 'judge only by action and have our doubts'.

In *Charles Darwin's Life with Birds: His Complete Ornithology* (2016), Clifford B. Frith has recently observed that 'in writing about birds, Darwin occasionally used anthropomorphic language, notably more often in his earlier publications, particularly in describing or discussing their behaviour'.[37] As an example of this anthropomorphising tendency, Frith cites Darwin's explanation of why robins sing in winter:

> Nothing is more common than for animals to take pleasure in practising whatever instinct they follow at other times for some real good. How often do we see birds which fly easily, gliding and sailing through the air, obviously for pleasure? ... Hence it is not at all surprising that male birds should continue singing for their own amusement after the season of courtship is over. (*Descent*, p. 419)

For Frith, this is a clear instance of Darwinian anthropomorphism: 'in fact', he swiftly retorts, 'the autumnal singing by these robins is territorial in function'.[38] If it is true, however, that we can never know what passes in the mind of an animal, then surely we cannot rule out the possibility that robins sing, at least in part, 'for their own amusement'. For natural historians from Pliny to Francis Allen, it has proved difficult to 'escape' the conclusion that the evolution of birdsong prefigures 'an aesthetic sense in the birds themselves'.[39] I am neither an ornithologist nor a philosopher, and my intention in this book is not to determine, one way or another, whether robins experience pleasure in singing. My approach is contextual and literary critical. I am concerned with the history and politics of a debate about animal language in the late eighteenth and nineteenth centuries; in tracing that history, I examine the ways in which scientific findings have been transmitted to and interpreted by philosophers, poets and the wider culture. In a recent volume of scientific essays forwarded by Noam Chomsky and entitled *Birdsong, Speech and Language: Exploring the Evolution of Mind and Brain* (2013), birdsong has re-emerged as an analogy 'particularly well placed to probe certain biolinguistic questions' regarding the origins of human speech and language.[40] Those questions partly inspired this book. But they are well beyond my remit and expertise. I cannot and do not intend to answer them here. In tracing the ways in which scientists, philosophers and poets have puzzled over these questions throughout the centuries, what I can do, and try to do in this book, is to pinpoint and analyse many of the deep-rooted assumptions which have shaped, and continue to shape, how we respond to the sounds and songs of other species in the Anthropocene.

III

Language, as Darwin observed, has long been recognised as 'one of the chief distinctions between man and the lower animals' (*Descent*, p. 106). 'Man alone of the animals is furnished with the faculty of language', declared Aristotle.[41] 'I think that men', Cicero agreed, 'although lower and weaker than animals in many respects, excel them most by having the power of speech'.[42] Throughout the eighteenth and nineteenth centuries, grammarians routinely began their treatises by extolling the transformative power of a faculty which, as Nathan Bailey observed in his *Universal Etymological Dictionary* (1721), 'makes so considerable a Difference between a Man and a Brute'.[43] In the introduction to his highly influential *English Grammar* (1795), Lindley Murray similarly identified 'the faculty of speech' as 'one of the distinguishing characters of our nature'.[44] Following the publication of Darwin's *On the Origin of Species* (1859), the opponents of evolution increasingly relied upon this faculty as the one remaining bulwark which might 'yet enable us to withstand the extreme theories of the Darwinians, and to draw a hard and fast line between man and the brute'.[45] To those who 'speak of development' and who 'think they discover the rudiments at least of all human faculties' among 'the lower animals', Müller replied in no uncertain terms: 'it admits of no caviling, and no process of selection will ever distil significant words out of the notes of birds or the cries of beasts'.[46] For Darwin and subsequent generations of evolutionary scientists, the evolution of language has remained the most vexing and perplexing question – or 'Darwin's problem', as it has become known.[47]

Introduction 13

Throughout the long nineteenth century, philosophers fiercely disputed definitions of language. Although the most prominent intellectuals could not agree among themselves on precisely what language was or where it came from, they did (and do) agree that, whatever language was, it represented a definitive leap in the evolution of the human animal.[48] As Ann Wierda Rowland observes in *Romanticism and Childhood: The Infantilization of British Literary Culture* (2012), childhood in eighteenth-century philosophy was broadly perceived as representing an intermediary stage in the process she terms 'becoming human'.[49] Prominent philosophers such as Jean-Jacques Rousseau, Johann Gottfried Herder and James Burnett Lord Monboddo noted 'significant continuities' between infants and animals: 'when we come into the world', wrote Herder, 'we are of course able to scream or cry, but not to talk or speak; we emit only animal sounds'.[50] Although human beings shared in common with other animals this universal 'language of nature', grammarians insisted upon a qualitative difference between the 'natural' voices of animals and the 'artificial' language of human beings. While Murray acknowledged that 'among irrational animals, there is something which, by a *figure*, we may call *Language*, as the instinctive economy of bees is figuratively called *Government*', he swiftly set out the 'proper' distinctions between human and non-human utterances (I, p. 23):

> Animal voices ... have no analogy with human speech. – For, *first*, men speak by art and imitation, whereas the voices in question are wholly instinctive .... *Secondly*, the voices of brute animals are not broken, or resolvable, into distinct elementary sounds, like those of man when he speaks; nor are they susceptible of that variety, which would be necessary for the communication of a very few sentiments: and it is pretty certain, that, previously to instruction, the young animals comprehend their meaning, as well as the old ones. *Thirdly*, these voices seem intended by nature to express, not distinct ideas, but such feelings only, as it may be for the good of the species, or for the advantage of man, that they should have the power of uttering; in which, as in all other respects, they are analogous, not to our speaking; but to our weeping, laughing, groaning, screaming, and other natural and audible expressions of appetite and passion. (I, pp. 23–4)

While Murray and others attempted to draw clear, dividing lines between the 'language' of human beings and the 'voices' of animals, such distinctions conflicted with the observed behaviour of various species and, most especially, birds. Songbirds possess many of the characteristics which Murray perceived as the distinguishing features of human speech. As distinctive, organised and highly complex patterns of sound, the songs of birds surely must represent an example of an animal 'voice' composed of 'distinct elementary sounds' (or 'notes', as men have been accustomed to call them). While Murray argued that animal voices were 'wholly instinctive', such general arguments conflicted with the fact that various species of birds could be, as they had been for centuries, *trained* to sing particular songs or in some cases to articulate human words. As scientists and philosophers began to recognise affinities between birdsong and human speech, they also, however, increasingly focused in on Murray's third and final set of criteria: animal voices expressed their passions and appetites, but only the human animal was able to conceptualise, frame and express 'distinct ideas'. Following the American psychologist Irene Pepperberg's study in the 1990s of an African grey parrot named Alex and other groundbreaking experiments in animal cognition, birds, primates and various other species have been proved capable of the kind of 'symbolic communication' routinely denied them throughout the long nineteenth century: not only could Alex label and identify particular objects, colours and shapes, but he was also able to distinguish whether one object was the 'same' as or 'different' from another.[51] Even as parrots and primates have appeared perfectly capable of forming such 'distinct ideas', scientists have rather suspiciously seemed to, as de Waal dryly points out, 'feel the need to raise the bar and add refinements such as that language requires syntax and recursivity'.[52] Our understanding of both human and animal cognition has developed significantly since the eighteenth and nineteenth centuries. What is clear, however, is that arguments about animal language (then as now) appear intimately bound up in larger questions regarding animal sentience and intelligence. This book delineates the twists, turns and contradictions that characterise this debate, and the larger questions which subsequently arose regarding the nature of thought and word, and their mysterious relation to each other.

In *Animal Musicalities: Birds, Beasts and Evolutionary Listening* (2018), Rachel Mundy has perceptively argued that to read responses to birdsong in the early twentieth century is to confront a 'host' of other questions: 'Who is valued when we evaluate musical difference? How are such evaluations performed? How are music's categories conditioned by the broad divide between humans and other animals?' And last, though by no means least, 'how are assumptions about race, gender, class, sexuality, and other forms of difference tied to assumptions about species?'[53] Similarly pertinent questions arise from an analysis of the study of language in the long nineteenth century. As studies of the 'politics of language' in this period have shown, linguistic theories are inseparable from the political context in which they were conceived and understood.[54] As they reflected on the continuities between birdsong and human speech, philosophers widely perceived primitive peoples and feral children as representing an intermediary stage in the process of 'becoming human'. Responding to these debates, Coleridge composed 'The Foster-Mother's Tale':

> And so the babe grew up a pretty boy,
> A pretty boy, but most unteachable—
> And never learnt a prayer nor told a bead,
> But knew the names of birds, and mocked their notes,
> And whistled, as he were a bird himself!
>
> (*Poetical Works*, I, ll. 28–32)

Coleridge's description of the 'pretty boy' exemplifies the tensions in how the languages of primitive peoples were judged and valued in the long nineteenth century. Closely associated with the birds whose notes he mocks, the boy speaks a language that is at once beautifully wild and dangerously subversive, aesthetically rich and heretically impervious to the religious mores of European societies. Simultaneously lauded and denigrated as 'pretty' modes of expression, the voices of savages were widely used as a useful foil by which to gauge and measure 'civilised' modes of speech. But conjectural histories of the savage in this period are, like the foster-mother's tale, anecdotal, contradictory and profoundly unreliable. Regardless of whether their speech bore any resemblance to the songs of birds, savages, wild children and other marginalised groups were indeed *like* the bird in the sense that philosophers routinely imposed onto them their own conjectural narratives about the origins of language and of poetry. This book explores how perceptions of the human and non-human boundary at once reflected and fed back into ideas about race, gender and class in the literature of the long nineteenth century. Writing on the borderlands of these larger debates, the poets discussed in this book perceived a connection between how their contemporaries viewed and valued other species and how they viewed and valued other races, genders and classes of human beings. With equal measures of humour and pathos, these writers delve deep into the ingrained prejudices, and insecurities, that led their contemporaries to perceive and censure dialect words as, in Hardy's phrase, 'those terrible marks of the beast'.[55]

IV

> 'Most musical, most melancholy' Bird!
> A melancholy Bird? Oh! idle thought!
> In nature there is nothing melancholy.
> —But some night-wandering man whose heart was pierced
> With the remembrance of a grievous wrong,
> Or slow distemper, or neglected love,
> (And so poor Wretch! fill'd all things with himself
> And made all gentle sounds tell back the tale
> Of his own sorrow) he, and such as he,
> First named these notes a melancholy strain.
> (Coleridge, 'The Nightingale', *Poetical Works*, I, ll. 13–22)

The long nineteenth century witnessed a heightened awareness of that 'irresistible' pressure of the figurative and the poet's propensity to make the sounds of nature, in Coleridge's phrase, 'tell back the tale | Of his own sorrow'. Although writers like Coleridge commonly critiqued these 'melancholy' tendencies in the poet, they also lived at a time when scientists were questioning some of their own established views about how and why birds sing. While the followers of Descartes continued to describe animals as machines wholly devoid of reason or even consciousness, an alternative school of thought began to recognise in birds the kind of artistic, skilful and self-aware animal minds from which they believed human music and speech had originally evolved. Placing the poetry of Coleridge, the Wordsworth siblings, Clare and Hardy in this context, this book argues that poetic renderings of birdsong in the period reflect this complex shift in how human beings came to perceive the art of birdsong, and how they came to perceive, measure and value their own art by the contrast.

The first two chapters sketch out the intellectual contexts which inform my approach to birdsong in Romantic and Victorian poetry. Chapter One traces the development of 'the science of birdsong' in the long nineteenth century. Although it was well known to bird-fanciers that various species could be trained to sing particular tunes, the fact that birds could self-evidently *learn* to sing was not directly used to challenge, or even necessarily perceived as challenging, an established tenet of British zoology: namely, that the 'natural' voices of animals bore no comparison with the 'artificial' language of human beings. With regard to birdsong and so many other areas of scientific inquiry, this period may be characterised by an ongoing struggle to square the known 'facts' with the general rule, to reconcile the mounting evidence with a vestigial belief in a divinely ordained universe. As this chapter argues, a generation of scientists, natural historians and observers may be seen as in the incipient stages of doing what a young Charles Darwin would do following his return from the voyage on the HMS *Beagle*: 'accumulating and reflecting on all sorts of facts'.[56] The chapter concludes by exploring how the many isolated facts about birdsong were collated, compared and actively used to draw an analogy with human speech in Darwin's *The Descent of Man*.

In Chapter Two, I delineate 'the science of language' as it developed from the philosophical speculations of Rousseau and Herder to the establishment of the 'New Philology' in the 1860s. As philosophers recognised significant continuities between birdsong, speech and poetry, they also, however, increasingly turned their attention to the internal, mental faculties as the distinguishing marks of an evolved and uniquely human language. This chapter examines the cultural and political implications of a developing equation of language and thought in the long nineteenth century. The apparent absence of language in animals was widely seen to reflect a lack of intelligence, reason or even consciousness. Since language reflected the unique faculties of the human mind, philosophers of all stripes raced to discover an intrinsic set of principles common to all human languages throughout time and across continents. According to this same principle, however, differences between languages were also seen to reflect or even determine differences in the minds of their speakers. Routinely, philosophers interpreted the speech of savages, rustics, women and other marginalised groups as reflecting a less developed or stunted mental capacity. As they responded to these larger debates, scientists and poets throughout this period reflected on their own experiences and the notorious *difficulty* they habitually encountered in attempting to translate thoughts into words.

The following chapters explore how poets in this period responded to and engaged with these larger questions surrounding birdsong, speech and poetry. In Chapter Three, I place the writings of Coleridge and the Wordsworths in the context of a heated debate regarding the origins of mind and language. While Coleridge throughout his life brooded over metaphysical arguments regarding 'the one life within us and abroad' ('The Eolian Harp', *Poetical Works*, I, l. 26), Dorothy Wordsworth's journals are filled with close, detailed descriptions of birds and their songs that are neither assimilated to nor inhibited by any overarching theory regarding the sentience of other creatures and our human relation to them. As he responded to his sister's lively observations and the philosophical arguments in which he found his friend so deeply embroiled, William

Wordsworth was led into larger discussions about what may be going on inside the heads of various human and non-human others. Drawing on his own experiences of composing and 'muttering' over his poems in daily walks with his sister, Wordsworth, throughout his writing, explores a subvocal language of thought that is patterned and shaped, though not always or exactly worded. Out of a deep personal recognition of a grave disjuncture between thinking and saying, Wordsworth explores the inner lives of others in ways that would prove crucial to Clare, Hardy and other poets writing in the following centuries.

Clare's transcription of the nightingale's song has recently been praised as 'the most accurate rendering in words of any bird's voice for nearly a century'.[57] Often compared with his Romantic predecessors and contemporaries in this respect, Clare's descriptions of birds and the natural world more generally have been widely recognised for their detail, accuracy and resolute focus on the thing itself. The so-called 'peasant poet', however, was not naïve. In Chapter Four, I argue that Clare's educational background and multifarious interests in poetry, science and natural history made him singly alert to the difficulties and dangers inherent within his own attempt to 'syllable the sounds' of the nightingale (*Natural History Prose*, p. 312). The chapter places Clare's writing in a pivotal though pre-Darwinian stage of the 'science of birdsong': a period in which all kinds of 'facts' about birdsong were being collected, compared and vigorously disputed. Watching the bird closely as it inwardly mutters its undersong, stammers or hurries over ill-remembered passages, Clare witnessed the kind of behaviour which would ultimately challenge the 'foolish lyes' uttered by both poets and naturalists regarding how and why birds sing (*Natural History Prose*, p. 110). By exploring the deep connections which Clare draws between the 'muttering' of the bird while practising its songs and his own processes of composition, the chapter seeks to extend and, in certain respects, redefine some of the binary terms which have framed responses to the writings of this so-called 'peasant poet': 'natural' and 'artificial', 'instinctive' and 'learned', 'spontaneous' and 'premeditated' art.

By the time that Hardy began publishing in the 1870s, the debate surrounding animal language had dramatically intensified following the publication of Darwin's *Origin of Species*. Chapter Five places Hardy's writing in the context of the heated dispute that arose between evolutionary scientists and philologists in this period regarding the relationship between language and thought. While Müller insisted on a close, coeval relationship between the ability to frame ideas and the ability to express those ideas in words, Darwin, throughout his writing, demonstrates a lively fascination with the diverse and dynamic kinds of thinking that human beings and other animals appear able to perform 'manifestly without the aid of language' (*Descent*, p. 110). Responding to these larger debates, Hardy's writing is centrally concerned with the tragic consequences of a world in which there is both language without thought and thought without language. While characters of all backgrounds are seen to 'pipe' the church catechism as mindlessly as the bullfinches which the heroine teaches to 'whistle tunes' in *Tess of the D'Urbervilles* (1891–2), Hardy outlines and affirms the inner, imaginative life of a milkmaid who, as the narrator describes Tess's responses to the music which she hears in church, 'thought, without exactly wording the thought'.[58] Writing against a tradition of novelistic 'realism' which accentuated the linguistic differences that separate class from class, region from region and epoch from epoch, Hardy calls attention to the underlying affinities between how milkmaids and university students ultimately think and feel. Increasingly frustrated by the dictates of novelistic realism, Hardy in his late years turned to poetry as the form that seemed 'to fit my thoughts better as I grow older, as it did when I was young also'.[59] This chapter examines Hardy's claim for poetry as a form better fitted to express both his own thoughts and the thoughts of others, and to generate sympathy with and between 'the whole conscious world collectively'.[60]

CHAPTER I

The Science of Birdsong
1773–1871

Voice is distinguished chiefly by its pitch, high or low; it does not differ in kind in one and the same sort of animal. But articulated voice, which one might describe as a sort of 'speech,' differs in different animals, and also within one and the same kind of animal according to locality: thus, some partridges cackle, others make a shrill noise. Among the small birds, some when singing utter a different voice from their parents, if they have been reared away from the nest and have heard other birds singing. A hen nightingale has before now been observed teaching her chick to sing, which suggests that the 'song' does not come naturally in the same way as the voice, but is capable of being trained. Men have the same voice the world over, but different varieties of speech.
Aristotle, Historia Animalium (?350 BCE)

Notes in birds are no more innate, than language is in man, and depend entirely upon the master under which they are bred, as far as their organs will enable them to imitate the sounds which they have frequent opportunities of hearing.
Daines Barrington, 'Experiments and Observations on the Singing of Birds'
(1773–4)

The sounds uttered by birds offer in several respects the nearest analogy to language, for all the members of the same species utter the same instinctive cries expressive of their emotions; and all the kinds which sing, exert their power instinctively; but the actual song, and even the call notes, are learnt from their parents or foster-parents.
Charles Darwin, The Descent of Man (1871)

Over two thousand years ago, Aristotle used the Greek word *dialektos* to register the striking parallels between birdsong and human speech.[1] Since birds had been kept and trained to sing for generations, the scientific studies of birdsong discussed in this chapter drew from an old and deep well of popular knowledge and experience. The market price of a nightingale in Pliny's Rome was determined by its individual powers of song or, by extension, its capacity to acquire and practise an 'Art' (I, p. 286). Throughout the eighteenth and nineteenth centuries, naturalists relied on a mass of supporting evidence from an ancient and evidently lucrative trade in singing (and some talking) birds. This chapter begins by examining a central, if somewhat overlooked, figure in the history of this developing science: the bird-catcher. In order to lure the birds into his snare, the bird-catcher learned to imitate the songs of his prey and, in turn, taught them to sing to his tune. Consequently, the bird-catcher provided much of the groundwork and the vocabulary for studies in ornithology. The practices of his trade fundamentally undermined a key theoretical distinction between the 'natural' sounds of animals and the 'artificial' language of human beings. I examine records of bird-catching and bird-fancying from eighteenth-century training manuals to Henry Mayhew's extended discussion of the metropolitan 'bird-trade' in *London Labour and the London Poor* (1851) and the eventual decline of the London chaffinch-fanciers as recounted in W. H. Hudson's *Birds in London* (1898).[2]

This traditionally working-class and highly competitive sport proved crucial to an emerging scientific method based on practical experience, direct observation and controlled experiment. Natural historians and scientists, from Daines Barrington to Charles Darwin, commonly called upon the bird-catcher as an authority in their discussions of birds, their songs and what Gilbert White controversially referred to as their 'language'.[3] This chapter outlines a tradition of the curious, whose investigations began to break down binary distinctions between human and non-human utterances. Examples range from Gilbert White's 'query' as to whether owls hoot in the key of B flat to Barrington's direct comparison of birdsong variations with human 'provincial dialects' (White, p. 119; Barrington, 'Experiments', p. 280). While such seemingly trifling studies were widely commented on in magazines and journals throughout the period, I observe an irregularity in their reception: Barrington's experiments were relegated to the footnotes and appendices of natural history throughout the eighteenth and early nineteenth centuries. The chapter concludes by showing how this wealth of material, compiled over centuries, was excavated from the footnotes and explicitly used to identify birdsong as 'the nearest analogy' to human speech in Darwin's *The Descent of Man* (p. 108).

I

Perhaps the most iconic representation of the bird-catcher, Papageno, in Mozart's *The Magic Flute* (1791), adorns himself in the plumage of his prey and learns to sing their songs (Figure 3). A conspicuous figure in art and

Figure 3 Papageno: 'I am the bird-catcher, yes! Always cheerful, fiddle-di-i, fiddle di-da!' Act I of *The Magic Flute* by Wolfgang Amadeus Mozart (1756–91), engraved by Friedrich Wilhelm Meyer Senior (b.c. 1770).

literature, the bird-catcher was also, however, a very real presence in European cities throughout the eighteenth and nineteenth centuries. Recent research has identified bird-fancying as something of a 'national fad' in England and Germany in this period, and has drawn attention to some of the core texts of the trade, particularly the set of tunes 'specifically designed to teach birds to sing' collected in *The Bird Fancyer's Delight* (1717).[4] As J. M. Bechstein explains in his *Naturgeschichte der Stubenvögel* or *Natural History of Caged Birds* (1795), 'a good bird catcher ought to know not only the different modes of taking birds, but also all the calls for attracting the different species and sexes'; the success of the bird-catcher's trade depended on his ability to distinguish the chaffinch's call to its companions, '*iack iack*', from '*treef treef*', an 'expression of sorrow'.[5]

Not only did the bird-catchers provide much of the groundwork and the vocabulary for studies in ornithology, but the 'science' of birdsong, in its early stages of development, was typically designed for and redirected back to those with a practical interest in training birds to sing – or 'improv[ing]' their notes, as Barrington put it ('Experiments', p. 289). Bechstein's *Natural History of Caged Birds* contained detailed instructions for the 'many people who like to keep birds' (p. i). On a deeper and more fundamental level, instructions for domestic management were built into the structure of ornithological works. Consider, for example, J. Macloc's description of the bullfinch in his *Natural History of the Most Remarkable Quadrupeds, Birds, Fishes, Serpents, Reptiles, and Insects in the Known World* (1815). Alongside the bird's physical attributes, its measurements and eye-colour, naturalists like Macloc commonly concluded their entries on popular domestic singers, such as the bullfinch, with a list of the relevant, recognised techniques for training. The layout is fairly typical of natural historical works at this time and includes, as a matter of course, precise instructions regarding the time at which the bird may be taken from the nest, the 'paste' of bread, milk and rapeseed with which the bird may be fed, and the 'pains' which must be taken with these birds 'in the early part of their education'.[6] As Oliver Goldsmith was led to complain with regard to the nightingale in particular, 'the greatest part of what has been written concerning it in our country, consists in directions how to manage it for domestic singing'.[7]

In *London Labour and the London Poor*, Henry Mayhew delineated the London 'bird-trade' of the 1840s and 50s (II, p. 65). Around the metropolis there was what Mayhew described as 'a perfect belt of men', each 'labouring to give city-pent men of humble means one of the peculiar pleasures of the country – the song of the birds' (II, p. 62). Although women are often figured alongside caged birds in the novels and portraiture of the long nineteenth century, Mayhew's research shows that singing contests in fact represented a highly popular sport among an urban and predominantly male working class.[8] Mayhew recorded in his interview with one of the most infamous figures of the trade, Mr Jack Black, 'the Queen of England's Rat-Catcher':[9]

'When I was about fifteen, sir, I turned to bird-fancying. I was very fond of the sombre linnet. I was very successful in raising them, and sold them for a deal of money. I've got the strain of them by me now ... I used to moult them off in the dark, by kivering [covering] the cages up, and then they'd learn from hearing the old ones singing, and would take the song. If any did not sing perfectly I used to sell 'em as cast-offs.

'The linnet's is a beautiful song. There are four-and-twenty changes in a linnet's song. It's one of the beautifullest song-birds we've got. It sings "toys," as we call them; that is, it makes sounds which we distinguish in the fancy as the "tollock eeke eeke eeke quake le wheet; single eke eke quake wheets, or eek eek quake chowls; eege pipe chowl: laugh; eege poy chowls; rattle; pipe; fear; pugh and poy."

'This seems like Greek to you, sir, but it's the tunes we use in the fancy. What we terms "fear" is a sound like fear, as if they was frightened; "laugh" is a kind of shake, nearly the same as the "rattle."

'I know the sounds of all the English birds, and what they say. I could tell you about the nightingale, the black cap, hedge warbler, garden warbler, petty chat, red start – a beautiful song-bird – the willow wren – little warblers they are – linnets, or any of them, for I have got their sounds in my ear and my mouth.'

As if to prove this, he drew from a side-pocket a couple of tin bird-whistles, which were attached by a string to a button-hole. He instantly began to imitate the different birds, commencing with their call, and then explaining how, when answered to in such a way, they gave another note, and how, if still responded to, they uttered a different sound.

In fact, he gave me the whole of the conversation he usually carried on with the different kinds of birds, each one being as it were in a different language. He also showed me how he allured them to him, when they were in the air singing in the distance, and he did this by giving their entire song. His cheeks and throat seemed to be in constant motion as he filled the room with his loud imitations of the lark, and so closely did he resemble the notes of the bird, that it was no longer any wonder how the little things could be deceived.

In the same manner he illustrated the songs of the nightingale, and so many birds, that I did not recognise the names of some of them. He knew all their habits as well as notes, and repeated to me the peculiar chirp they make on rising from the ground, as well as the sound by which he distinguishes that it is 'uneasy with curiosity,' or that it has settled on a tree. Indeed, he appeared to be acquainted with all the chirps which distinguished any action in the bird up to the point when, as he told me, it 'circles about, and then falls like a stone to the ground with its pitch.'

'The nightingale,' he continued, 'is a beautiful song-bird. They're plucky birds, too, and they hear a call and answer to anybody .... I can ketch a nightingale in less than five minutes; as soon as he calls, I calls to him with my mouth, and he'll answer me (both by night or day), either from a spinny (a little copse), a dell, or a wood, wherever he may be. I make my scrapes (that is, clear away the dirt), set my traps, catch 'em almost before I've tried my luck. I've ketched sometimes thirty in a day, for although people have got a notion that nightingales is scarce, still those who can distinguish their song in the daytime know that they are plentiful enough .... You see persons fancy that them nightingales as sings at night is the only ones living, but it's wrong, for many of them only sings in the day'. (III, pp. 14–15)

These kinds of traditional bird-sound mnemonics may be relatively crude and approximate, but they serve a purpose: they enable the bird-catcher to 'distinguish' between the 'four-and-twenty changes' in a linnet's song. Black is able to distinguish specific, coded 'meanings' within the sounds. At times, the bird's call is matched with a specific 'action', such as the 'peculiar' chirp which the bird makes when settling on a tree or rising from the ground. At others, the modulations are understood to express subtle shades of meaning, or states of being, such as that of being 'uneasy with curiosity'. With the aid of their tin whistles, figures such as Jack Black substantiated the claim, to the astonishment of their auditors, that they 'in the fancy' had discovered the secret that eluded each and every Romantic poet: 'I know the sounds of all the English birds, and what they say'.

Mayhew's presentation of Black reflects the bird-catcher's shifting status in the long nineteenth century. At various points in the interview, Mayhew shows sincere admiration of, and respect for, the peculiar expertise of bird-catchers. Black is able to recite the songs of 'so many birds' that, the journalist admits, 'I did not recognise the names of some of them'. Mayhew further asserts the authority of the bird-catcher in a larger scientific debate about the nightingale's song: the debate which Clare's publisher, James Hessey, summarised as the 'solemn trifling' of naturalists regarding whether these birds sing by night or by day, and whether their notes express joy or melancholy.[10] Whether Mayhew contrived to ask these specific questions regarding the nightingale or subsequently framed the interview in these terms, his description asserts the 'knowing' of a working-class animal trader in a larger intellectual debate: 'you see persons fancy that them nightingales as sings at night is the only ones living', explains Black, 'but it's wrong'.

Mayhew's admiration for the bird-catcher's arts of deception is, however, counterbalanced by his concern for the 'little things' so deceived. As Mayhew discovered, the bird-catcher showed himself 'unwilling to admit' the rate of mortality among nightingales, nor would he accept that this bird's habits necessarily 'unfit him for a cage existence' (II, p. 60). Jack Black may have recognised the call as an expression of being 'uneasy with curiosity', but he could not or would not acknowledge the 'symptoms of great uneasiness' which Mayhew perceived in the nightingale during the migratory season, 'dashing himself against the wires of his cage or his aviary, and sometimes dying in a few days' (II, p. 60). In this respect, Mayhew's writing at once reflects and anticipates the changing social attitudes which would ultimately lead to the prohibition of the bird-catcher's trade under the Wild Bird Protection Acts of the 1880s.

In *Nature Near London* (1883), Richard Jefferies expressed a growing 'detestation for the bird-catcher'.[11] Although Jefferies did not himself 'fear the extinction of small birds', he drew attention to the 'fate that awaits the captive': 'far better for the frightened little creature to have its neck at once twisted and to die than to languish in cages hardly large enough for it to turn in behind the dirty panes of the windows in the Seven Dials' (p. 93). Richard Rowe considered the issue from the bird-catcher's perspective in *Life in the London Streets; Or, Struggles for Daily Bread* (1881):

> No: I dont 'old with this new hact about Small Birds. It's on'y another bit o' the swells' spite ... No: they must keep poor men from 'avin' singin' birds, and other poor men from makin' their livin' by ketchin' on 'em.[12]

To the bird-catcher, these 'new hacts' seemed little more than the snobbish elitism of a wealthy and patronising elite; the poor man's access to the countryside was being rapidly reduced by a series of trespassing and wildlife-protection laws. As W. H. Hudson reflected in *Birds in London*, increased policing of the London parks had left the East End chaffinch-fanciers in the rather undignified position of 'slouching about among the shrubberies, each with a small cage covered with a cotton handkerchief or rag, in quest of a wild bird for his favourite to sing against'.[13] Although Hudson supposed that significant decreases in the number of chaffinches at Victoria Park were most likely the result of the bird-catcher's own practices, he also recognised that this 'great loss' was nonetheless most keenly felt by those who valued these songsters the most dearly and did not enjoy the privilege of living in leafy suburbs (p. 199).

The bird-catcher proved a vital source of information for the developing 'science of birdsong' in the long nineteenth century; ironically, however, his practices seemed increasingly at odds with what Hardy recognised as the 'ethical' implications of that science (*Later Years*, p. 141). 'In thought and wish', wrote Wordsworth, in *The Prelude*

(1798–1839), of his own boyhood exploits, 'my shoulder all with springes hung, | I was a fell destroyer'.[14] For all his intimate knowledge of the natural world, the hunter of birds is increasingly seen to lack sympathy for the lives of the creatures he so skilfully tracks, captures and destroys. In the 1820s, Clare recorded a common practice of bird-catchers: when they took 'a nest of young ones', they would place it in a cage and 'hang it up' close to where they had taken it 'for the old birds to come & feed them'; although the old ones would come to feed the young, the nestlings would rarely survive, which led the bird-catchers to believe that the parent birds would bring food to deliberately 'poison' their young (*Natural History Prose*, p. 45). In a letter to *The Times* newspaper in 1913, Hardy recalled these popular schoolboy traditions in order to protest the inhumane treatment of caged skylarks and other animals.[15] In the late eighteenth and early nineteenth centuries, the experiences of bird-catchers, both amateur and professional, seemed to provide tantalising glimpses into the complex emotional and social lives of birds. By the time that Hardy was writing to *The Times* in the early twentieth century, however, the Secretary of the Cage Birds League, Henry J. Fulljames, derided the ignorance of such 'sentimental' tales.[16] In a Hardyan twist of fate, the bird-catcher's knowledge and expertise contributed to a shift in cultural attitudes that would ultimately lead to the decline and prohibition of his 'ancient hobby'.[17]

II

Following his extensive interviews with pigeon-fanciers in the *Origin of Species*, Darwin expressed his surprise at their inability, or unwillingness, to recognise the wider implications of their own practices: relentlessly focused on the job in hand, 'they ignore all general arguments, and refuse to sum up in their minds' (*Origin of Species*, p. 25). Although it was well known to bird-catchers that birds could be trained to sing, their expertise was not incorporated into a larger hypothesis about birdsong, speech and the origins of language. In a gradual process of summing up, studies specifically dealing with the singing of birds began to appear in the late eighteenth century. In his *Natural History of Selborne*, White noted the remarks, seemingly off-hand, of a 'musical friend' who 'has tried all the owls that are his near neighbours with a pitch-pipe set at concert pitch, and finds that they all hoot in B flat' (p. 119). The letter concludes abruptly, with the assurance that the musical friend 'will examine the nightingales next spring' (p. 119). White picks up the theme again in the next letter, which nonetheless remains in a kind of note-form, as part of a process of observation and discovery:

> From what follows, it will appear that neither owls nor cuckoos keep to one note. A friend remarks that many (most) of his owls hoot in B flat; but that one went almost half a note below A. The pipe he tried their notes by was a common half-crown pitch-pipe, such as masters use for tuning of harpsichords; it was the common London pitch.
>
> A neighbour of mine, who is said to have a nice ear, remarks that the owls about this village hoot in three different keys, in G flat or F sharp, in B flat, and A flat. He heard two hooting to each other, the one in A flat, and the other in B flat. Query: Do these different notes proceed from different species, or only from various individuals? The same person finds upon trial that the note of the cuckoo (of which we have but one species) varies in different individuals; for, about Selborne wood, he found they were mostly in D; he heard two sing together, the one in D, and the other in D sharp, which made a disagreeable concert; he afterwards heard one in D sharp, and about Wolmer Forest some in C. As to nightingales, he says that their notes are so short, and their transitions so rapid, that he cannot well ascertain their key. Perhaps in a cage and in a room, their notes may be more distinguishable. This person has tried to settle the notes of a swift, and of several other small birds, but cannot bring them to any criterion. (pp. 119–20)

Structurally, White's remarks and observations seem relatively disjointed, shifting between questions of migration and musical keys without apparent reason or explanation. Yet a seemingly incidental connection is brought out in the 'query': White is exploring the connections between place or locality and variations in hooting. The process of distinguishing depends on the 'nice ear' of a musical friend, the limits of which White fully acknowledges (particularly with regard to the rapid 'transitions' of the nightingale). The very act of distinguishing, however, represents a critical shift. Rather than asserting a general principle, the particular instance leads to a general 'query' which is nonetheless left open, undecided, in White's way of thinking and discovering. In this respect, he embodies a mode of listening and responding to the natural world which would become increasingly significant to his admirers in the following centuries. In such 'amusingly eccentric' episodes, White has been credited with 'one of the earliest instances of a scientific approach to animal communication'.[18]

These 'important sounds' are related to the complex and often heated social lives of birds. From careful study of a bird's behaviour, White matches the sound with a particular object or action, while he also appears to have conducted some ad hoc experiments: 'take a chicken of four or five days old, and hold it up to a window where there are flies, and it will immediately seize its prey, with little twitterings of complacency; but if you tender it a wasp or a bee, at once its note becomes harsh, and expressive of disapprobation and a sense of danger' (p. 192). The descriptions are generally light, comic, often smiling at the 'strange and ridiculous' nature of birds and presenting the high passions at play in mock-heroic terms: 'the cock turkey struts and gobbles to his mistress in a most uncouth manner' (p. 192). The wonderfully detailed and, at the same time, richly imaginative descriptions of the sounds themselves often register the subtlety of the distinguishable tones of a bird's 'vocabulary' (p. 193): the 'little inward moan' of the hen, for example, at the sight of a predator (p. 192). Perhaps the most notable and influential aspect of White's writing derives from his recognition, and celebration, of the expressive qualities of the language of birds – the passions and frustrations of the turkey-cock and the tremulous life of the hen. In his description of the 'very sweet, but inward melody' of the blackcap (p. 84), White observes the kind of behaviour that his friend Barrington would subsequently connect with a larger theory regarding how birds learn to sing. Characteristically, however, White's writing focuses on the 'inward' quality of a song that appears to offer tantalising glimpses into the inner lives of birds, to hint at the kind of complacency, self-satisfaction and enjoyment that, as Darwin would later maintain, robins and other birds experience in singing. In an oft-quoted passage, White described 'the language of birds' as 'very ancient, and, like other ancient modes of speech, very elliptical: little is said, but much is meant and understood' (p. 191). As will be discussed in more detail in Chapter Two, White here hints at a connection which philosophers explored throughout the long nineteenth century: the connection, that is, between 'the language of birds' and an ancient, tonal and 'elliptical' mode of human speech.

Many of the letters included in White's *Natural History* are addressed to Barrington, as well as another naturalist friend, Thomas Pennant. First given as a series of lectures to the Royal Society in the spring of 1773, Barrington's 'Experiments and Observations on the Singing of Birds' was published in an article later that year in the society's journal, *Philosophical Transactions*, and was subsequently reprinted in an appendix to Pennant's *British Zoology* (1776). The insights of Barrington's article are partly owing to the prolific and interdisciplinary nature of his research on various and miscellaneous subjects; trained as a barrister, Barrington was also the Vice President of the Royal Society, as well as a prominent figure in the diverse fields of natural history, anthropology, philology and particularly the history of provincial dialects.[19] Practically speaking, Barrington's 'experiments' were very similar to what the bird-fanciers had been doing for centuries. Yet his findings are significant in so far as they adhere to an established 'scientific method', often attributed to Francis Bacon's *Novum Organum* (1620), which consisted in 'systematic observation, measurement, and experiment, and the formulation, testing, and modification of hypotheses' (*OED*). Barrington often references the bird-fanciers as an authority throughout the article, but their 'authority' is related to a scientific argument or hypothesis – a hypothesis which, more crucially, drew significant behavioural parallels between song-learning in birds and speech-acquisition in infants.

In what he initially defended, in Lord Bacon's terms, as rather '*experiments of light, than of fruit*', Barrington removed three linnets from the nest when they were three weeks old and 'educated' them under the 'three best singing larks' ('Experiments', pp. 288, 254). Since each of the linnets 'adhered entirely to that of their respective instructors', Barrington concluded that the songs of birds were 'no more innate, than language is in man; and depend entirely upon the master under which they are bred, as far as their organs will enable them to imitate the sounds which they have frequent opportunities of hearing' (pp. 254, 252). Taking his terms from the bird-catchers, Barrington also identified the process of '*recording*' in which the nestling begins to listen to, remember and imitate the song of its parents, until it can recite the whole in full without mistake or '*sing his song round*' (pp. 250–1). In a comparison often cited in subsequent examinations of birdsong, Barrington went on to draw a key parallel between these early attempts at song and 'the imperfect endeavour in a child to babble' (p. 250). As he describes the first, imperfect assays of the bird in 'endeavouring to form his song', Barrington is drawn into a more speculative line of thinking and interpreting: the bird 'hurries over' any imperfectly remembered passages, 'as if', Barrington reflects, 'he did not wish to be heard, and could not yet satisfy himself' (p. 251). Barrington's comments stand on the brink between the opposing forces of anthropomorphism and anthropodenial: the scientist is unable to prove, yet seems reluctant to ignore, what it seems 'as if' the bird is doing. Although Barrington could not call to mind 'a passage in any writer, which seems to relate to this stage of singing' (p. 251), writers throughout the Romantic and Victorian periods would use descriptions of 'shy come nightingales' to reflect on their own processes of 'muttering o'er their songs' (Clare, 'When first we hear the shy come nightingales', *Middle Period*, V, ll. 1–2).

Barrington also reflects on the possible 'origins' and development of birdsong variations, though he concludes that 'the origin of the notes of birds, together with its gradual progress, is as difficult to be traced, as that of the different languages in nations' (p. 287). Since birdsong variations may only be heard by those who have most carefully 'attended' to the song of birds, Barrington consults the authority of those whose trade depended on such precision: as he explains, 'the London bird-catchers prefer the song of the Kentish goldfinches, but Essex chaffinches; and when they sell the bird to those who can thus distinguish, inform the buyer that it hath such a note, which is very well understood between them' (pp. 279–80). This common understanding between professionals is then applied to a broader theory of how the songs of birds, like the 'provincial dialects' with which Barrington compares then, may gradually change or drift from that of their ancestors 'from generation to generation' (pp. 280, 287).

Barrington in many ways established a more scientific method of experimentation and inquiry, yet his comments are inflected by wider cultural concerns. According to Barrington, the wild nightingale lacks the vocal control and sustained attention acquired through training or tuition under a human 'master': the bird in its wild state 'seldom sings anything but short and loud jerks, which consequently cannot be compared to the notes of a caged bird, as the instrument is overstrained' (p. 283). As human beings 'have not more musical ideas which are innate, than we have of language', he further argues that even those blessed with 'this sixth sense (as it hath been called by some) require, however, the best instruction'; since 'the orchestra of the opera, which is confined to the metropolis, hath diffused a good stile of playing over the other bands of the capital', Barrington reasoned that the singing of a 'London blackguard' was nonetheless 'infinitely' superior to that of a 'ploughman in the country' (pp. 259–60). Although Barrington admits he does not 'mean by this, to assert that the inhabitants of the country are not born with as good musical organs', his criticisms are rooted in an eighteenth-century obsession with 'improvement' and more specifically improvement by 'learning from others' (p. 260).

At the conclusion, Barrington gestures towards the potential wider implications of his 'trifling' study (p. 291): 'there is no better method of investigating the human faculties', he argues, 'than by a comparison with those of animals' (p. 288). Yet Barrington appears reluctant to press any 'comparison' further; instead, he somewhat abruptly concludes by emphasising the apparent and unassailable differences between the human and non-human animal. Such a 'comparison', he insists, may only be made on the condition that 'we make it without a most ungrateful wish of lowering ourselves, in that distinguished situation in which we are placed' (p. 288). Barrington's 'curious' and 'ingenious' essay was widely commented on in natural historical works and magazines throughout the period.[20] Yet the word 'ingenious' brings out some of the tone of the response. In a footnote to his entry on the linnet, the Comte de Buffon stated his agreement with 'the Honourable Daines Barrington, that birds have no innate song'.[21] In a prefatory essay on 'Birds in General' attached to John Wright's English edition of *Buffon's Natural History* (1831), however, there is no mention of either Barrington's arguments or de Buffon's noted agreement with them; here, the writer insists upon a broad general distinction between 'the instincts of animals' and 'the *teachableness* which is the characteristic of man'.[22] In *The Temple of Nature* (1803), Erasmus Darwin described how the nestling birds 'whisper to the song', but the scientific evidence and its implications are relegated to the footnotes: it is not in the main body of the poem that the scientist expresses his suspicion that 'the singing of birds, like human music, is an artificial language rather than a natural expression of passion'.[23] It would be almost a century before Barrington's 'ingenious' findings appeared as more than a footnote or an appendix to British zoology, although his words would be quoted practically verbatim by Erasmus's grandson, Charles Darwin, in *The Descent of Man*.

III

'Language is our Rubicon', declared Max Müller in his *Lectures on the Science of Language* (1861), 'and no brute will dare to cross it' (I, p. 340). Since Darwin's opponents had 'already ceded the point that animals have memory, experience emotions, and so on', it may readily be assumed that Darwin's chapter on language in *The Descent of Man* would have aroused the 'considerable anticipation of both pro- and anti-Darwinian readers'.[24] On the one hand, it is true that Darwin's opponents appeared to recognise that animals possessed basic cognitive faculties; on the other, however, these same opponents simultaneously argued that language was dependent upon the possession of those faculties – memory, reason and, most particularly, the ability to form abstract concepts. Darwin's chapter on the mental faculties of animals is structured to take on and pull apart Müller's infamous equation: 'no animal thinks, and no animal speaks, except man' (*Science of Language*, I, p. 369).

In *The Descent of Man*, Darwin drew together the research of Barrington, Bechstein, White and an extensive range of other sources, including the lived experience of bird-fanciers. Although he was drawing from this wealth of material, the material itself is arranged and brought together in an extensive assemblage of what might now be called 'comparative data'.²⁵ Starting on relatively safe ground, Darwin begins by observing a fact 'so well established, that it will not be necessary to weary the reader by many details' (pp. 89–90). As was common knowledge to natural historians, animal trainers and, due to the significant rise in pet-keeping in the long nineteenth century, a broad spectrum of the general public, animals could 'manifestly feel' and experience the same basic emotions and instinctive drives as their human masters: pain, pleasure, fear, desire, the maternal instinct and so on (p. 89).²⁶ Darwin widens the issue to include those 'lower' classes of animals normally denied these capabilities, such as birds, fish and insects, and notably the ants which 'that excellent observer', P. Huber, had observed 'chasing and pretending to bite each other, like so many puppies' (p. 89). He further shows the more complex emotions evident in animals, such as 'suspicion' and 'courage', which allow a greater degree of individual personality and subversive agency to animal minds capable of 'long-delayed and artful revenge' (p. 90). The 'jealous' behaviour and 'sense of humour' exhibited by dogs are cited with a kind of inverted anthropomorphism, which does not so much impose human thoughts or values onto an animal mind as allow complex feeling and individuality to an animal neither so different, nor so distinguishable, from the human (p. 92).

Darwin then turns his attention to the 'more intellectual emotions and faculties' (p. 92). He recognises not only the capacity for 'memory' among animals, but also its corollary: *'Imagination'* (p. 95). In Darwin's definition, imagination is the offspring of memory: the ability not only to remember past harm, but consequently also to anticipate or imagine oncoming disaster; since the 'sounds uttered' by 'all the higher animals' and 'even birds' in their sleep suggest that each has 'vivid dreams', Darwin concluded that 'we must admit that they have some power of imagination' (pp. 95–6). In the next section, Darwin develops and builds upon these fundamentals in order to confront the term and the 'faculty' which he perceives as the highest among the mental powers, and prized as 'the summit' of human intelligence: *'Reason'* (p. 96). He recognises the necessity of scientific method in controlling the 'circumstances' by which alone the scientist may 'judge' whether the action performed is 'due to instinct, or to reason' (p. 97). As one such 'experiment', Darwin cites the findings of one 'most careful observer', Dr Rengger; when Rengger gave hard-boiled eggs to monkeys in Paraguay, they apparently at first 'smashed them' and consequently 'lost much of their contents'; afterwards, however, the monkeys learned to 'gently hit one end' of the egg 'against some hard body, and picked off the bits of shell with their fingers' (p. 99). Darwin also supplies anecdotal evidence, recalling the recent experiences of himself 'and I daresay others' at the London Zoological Gardens, where elephants had been seen blowing their trunks, and bears pawing in water, to drive or float objects through the bars of their cages (p. 98). After several pages of carefully collected and organised examples, taken from a variety of sources and authorities, Darwin concludes with a direct and unflinching challenge to the 'philosophers' who attempt to 'explain away all such fact as those given above' with what 'appears to be mere verbiage' (p. 100). It is not the arguments of 'speculative philosophy', but the 'popular expression', derived from the 'long experience' of the muleteers in South America, with which Darwin concludes: 'I will not give you the mule whose step is easiest, but *la mas racional* – the one that reasons best' (p. 100).

Having shown the various kinds and degrees of 'mental powers' among animals, Darwin, in the following section, goes on to examine the 'faculty' widely considered to be the expression of those powers: '*Language*' (p. 106). Although he does not dispute that the 'habitual use of articulate language is peculiar to man', he cites the arguments of Archbishop Whatley: 'man is not the only animal that can make use of language to express what is passing in his mind, and can understand, more or less, what is so expressed by another' (p. 106). Darwin begins by giving a series of examples, in which he opens out the term 'language' to include a variety of forms of communication, including non-verbal facial gestures and 'inarticulate' cries that express passion (pp. 106–7). In this respect, Darwin is not so much suggesting that animals have a 'language' approaching human language as that human language itself retains the traces of such expressive emotional cries. Echoing the theories of Rousseau, Herder and other eighteenth-century philosophers (discussed in more detail in the following chapter), Darwin argues that 'man ... uses, in common with the lower animals, inarticulate cries to express his meaning, aided by gestures and the movements of the muscles of the face' (p. 107). As White commented on the 'elliptical' nature of the language of birds (p. 191), similarly, Darwin emphasises the expressive qualities of such inarticulate sounds and gestures: 'our cries of pain, fear, surprise, anger, together with their appropriate actions, and the murmur of a mother to her beloved child, are more expressive than any words' (p. 107).

Darwin subtly unpicks various and conflicting definitions of language. He refers to several of these definitions, though in each case he gives an example of that capacity among 'the lower animals': 'that which distinguishes man ... is not ... is not ... nor is it ...' (pp. 107–8). He observes the dog's capacity to 'understand many words and sentences', as well as the capacity for 'articulation' among parrots and several other birds (p. 107). For Darwin, the 'peculiar' nature of articulate language arose not so much from a single ability, a single attribute, as from an 'infinitely larger' capacity 'of associating together the most diversified sounds and ideas' (pp. 107–8). In response to the 'various articles which have been published lately', Darwin addressed the issue of the 'supposed entire absence in animals of the power of abstraction, or of forming general concepts' (p. 105). He begins by acknowledging the limitations of his own knowledge on the subject at the same time that this element of doubt or uncertainty is also quietly used to undermine the 'sure' and certain arguments of his opponents; for either side, the main difficulty 'arises from the impossibility of judging what passes through the mind of an animal' – that which cannot be ruled in, Darwin subtly suggests, also cannot be ruled out (p. 105). Acknowledging the further difficulty arising from scholastic disputes and differences over the 'meaning which they attribute to the above terms', Darwin places his own emphasis on the most rudimentary definition of abstraction that may be discovered among the lower animals (p. 105). When 'a dog sees another dog at a distance', he explains, 'it is often clear that he perceives that it is a dog in the abstract; for when he gets nearer his whole manner changes, if the other dog be a friend' (p. 105). Citing a letter addressed to Max Müller, published in the *Birmingham News*, Darwin argues that it is 'pure assumption to assert that the mental act is not essentially of the same nature in the animal as in the man. If either refers what he perceives with his senses to a mental concept, then so do both' (p. 105).

Darwin further challenges a common distinction between animal and human communication, derived from Aristotle's fourfold structure of verbal communication in *De interpretatione*; according to this structure, words first acted as the signs of 'things'.[27] Anticipating Pepperberg's research on Alex the grey parrot, Darwin suggests that parrots could not only imitate human words but were further able to 'connect unerringly words with things, and persons with events' (p. 107). Darwin's evidence is provided in a footnote, perhaps reflecting a certain nervousness around such a highly controversial subject. Here, he cites the account of an established figure, the Admiral Sir J. Sulivan, whose father kept a parrot which 'invariably, called certain persons of the household, as well as visitors, by their names' (p. 107; n. 52). According to the report, this bird 'said "good morning" to everyone at breakfast, and "good night" to each as they left the room at night, and never reversed these salutations' (p. 107; n. 52).

Darwin cites Barrington at length, though in many ways his arguments indicate crucial and significant steps beyond his predecessor. He observes his predecessor's comment that the songs 'are no more innate than language is in man', that the first attempts at song 'may be compared to the imperfect endeavour in a child to babble', that the young males 'practise' their songs in what the bird-catchers called the '*recording* phrase' and that variations between songbirds of the same species, but inhabiting different districts, may be compared to 'provincial dialects' (pp. 108–9). Whereas Barrington had discovered 'apposite' similarities between birdsong and human language, Darwin used his research to argue that the 'sounds uttered by birds' represented the 'nearest analogy to language' (p. 108). Perhaps more significant, however, are Darwin's remarks on the relationship between 'instinct' and 'learning'; while 'all the kinds which sing exert their power instinctively', Darwin distinguished between these 'instinctive' powers and the 'actual song' of the nestlings, which is 'learnt from their parents or foster-parents' (p. 108). Birdsong, in this respect, was significant not so much as an example of animal learning as an example of a faculty which Darwin recognised as common to both bird and infant: 'an instinctive capacity to acquire an art' (p. 109). Darwin's phrase anticipates modern studies of both language and birdsong – or what has become known as the 'instinct to learn'.[28]

Darwin further reflects on the relationship between language and the mind. He argues that the 'peculiar' nature of human language arose from a complex relationship between the development of language and the development of the 'brain'; he observes the significance of the physical aspects of speech, the vocal organs and their continued 'use', but suggests that 'the relation between the continued use of language and the development of the brain, has no doubt been far more important' (p. 110). He referred back to his previous arguments, which he at this stage explicitly uses to challenge Müller's equation: 'we have . . . seen that animals are able to reason to a certain extent, manifestly without the aid of language' (p. 110). While in this sense his evidence had been arranged to show that there could be thought without language, he recognised the significance of words in 'carrying on a complex train of thought' (p. 110). Although 'the mental powers in some early progenitor of man must have been more highly developed than in any existing ape, before even the most imperfect form of speech could have come into use', Darwin emphasised the mutual interaction between language and the mind: 'we may confidently believe that the continued use and advancement of this power would have reacted on the mind itself, by enabling and encouraging it to carry on long trains of thought'. In this respect he suggested a subtle interrelationship between the 'continued use' of the 'vocal organs' and the development of the 'mental powers' as they act and react upon each other (p. 110).

In his discussions of the possible origins of language, Darwin draws on eighteenth-century theories of primitive man, as Alexander von Humboldt described him, as 'a singing creature, only associating thoughts with the tones'.[29] Adapting the various theories and ideas of his predecessors (discussed in more detail in the following chapter), Darwin concludes from a 'widely-spread analogy' that language 'probably' owes its origin to a process of sexual selection:

> primeval man, or rather some early progenitor of man, probably first used his voice in producing true musical cadences, that is in singing ... and we may conclude ... that this power would have been especially exerted during the courtship of sexes – would have expressed various emotions, such as love, jealousy, triumph – and would have served as a challenge to rivals. (p. 109)

For Darwin, the next step involved a process of onomatopoeic imitation of natural sounds, which he suggests represents a kind of primitive mode of symbolic communication. Darwin does not go so far as to suggest that the language of birds has a 'semantic' content, but he does observe that they have 'distinct warnings for danger on the ground, or in the air from hawks' (p. 110). Combined with the mocking proclivities of monkeys and 'vocal imitation' in birds, Darwin suggests that such animal capacities might explain 'the first step' towards articulate language (pp. 109–10). In an admittedly speculative theory, he concludes: 'may not some unusually wise ape-like animal have imitated the growl of a beast of prey, and thus told his fellow-monkeys the nature of the expected danger?' (p. 110).

CHAPTER 2

The Science of Language:
1755–1873

> Thro all the Woods they heard the charming noise
> Of chirping birds; and try'd to frame their voice,
> And *imitate*; thus *Birds* instructed *Man*,
> And taught him *Songs*, before their Art began.[1]

Philosophers and poets have often speculated on the natural, animal origins of human speech. While many remained sceptical of what Johann Gottfried Herder dismissed as the Lucretian 'monstrosity' of primitive man 'ap[ing] the nightingale', in the late eighteenth and nineteenth centuries there emerged a broad consensus that the first humans communicated through a form of musical proto-language that was closer to the expressive prosody of birdsong than it was to the grammatical discourse of modern societies.[2] This chapter explores the increasingly dominant view that sound preceded sense, and that poetry came before prose. I outline this theory as it developed from the works of eighteenth-century philosophers, such as Jean-Jacques Rousseau and James Burnett Lord Monboddo, to late nineteenth-century hypotheses on the origins of music, speech and language by Herbert Spencer and Charles Darwin.

The long nineteenth century witnessed a major shift in focus from the divine to the animal, passionate and sexual origins of language. As philosophers recognised significant continuities between birdsong and human speech, they also, however, increasingly turned their attention to the internal, mental faculties as the distinguishing marks of an evolved and uniquely human language. This chapter examines the political and ethical implications of a developing equation of language and thought in the long nineteenth century. The absence of language in animals was widely seen to reflect a lack of reason, reflection or even consciousness, and was (as it continues to be) covertly used to justify the ubiquitous mistreatment of 'dumb' creatures that Hardy decried as both illogical and inhumane, and 'in strictness a wrong' (*Later Years*, p. 138). Anticipating current forms of 'linguistic universalism', philologers throughout this period sought to uncover a defining set of mental capabilities unique to the human mind and therefore common to all peoples at all times and in all places. According to the same principle, however, a kind of creeping 'linguistic relativism' interpreted linguistic differences as reflecting or even determining differences in the minds of their speakers. Routinely, a small, elite group of white male intellectuals in Western societies deemed the 'inferior' speech of savages, women, the uneducated and other marginalised groups as reflecting a less highly developed or stunted mental capacity. If it is true, however, that thought is dependent on language, why then do poets, philosophers and human beings in general commonly experience the struggle and frustration of not being able to express their ideas in words? As they responded to these larger debates, scientists and poets in this period, from Wordsworth to Darwin, reflected on their own experiences and provided many of the richest insights into a subvocal 'language of the mind' – or 'mentalese', as it is now known.[3]

I

'Man's first language, the most universal and energetic language', declared Rousseau in *A Discourse on Inequality* (1754), 'and the only one he needed before it became necessary to make persuasive speeches to assemblies of men, is the cry of nature'.[4] While Rousseau did not wholly idealise the state of solitary, nomadic and inarticulate man, he did emphasise both the emotional force and usefulness of a cry that was the 'only' form of expression 'needed' in such a state. He encouraged his readers to 'suspend' their judgement of 'men in the state of nature' and to question whether the 'progress' of human 'knowledge' is 'an adequate compensation for the harm' that so-called civilised men routinely 'do each other as they learn of the good they ought to do each other' (p. 98). With its marked emphasis on the expressive power of inarticulate cries and highly sceptical attitude towards progress, Rousseau's theory of the origins of language were widely perceived as threatening the primacy of human language and therefore man's place in the order of things. As Herder would later famously say of another French philosopher, Étienne Bonnot de Condillac, and Rousseau respectively, 'the former turned animals into men and the latter men into animals' (*Two Essays*, p. 103).

In his posthumously published *Essay on the Origin of Languages* (1781), Rousseau expanded on many of the arguments originally set out in the *Discourse on Inequality*. 'The first languages', he argued, 'were singable and passionate before they became simple and methodical'.[5] While Rousseau did not suggest that 'verse, speech and singing' were 'initially the same thing', he did argue that they shared a 'common origin' and that they had gradually evolved into separate forms:

> The periodic recurrences and measures of rhythm, the melodious modulations of accent, gave birth to poetry and music along with language .... The first tales, the first speeches, the first laws, were in verse. Poetry was devised before prose. That was bound to be, since feelings speak before reason (*Two Essays*, pp. 50–1).

In this passage, Rousseau presents an early version of the theory of a 'musical proto-language'. A language composed of irregular rhythms, pauses and 'melodious modulations of accent', this earlier form of communication would 'deemphasize grammatical analogy for euphony, number, harmony, and beauty of sounds. Instead of arguments, it would have aphorisms. It would persuade without convincing, and would represent without reasoning' (*Two Essays*, p. 15). By contrast, 'modern tongues' had become 'more regular and less passionate'; in substituting 'ideas for feelings', language had become 'more exact and clearer', but also 'more prolix, duller and colder' (*Two Essays*, p. 16). If reason and grammar had developed in tandem with each other, man's language had in this process lost an alternative mode of signification – 'the sounds of a melody' which, Rousseau insisted, 'do not affect us merely as sounds, but as signs of our affections, of our feelings' (*Two Essays*, p. 59). Throughout the eighteenth and nineteenth centuries, philosophers commonly recognised this distinction between the sound and sense of words, and it was this 'reaction', not to 'thoughts but to syllables', in which Herder perceived the 'magic power of the orator, of the poet, that returned us to being children' (*Two Essays*, p. 98).

Anticipating Wordsworth, Coleridge and other Romantic poets, Rousseau reflected on the relationship between words and things, between the signifier and the thing signified. He compared the original 'language of nature' with the 'duller' and 'more prolix' languages of developed societies:

> Even in its mechanical part it would have to correspond to its initial object, presenting to the senses as well as to the understanding the almost inevitable impression of the feeling that it seeks to communicate .... Most of the root words would be imitative sounds or accents of passion, or effects of sense objects. It would contain many onomatopoeic expressions. (*Two Essays*, p. 15)

The first language would 'contain many onomatopoeic expressions', although the mimetic qualities of this language are also rooted in musical tones as 'signs of our affections, of our feelings' (p. 59). Such language is characterised not only by 'imitative sounds', but also by the 'accents of passion'; it is not simply that 'root words' would correspond to the object itself, but that the sound of the word would 'accent' and communicate the human 'feeling' inspired by these 'sense objects'. In this contribution to the 'onomatopoeic' theory of the origins of language, Rousseau draws a subtle distinction between nature and its 'impression' on the human mind that would prove crucial to the writings of the Romantic poets.

Rousseau's ambivalence with regard to human intellectual progress was inevitably met with accusations of hypocrisy from his critics. In the 1752 preface to his play *Narcisse*, he defiantly declared his intention to continue writing plays, novels and essays 'while at the same time saying all the ill I can about literature and those who practise it'.[6] In his classic study of Rousseau in *Blessings in Disguise; Or, the Morality of Evil* (1993), Jean Starobinski argues that such apparent contradictions are best understood in the context of Rousseau's insistence that the remedy, or at least the palliative, may only be extracted from the poison.[7] The cure for the arts can only be found in the arts themselves. Or, as Rousseau himself put it, we must look to 'perfected art for the cure of the ills that inchoate art (*l'art commencé*) inflicts on nature'.[8] For Starobinski, a curious instance in which Rousseau appears to achieve this ideal of 'perfected art' appears in his autobiographical *Confessions* (1782). At the first performance in court of his opera *The Village Soothsayer* (1792), Rousseau sits in among the crowd, observing the effects of his music on the audience and most especially its female members:

> From the first scene, which is truly a scene of touching naïveté, I heard high up in the lodges a murmur of surprise and applause unprecedented in performance of this genre. The growing ferment was soon perceptible throughout the hall and, as Montesquieu might put it, its effect only enhanced its effect .... All around me women who to me seemed as beautiful as angels spoke in half-whispers: 'This is charming, this is delightful. There is not a sound in it that does not speak to the heart.' The pleasure of giving emotion to so many kind people moved me to tears myself, and at the first duet, when I noticed that I was not the only person crying, I could no longer contain myself.
>
> I am nevertheless certain that at that moment the concupiscence of sex had much more to do with my feelings than did the vanity of the author, and surely if only men had been present I would not have been consumed, as I was continuously, by the desire to gather up with my lips the delicious tears that I caused to flow.[9]

For Starobinski, what is crucial about this episode is that Rousseau is employing 'the labour of art' in order to re-create those primordial sighs that were once spontaneously uttered beneath 'ancient oaks'.[10] A paradox to which Romantic poets would return repeatedly throughout their writings, the purpose of art is to recapture a state *before* art existed. With its pronounced sexual overtones, this passage also, however, raises deeper and more troubling questions about the power of music. More explicitly than in any of his philosophical writings, Rousseau here acknowledges the 'concupiscence of sex' and its intimate connection with the origins of human music, speech and language. As the rhythms of his own prose trace the 'gradual ferment' as it develops from a 'murmur of surprise' to 'half-whispers' to a climax of flowing 'tears', Rousseau draws attention to music's ability to, in his own phrase, 'persuade without convincing' (*Two Essays*, p. 15). Anticipating Darwin's theory of sexual selection, the passage also foreshadows Hardy's more ambivalent presentations of music and its effect upon heroines such as Tess Durbeyfield, who finds herself irresistibly drawn to Angel Clare's harp music 'like a fascinated bird' (*Tess*, p. 122).

Reviewed by the Scottish Enlightenment thinker Adam Smith in 1756, Rousseau's *Discourse on Inequality* and its essential arguments regarding the origin of music, speech and language reached Edinburgh and another crucial figure in this debate, Lord Monboddo.[11] If, as Herder insisted, Rousseau 'made human beings into animals', then Monboddo went considerably further in arguing that man originally existed in a state of nature practically indistinguishable from that of the primates. Indeed, the 'Orang Outang' (a term which generically referred to all primate species) so closely resembled human beings 'inside as well as outside' as to be counted as one and the same species.[12] Anticipating much of the vitriol that such arguments were likely to receive from eminent figures such as Samuel Johnson, Monboddo confided in his friend, James Harris, in 1772:[13]

> I believe that I shall be thought by many to have sunk our nature too low. For though nobody has a higher idea than I of Human Nature, when it is improved by the arts of Life and exalted by Science and Philosophy, I cannot conceive it – before the invention of language – to have been in a state much superior to that of the brute.
>
> In short the *mutum ac turpe pecus* of Horace is my notion of man in his natural and original state; and in support of my Philosophy, I have appealed to History – both ancient and modern – for proof of the brutal condition in which many nations have been found and are still to be found even though they have some use of speech. From which we may justly infer how much more abject and brutish their condition must have been before they had the use of speech at all.[14]

Conscious that he would be judged to have 'sunk' the human animal even lower in the scale than even Rousseau had dared, Monboddo, in direct contrast with his predecessor, emphasised the improving influence of the arts, sciences and philosophy. While he observes significant continuities between man and 'the brute', Monboddo offsets this argument by accentuating the contrast between the 'abject and brutish' condition of savages and the dramatically 'improved' status of a small, elite group of white male intellectuals in Western societies. For all that Monboddo's theories have been seen to anticipate modern arguments in both evolutionary science and the study of language, the philosopher's fascination with man's animal origins are counterbalanced, as Olivia Smith observes in her seminal study *The Politics of Language: 1791–1819* (1984), 'by an impulse to differentiate some men from the animal nature of the majority'.[15]

'Man ... did not, in his natural state, speak', declared Monboddo in *Of the Origin and Progress of Language* (1773–92), 'but he sung' (VI, pp. 136–7). In perhaps the most literal interpretation of the Lucretian myth, Monboddo cited the authority of 'an ingenious man' (I, p. 469), Thomas Blacklock of Edinburgh, who argued that 'the first language among men was *music*, and that, before our ideas were expressed by articulate sounds, they were communicated by tones, varied according to different degrees of gravity or acuteness ... which we first learned by imitation of the birds' (I, pp. 469–70). Monboddo builds on several existing theories of man's linguistic origins: firstly, the 'interjectional' theory, according to which language developed from the 'inarticulate cries' that human beings share with other animals; secondly, the 'musical' theory, which postulated that the first men learned to modulate these inarticulate sounds into 'musical tones' comparable to, if not directly derived from, the singing of birds; and thirdly, the 'onomatopoeic theory', which argued that the first human words were formed by imitating the sounds of the 'inanimate, as well as animated things' thus signified (I, pp. 493–4). More than any other figure in the eighteenth century, Monboddo recognised significant continuities between human and non-human utterances. He does not, however, simply suggest a resemblance between birdsong and human speech in general. More precisely, he emphasises the similarities between birdsong and primitive speech, while accentuating the differences between 'barbarous languages' and 'the regular languages of art' as developed in 'the several countries of Europe' (I, p. 499).

The Lucretian theory 'of the invention of music' was apparently 'confirmed' to Monboddo 'by what I learned from the wild girl that I saw in France' (I, p. 493). Marie-Angélique Memmie Le Blanc, 'The Wild Girl of

Champagne', was captured in Songy in France in 1731. Thought to have been of Native American ancestry, she was brought to Marseille in 1720. Following her escape to the forests in which she survived in a wild state, Marie-Angélique was eventually captured and, perhaps uniquely among feral children, learned to read and write as an adult. Monboddo conducted interviews with her and wrote a preface to the English edition of Marie-Catherine Hommasel-Hecquet's original pamphlet, *An Account of a Savage Girl, Caught Wild in the Woods of Champagne* (1768). In the preface, Monboddo notes the savage girl's proficiency in 'imitating the notes of singing birds, such as the nightingale, and that so naturally, as often to deceive' the inhabitants of the Chalon convent where the feral girl was temporarily placed.[16] Not only had she 'learnt to imitate the notes of birds, which was the only music known in her country', but her language, like the songs of birds, was also 'spoken all from the throat, with little use of the tongue, and none at all of the lips' (pp. viii, ix–x). Monboddo believed the girl to have originated from the Huron tribe, whose language, he insisted, bore the closest resemblance to the song of birds. Not only did the Huron peoples speak 'from the throat', but the 'music of savages' also had 'a very small compass'; the musical scale of the Hurons, according to Monboddo, was said not to 'rise above a fourth, the ordinary compass of the music of the birds, from which, in all probability, it was copied' (*Origin and Progress*, I, p. 473). Whether or not philosophers concurred with Monboddo's argument regarding birdsong, speech and language, the 'guttural' accents of savages and rustics were nevertheless routinely contrasted with the 'proper' pronunciation of 'polite' society throughout the long nineteenth century. As Mrs General explains to her young ward in Charles Dickens's *Little Dorrit* (1857), 'papa, potatoes, poultry, prunes, and prism, are all very good words for the lips'.[17] The speech of primitive peoples not only suggested a limited capacity for articulation but also, as we shall see, was widely seen to lack the inward, intellectual capacities that marked the languages of their 'civilised' neighbours.

II

Since Aristotle, linguists have broadly distinguished between the external speech of the voice (*logos prophorikos*) and the internal speech of reason (*logos endiathetos*).[18] Following this general tenet, Universal Grammarians throughout the eighteenth century presented language as a 'painting' or copy of the mind: 'la parole est une peinture de l'espirit'.[19] Although philosophers broadly recognised the capacity for vocal mimicry among songbirds and parrots, the 'lower' animals were generally seen to lack the power of reason and the ability to form abstract concepts widely perceived as the distinguishing marks of a uniquely human language. Since 'all general ideas are purely intellectual' and 'can only be introduced into the mind with the assistance of words', this essential principle explained, Rousseau argued, 'why animals cannot formulate such ideas and can never acquire that capacity for self-improvement which depends on them' (*Discourse on Inequality*, p. 95). Despite the fact that Rousseau openly acknowledged these apparent and unbridgeable differences, his depictions of primitive, singing man were perceived by Herder as obscuring both the nature and scale of those differences: 'the human species', Herder insisted, 'stands above the animals not by stages of more or less but in kind' (*Two Essays*, p. 108).

Herder begins his 'Essay on the Origin of Language' (1772) by stating his agreement with the general tenet that 'while still an animal, man already has language' (*Two Essays*, p. 87). For Herder, the 'most delicate chords of animal feeling' are struck for one common purpose: the cry, as Herder understands it, is 'a going out toward other creatures ... it calls for an echo from one that feels alike' (p. 87). However much theologians may insist upon the complexity and apparent design of 'our artful language' (p. 88), Herder insists that language did not arise from 'the grammar of God' but from 'the untutored sounds of free organs' (p. 96). Although 'Condillac, Rousseau and others did halfway find the road in that they derived the prosody and the song of the oldest languages from our cries of emotion', Herder insists that 'mere tones of emotion could never be the origin of language' (p. 137). As Rowland points out, the 'hidden forces' that Herder perceived 'dormant' or sleeping within the infant are central to his understanding of the qualitative differences between human language and 'the trills of the nightingale' (pp. 107, 136): 'children, like animals, utter noises of sensation. But is not the language they learn from other humans a totally different language?' (p. 99).[20] In a passage which foreshadows the imagery of Wordsworth, Coleridge and many other Romantic poets, Herder explains his theory: 'man manifests reflection when the force of his soul acts in such freedom that, in the vast ocean of sensations which permeates it through all the channels of the senses, it can, if I may say so, single out one wave, arrest it, concentrate its attention on it, and be conscious of being attentive' (p. 115). Commenting on this passage, Rowland neatly summarises that Herder perceives 'the distinctive feature of human beings' as 'something like the capacity for self-consciousness': not only does man uniquely possess a 'capacity to reflect', but also 'to be conscious of that act of reflection'.[21] Although he recognises the capacity for vocal mimicry among parrots and blackbirds, Herder insists that this unique capacity for reflection or awareness enabled human beings not simply to imitate the sounds of another animal but to consciously recognise that sound as the 'distinguishing mark' of the creature thus signified (p. 117). 'Parrots and starlings have learned enough human sounds', Herder concludes, 'but have they ever thought a human word?' (p. 126).

Although Herder insisted upon a difference of kind rather than degree between human and non-human utterances, his disagreement with figures like Rousseau does not, as Rowland dryly points out, 'prevent him from making frequent comparisons between primitive languages and animal sounds'.[22] 'Easterners have not entirely left behind bird language', Herder remarks, rather casually.[23] In his speech 'On the Education of Students in Language and Speech', Herder's arguments at once reflect and feed back into wider and politically charged debates regarding both primitive languages abroad and vernacular dialects at home:

> These animal sounds remain with some people and races throughout their entire lives. One has only to stand at a distance from which the sound of the voice and accent can be heard without the meaning of the words being conveyed: in some people one will hear the turkey, the goose, the duck; in many speakers it will be the peacock, the bittern; in pretentious dandies it will be the canary; it will be anything but the human voice.... Youths who have acquired this unpleasant dialect of merely animal sounds, whether they come from the cities or the country, should make every effort in school to acquire a human, natural speech possessed of character and soul and to rid themselves of their peasant or shrieking back-alley dialects. They should leave off the barking and yelping, the clucking and cawing, the swallowing and the dragging together of words and syllables and speak human rather than animal language.[24]

Placing this passage in the context of the 'methodological purification' of German speech in the late eighteenth century, Friedrich Kittler observes that vernacular speakers are here 'relegated to the mere animal'.[25] But the passage also sets up the problem that is the subject of this chapter: the problem of 'distance', by which the 'meaning of the words' is lost and strange or unfamiliar forms of speech consequently disregarded by the outsider as the gobbling of turkeys, the booming of bitterns or the singing of canaries. Listening from a distance, and preoccupied with their own cultural anxieties, philosophers such as Herder routinely interpreted and dismissed 'peasant and shrieking back-alley dialects' in this way. For all that Herder insisted upon a qualitative difference between 'animal sounds' and 'human language', various races and classes of human beings are frequently denied the inward, intellectual capacities – the 'character' and 'soul' – that, according to Herder's own logic, are what separates human from 'animal language'.

In Britain, the study of language was dominated throughout this period by a theory of Universal Grammar. According to the theory, the deep, structural resemblances between languages were key to understanding a unique set of mental capabilities intrinsic to the human mind: reason, reflection, the ability to form abstract concepts. One of the most prominent practitioners of Universal Grammar, James Harris, in *Hermes* (1751) turns his attention to '*that Grammar, which without regarding the several Idioms of particular Languages, only respects those Principles that are essential to them all*'.[26] Although all languages 'were fundamentally alike in that they represented the mind', they also, as Olivia Smith points out, 'were fundamentally different in the quality of mind and civilisation that they represented'.[27] Philosophers in this period broadly separated the mind into two basic faculties, 'reflection and sensation', and used these categories to separate human speakers into two general classes: 'those who think' and 'those who sense'.[28] As Smith broadly summarises, 'vulgar' speech was characterised by an inability 'to transcend the concerns of the present, an interest in material objects, and the dominance of the passions'.[29] This inability to look or think beyond present conditions and material wants represented the most 'degraded' form of human intelligence because, as Harris remarked, 'it is necessarily common to all *animal* Beings, and reaches even to Zoophytes, as far as they possess *Sensation*' (p. 113). Although primitivists might appear to challenge such hegemonic views of language, Rousseau's account of an original, musical proto-language, as Smith points out, conforms to this broad stereotyping of primitive languages: 'concrete terms, emotional expressions, syntactic simplicity, an abundance of metaphors, and a paucity of terms' are consistently seen to mark the speech of the uncivilised, the uneducated and other minorities.[30] 'Rather than challenge the basic construct of ideas about language', primitivists thus 'maintain it while arguing that primitive languages are of more value than was generally recognised'.[31] Responding to Smith's research, Leonora Nattrass shrewdly points out that this common characterisation of 'vulgar' speech as 'imbruted' in the material world lingers behind criticism of the so-called 'peasant poet' John Clare's 'descriptive' poetry.[32]

For all the apparent differences between Monboddo's theories of language and those of his contemporaries, his writings conform to the general separation of sense and reflection derived from his 'worthy and learned friend' James Harris (*Origin and Progress*, I, p. 8). This separation enabled him to draw distinctions not only between men and other animals, but also 'betwixt our animal and intellectual nature' (V, p. 363). Along the gradients of evolutionary and social progress, 'barbarous' nations are consistently seen to represent an intermediary link between the 'animal' and the 'intellectual' aspects of human nature: 'from savage men', writes Monboddo, 'we are naturally led to consider the condition of the brutes; betwixt whom and the savages there is such a resemblance, that there are many who will hardly admit of any difference' (I, p. 146). Although the 'vulgar among us' are seen to have derived some 'advantage' from 'being educated among thinking and speaking men', Monboddo deemed the working classes of his own country incapable of forming the abstract philosophical concepts widely perceived as the distinguishing mark of human 'intellect' (I, p. 162). Only an elite class of liberal philosophers were able to use and understand general terms, 'forms' wholly abstracted from the 'matter' or material objects (I, pp. 162–3). If the capacity for abstract thought separates man from the animals, the 'lower' classes were seen to 'make this abstraction of the matter from the form very clumsily, and, if I may be allowed to use the expression, leave always some of the matter *sticking* to the form' (I, pp. 162–3). Where they are able to show 'any clear conception' of a term 'denoting any general quality', this ability is restricted to terms that denote 'a *sensation*, as *sweet, bitter, painful, pleasant*'; in this respect, 'the vulgar may be said to continue children ... all their lives' (I, p. 96).

Since these 'ideas about language were applied by courts of law and members of Parliament to justify repressive measures', Smith observes that radical writers, such as Thomas Paine and William Cobbett, were presented with 'the difficult task of not only justifying the capabilities of the disenfranchised, but also of redefining the nature of language'.[33] Repeatedly throughout his *Grammar of the English Language* (1819), Cobbett insists that those trained in the art of polite speech do not by any means demonstrate a superior intellect or understanding. Wittily turning the arguments of his opponents back upon themselves, he draws the distinction between sound and sense:

> *Pronunciation* is learned as birds learn to chirp and sing. In some counties of England many words are pronounced in a manner different from that in which they are pronounced in other counties; and, between the pronunciation of Scotland and that of Hampshire the difference is very great indeed .... Children will pronounce as their fathers and mothers pronounce; and if, in common conversation, or in speeches, the matter be

good and judiciously arranged, the facts clearly stated, the arguments conclusive, the words well chosen and properly placed, hearers whose approbation it is worth having will pay very little attention to the accent. In short, it is *sense*, and not *sound*, which is the object of your pursuit.[34]

Although Cobbett's views on dialect are relatively simplistic in so far as they suggest a difference only regarding sound and pronunciation, unquestionably his bold, unflinching insistence upon the perfect *naturalness* of accents, learned from the nursery, encouraged labouring poets such as Clare: no matter how the words were sounded, the accent and style, Cobbett is at pains to show, were nothing to be embarrassed about. What matters is the *substance* of the argument.

All too frequently, Cobbett further implies, educated men put style over substance, dismissing the arguments of the 'vulgar' based purely on their accent and a use of dialect words which Cobbett so staunchly defends as good and proper Saxon English. Cobbett refused to countenance the idea that a use of dialect reflected a lesser intelligence; conversely, he observed a tendency among the 'learned' to repeat words musically, melodiously, without regard for their semantic or discursive content. 'Never attempt to *get by rote* any part of your instructions', he urges his readers:

> Whoever falls into that practice soon begins to esteem the powers of *memory* more than those of *reason*; and the former are despicable indeed when compared with the latter. When the fond parents of an eighth wonder of the world call him forth into the middle of the parlour to repeat to their visitors some speech of a play, how angry would they be if any one were to tell them that their son's endowments equalled those of a parrot or a bullfinch! Yet a German bird-teacher would make either of these more perfect in his species of oratory. It is this mode of teaching, which is practised in the great schools, that assists very much in making dunces of Lords and Country Squires. They '*get their lessons;*' that is to say, they repeat the *words* of it; but, as to its sense and meaning, they seldom have any understanding. (pp. 73–4)

Whatever 'species of oratory' the individual may be trained in, men of all classes – philosophers, politicians and poets – all too frequently demonstrated this tendency to mindlessly repeat the words of others. In the most learned circles, Cobbett perceived a widening and deeply troubling separation between word and idea, grammar and logical reasoning. Although scholars have recognised significant advances in the study of language in the following century, an ongoing dispute regarding the relationship between language and thought would continue to reverberate through the political and class conflicts of Victorian England.

III

The origin of language was a central preoccupation for Rousseau, Monboddo and other eighteenth-century philosophers. By the 1860s, however, the Paris Société Linguistique had banned all papers on the subject of linguistic origins.[35] In place of what the Scottish Enlightenment thinker Dugald Stewart dismissed as the 'etymological metaphysics' of the previous age, studies in comparative grammar established what was newly and more respectably known as 'The Science of Language' or 'The New Philology'.[36] Historians agree on two main distinctions between approaches to the study of language in the eighteenth and nineteenth centuries: the 'decisive turn', as Hans Aarsleff summarises, 'occurred when the philosophical, a priori method of the eighteenth century was abandoned in favour of the historical, a posteriori method of the nineteenth'.[37] Although respected philologers such as Max Müller rejected earlier 'conjectural' and 'metaphysical' approaches, the concern with origins did not so much disappear as move to another discipline. Investigations into the origins of music, speech and language became the subject not of philologists, but of zoologists and evolutionary scientists. And increasingly, these divided disciplines met in fierce public debate, most notably in the heated and bristling exchanges between Müller and Darwin.

Evolutionary scientists drew heavily from the speculative writings of Rousseau, Herder and other philosophers. Since 'variations of voice are the physiological results of variations of feeling', Herbert Spencer concluded his essay on 'The Origin and Function of Music' (1857) by stating that 'each inflection or modulation is the natural outcome of some passing emotion or sensation; and it follows that the explanation of all kinds of vocal expression, must be sought in this general relation between mental and muscular excitements'.[38] In *The Expression of the Emotions in Man and Animals* (1872), Darwin similarly observed the 'intimate' connection between 'emotional' speech and 'vocal music', though he disagreed with Spencer's theory in one key respect.[39] While Spencer argued that music had developed out of a kind of broken, interjectional or elliptical mode of human speech, Darwin maintained the opposite; he argued that 'the habit of uttering musical sounds was first developed, as a means of courtship, in the early progenitors of man, and thus became associated with the strongest emotions of which they were capable, – namely, ardent love, rivalry and triumph' (*Expression*, p. 87).

Many of the prejudices of their eighteenth-century predecessors persist in the writings of Spencer and Darwin. Since music represented an 'elaborated' form of emotional speech, Spencer was further led to emphasise the importance of education or cultivation in the production of 'the highest form of vocal music' (p. 417). According to the Spencerian trajectory of progress, the 'recitative' or the 'chant' preceded the melody or musical air:

> Between the comparatively level recitative of ordinary dialogue, the more varied recitative with wider intervals and higher tones used in exciting scenes, the still more musical recitative which preludes an air, and the air itself, the successive steps are but small; and the fact that among airs themselves gradations of like nature may be traced, further confirms the conclusion that the highest form of vocal music was arrived at by degrees. (p. 417)

While the 'dance-chants' of savages are deemed 'very monotonous' in character, the more varied, elaborate forms of melody distinguished the 'songs of the civilised races' (p. 414). Whereas Rousseau had earlier praised the more musical qualities of primitive languages, Spencer perceives the ancient tonal languages of the Chinese and the Hindoos as demonstrating their speakers' apparent failure to have progressed or 'advanced' beyond the ordinary recitative (p. 416).

Spencer argues that musical forms developed out of emotional speech; conversely, he also suggests that 'musical culture' had in turn influenced the character of speech in 'civilised nations' (p. 424). Since 'the Scotch' are 'confined almost exclusively' to their 'national airs', Spencer reasons that this 'limited range of musical expression' explains the 'unusually monotonous' character of the 'modulations and intervals in their speech' (p. 424). Not only does he observe the differences between nations in this respect, but Spencer further remarks on the difference between classes within the same nation: 'listen to the conversation of a servant-girl, and then to that of a refined lady', he writes, 'and the more delicate and complex changes of voice used by the latter will be conspicuous' (p. 381). Spencer is known to have directly influenced Hardy's 'metaphysical' approach to music and speech, but the class prejudices inherent within his arguments contrast starkly with the novelist's own appreciation of Dorset accents – that 'syllable UR' which Hardy so staunchly defends as 'probably as rich an utterance as any to be found in human speech' (*Tess*, p. 15).

In *The Descent of Man*, Darwin falls into familiar patterns of prejudice. 'The chief distinction in the intellectual powers of the two sexes', he declares, 'is shown by man's attaining to a higher eminence, in whatever he takes up, than can woman – whether requiring deep thought, reason, or imagination, or merely the use of the senses and hands' (p. 629). Judging by 'the hideous music admired by most savages', Darwin could understand, if he did not fully adhere to, the reasoning of those who 'argued that their aesthetic faculty was not so highly developed as in certain animals, for instance, as in birds' (p. 116). Since 'high tastes are acquired through culture, and depend on complex associations', he readily concludes, seemingly without question, that such pleasures cannot 'be enjoyed by barbarians or by uneducated persons' (p. 116). Although Darwin's writing is littered with such assumptions about the intellectual and artistic proficiency of women, savages and the uneducated, his writing shows an awareness of the *subjective* nature of aesthetic appreciation as evidenced by 'capricious changes of customs and fashions' from place to place, and from epoch to epoch (p. 116). Darwin cautions against judging such 'strange antics' as those displayed by birds in the mating season by 'the standard of man's taste' (pp. 245, 429). Throughout his writing, he emphasises, indeed celebrates, the diversity of taste in the avian world: 'it is a curious fact', he observes, 'that in the same class of animals, sounds so different as the drumming of the snipe's tail, the tapping of the woodpecker's beak, the harsh trumpet-like cry of certain water-fowl, the cooing of the turtle dove, and the song of the nightingale, should all be pleasing to the females of the several species' (p. 429). For Darwin, man and the lower animals are 'likewise capricious in their affections, aversions, and sense of beauty' (p. 116). What connects human beings with other species, and with each other, is not a common standard of beauty, but a 'sense of beauty' (p. 116). With greater humour and humility than many of his predecessors had erstwhile shown, Darwin concluded that there is simply no accounting for the taste of birds and humans alike.

IV

In his *Lectures on the Science of Language* (1861), Müller used the principles of comparative grammar to directly refute evolutionary arguments. Müller ridiculed the 'conjectural' or 'metaphysical' theories of eighteenth-century philosophers: the onomatopoeic theory, which contended that the first words arose through direct imitation of the formal aspects and sounds of the natural objects they sought to portray, was categorically rejected as the '*Bow-wow*' theory; the 'interjectional' theory, which argued that language had developed from expressive emotional cries, was similarly lambasted as the '*Pooh-pooh*' theory (I, p. 344). Following the established principles of comparative grammar, Müller argued that all human languages could be traced back to '*roots*', which he variously described as irreducible, chemical elements or, in a geological metaphor presumably aimed at Darwin, 'the granite' which 'underlies all other strata of human speech' (I, p. 343). Following the publication of *The Descent of Man* in 1871, Müller gave a second series of lectures 'On Mr Darwin's Philosophy of Language' (*Fraser's Magazine*, 1873). Accusations of anthropomorphism are used to quell all speculation about the mental powers of animals:

> [I]f there is a *terra incognita* which excludes all positive knowledge, it is the mind of animals. We may imagine anything we please about the inner life, the motives, the foresight, the feelings and aspirations of animals – we can *know* absolutely nothing . . . it may be so, or it may not be so, for there is no limit to an anthropomorphic interpretation of the life of animals. (lect. 2, p. 660)

Despairing of the 'innumerable anecdotes' (lect. 2, p. 660) about animals that appeared following Darwin's own practices in *Origin of Species*, he repeated his equation: '*there is no thought without words, as little as there are words without thought*'.[40]

Throughout the 1860s, Darwin was thinking over the problem; as he told Joseph Dalton Hooker in a letter of 1863, 'I rather doubt about man's mind and language' (*Correspondence*, XI, pp. 35–9). When Müller sent a copy of his second series of lectures to Darwin, his adversary replied politely and respectfully, though his annotations reveal more pointed criticisms. Beside Müller's emphatic statement that '*there is no thought without words, as little as there are words without thought*', Darwin wrote 'Monstrous sentence'; in an accompanying note, he explains his objection: 'One often utterly forgets name of man, animal or substance & yet can think about it definitely. – I am sure that I have when writing forgotten word for complex feeling. (for instance Emulation) & yet have had a definite notion in my head'.[41] While this note clarifies Darwin's scientific or intellectual objections, the remark does not entirely explain why he described Müller's sentence as 'Monstrous'. In many ways, the single word is more revealing than the accompanying note; it suggests that Darwin did not simply disagree with his opponent on intellectual grounds, but that his objection had a moral or ethical aspect. As John Muir would later summarise the full ethical implications of the arguments that Müller was making, the 'loveless doctrine' that 'animals have neither mind nor soul, have no rights that we are bound to respect' had broadly enabled the mistreatment of them as beings 'made only for man, to be petted, spoiled, slaughtered or enslaved'.[42]

Darwin expressed his private distaste; by contrast, the American linguist William Dwight Whitney emerged in the 1870s as Müller's most outspoken adversary. In subsequent editions of *The Descent of Man*, Darwin himself referenced Whitney as a 'distinguished philologist' whose 'judgement' he believed would carry 'far more weight on this point than anything I can say' (*Descent*, p. 111; n. 63). Like Darwin, Whitney recognised language 'on the grand scale' as 'an auxiliary of thought', but he also observed that Müller's equation had led to one of the philologer's 'worst paradoxes'; by Müller's own logic, 'an infant (*in fans*, not speaking) is not a human being, and ... deaf-mutes do not become possessed of reason until they learn to twist their fingers into imitation of spoken words'.[43] Radick has found it 'difficult to see just what Müller had done so to irritate Whitney', though the anger, I would suggest, is ethically and politically charged; it comes from the same place as Darwin's 'Monstrous sentence'.[44] While Darwin in the early 1860s had expressed his 'doubt about man's mind and language', in his subsequent works he began to pick apart Müller's equation from both sides. As I argued in Chapter One, Darwin's study of the 'Mental Powers' in *The Descent of Man* is structured to show that there may be thought without words – that monkeys, elephants and various animals 'may constantly be seen to pause, deliberate, and resolve' and this 'manifestly without the aid of language' (*Descent*, pp. 96, 110). Conversely, as he argued in *The Expression of the Emotions in Man and Animals*, gestural movements and facial expressions could in one sense be said to 'reveal the thoughts and intentions of others more truly than do words, which may be falsified' (p. 333). As scientists and poets debated these larger questions concerning the relationship between language and the mind, they also reflected on their own experiences of thinking, speaking and composing.

V

Centuries earlier, in *An Essay concerning Human Understanding* (1689), John Locke used the example of 'birds learning of tunes' to argue that human beings share basic cognitive functions in common with other animals:

> [T]he endeavours one may observe in them, to hit the notes right, put it past doubt with me, that they have perception, and retain ideas in their memories, and use them for patterns ... It cannot with any appearance of reason, be supposed (much less proved) that birds, without sense and memory, can approach their notes, nearer and nearer by degrees, to a tune played yesterday; which if they have no idea of in their memory, is now nowhere, nor can

be a pattern for them to imitate, or which any repeated essays can bring them nearer to. Since there is no reason why the sound of a pipe should leave traces in their brains, which not at first, but by their after-endeavours, should produce the like sounds; and why the sounds they make themselves, should not make traces which they should follow, as well as those of the pipe, is impossible to perceive.[45]

In a direct challenge to the Cartesian view of animals as machines devoid of reason and consciousness, Locke insists that the 'endeavours' that one may observe in birds 'to hit the notes right' demonstrate their ability to retain 'ideas in their memories' and to 'use them for patterns'. Locke's argument is primarily aimed at the 'senseless' reasoning of Cartesian philosophers, but his language goes further in suggesting a mode of thought that does not involve or depend on words: a mental image or 'pattern' of sound, the 'trace' of a tune imperfectly remembered. As recent scientific studies have increasingly turned their attention to the kinds of thinking that other species appear able to perform without the aid of words, they have also more deeply questioned whether language is truly the sole medium of human thought.

Most vociferously, de Waal disputes the longstanding 'assumption that language is at the root of human thought'.[46] In response to broad dismissal of 'anthropomorphic' accounts of animal behaviour throughout the nineteenth and twentieth centuries, de Waal notes countless scientific studies and experiments in which animals without any apparent linguistic ability in the human sense have been proven to perform complex cognitive tasks. Another keen observer of primate behaviour, Robert Yerkes, described the problem-solving capabilities of our closest, though apparently speechless, relative, the chimpanzee:

> Frequently I have seen a young chimpanzee, after trying in vain to get its reward by one method, sit down and reexamine the situation as though taking stock of its former efforts and trying to decide what to do next. Usually this pause, for what looks amazingly like consideration or reflection, is followed by an especially vigorous or determined attack upon the problem.[47]

In the behaviour of chimpanzees, octopuses, dolphins, crows and many other species as they appear to be working out the problem 'in their minds', de Waal perceives a 'hint at the kind of mental activity that we refer to as "thinking," even though its precise nature was (and still is) barely understood'.[48] 'One cannot', de Waal insists, 'watch a parrot successfully count up items in his head and still believe that the only thing these birds are good at is parroting'.[49] As Pepperberg concluded after studying Alex the parrot for three decades, 'for far too long, animals in general, and birds in particular, have been denigrated and treated merely as creatures of instinct rather than as sentient beings'.[50] Although de Waal does not dispute 'how special the language capacity is' or its importance as an auxiliary of thought, he remains deeply sceptical of the idea that animals, including human animals, 'need language in order to think'.[51]

The arguments of ethologists such as de Waal are supported by studies of the human mind in cognitive psychology. In *The Language Instinct: The New Science of Language and Mind* (1994), Stephen Pinker roundly dismissed 'the idea that thought is the same thing as language' as a 'conventional absurdity'.[52] He questions the reasoning of those philosophers who 'argue that since animals lack language, they must also lack consciousness' and 'therefore do not possess the rights of conscious beings'.[53] In response to the arguments of Bertrand Russel, Pinker argues that a dog 'may not be able to tell you that its parents were honest though poor, but can anyone really conclude from this that the dog is *unconscious*?'[54] With regard to the internal workings of the human mind, Pinker urges his readers to reflect on their own experiences:

> Think about it. We have all had the experience of uttering or writing a sentence, then stopping and realising that it wasn't exactly what we meant to say. To have that feeling, there has to be a 'what we meant to say' that is different from what we said.[55]

As scientists, philosophers and poets have acknowledged since time immemorial, experience dictates that words all too frequently fail to express all that is going on inside our heads. While 'any particular thought embraces a vast amount of information' rapidly transferred through the interconnecting 'thick cables' of the brain, any attempt to communicate that thought to another person is inevitably complicated by the fact that 'attention spans are short and mouths are slow'.[56] Not only can a speaker 'encode only a fraction of the message into words', but he or she also faces the added problem of having to rely on 'the listener to fill in the rest'.[57] Considering the comically ambiguous phrases that routinely appear in newspaper headlines ('Drunk Gets Nine Months in Violin Case'), Pinker concludes that the English language, or indeed any language, 'is hopelessly unsuited to serve as our internal medium of computation': 'if there can be two thoughts corresponding to one word, thoughts can't be words'.[58] Pinker disputes the assumption that animals that lack language also lack basic cognitive abilities. But he also calls into question a no less pervasive tendency to view linguistic differences between human beings as reflecting, or even determining, 'differences in the thoughts of their speakers'.[59] Adamantly opposed to the kind of linguistic relativism which led the American psychologist Benjamin Lee Whorf to conclude that the grammatical structure of the Hopi language reflected a fundamentally different concept of time, Pinker insists human beings the world over 'do not think in English or Chinese or Apache; they think in a language of thought'.[60] Tacitly acknowledging the longstanding link between the science and the politics of language that is the subject of this chapter, Pinker actively seeks to dislodge many of the intellectual and cultural biases which pervaded the study of language throughout the long nineteenth century.

In support of his arguments, Pinker cites the experiences of scientists and creative people who 'insist that in their most inspired moments they think not in words but in mental images'.[61] A visual artist working in a medium that in and of itself challenges the idea that thought is dependent on words, the sculptor James Surls claims to be able to 'manipulate the sculptures in his mind's eye ... putting an arm on, taking an arm off, watching the images role and tumble'.[62] Perhaps 'the most famous self-described visual thinker', Albert Einstein reflected on the 'combinatory play' at work within the mind of a physical scientist:

> The psychical entities which seem to serve as elements in thought are certain signs and more or less clear images which can be 'voluntarily' reproduced and combined.... This combinatory play seems to be the essential feature in productive thought – before there is any connection with logical construction in words or other kinds of signs which can be communicated to others. The above-mentioned elements are, in my case, of visual and some muscular type. Conventional words or other signs have to be sought for laboriously only in a second state, when the mentioned associated play is sufficiently established and can be reproduced at will.[63]

Einstein's description of the 'combinatory play' by which the 'elements in thought' may be '"voluntarily" reproduced and combined' echoes various accounts of the imagination by Coleridge, Wordsworth and many other writers in the long nineteenth century. It is not my intention in this book to interpret such accounts, as a scientist might interpret them, as evidence that proves or disproves a particular theory or hypothesis of mind; my intention is neither to substantiate nor to challenge, but rather to pay close, patient attention to how Coleridge, the Wordsworth siblings, Clare and Hardy described and understood their own creative practices. In exploring a mysterious and even now only vaguely understood 'language of the mind', these writers were inevitably led into wider philosophical and politically charged discussions about what may be going on inside the heads of various human and non-human others.

An interest in the processes of the mind during composition is a central, if not defining, aspect of Romantic poetry. Notoriously, Wordsworth's creative practices became the stuff of legend. In *Reminiscences of Wordsworth among the Peasantry of Westmoreland* (1882), H. D. Rawnsley painted a memorable picture of the poet 'continually murmuring his undersong' as he passed over field and woodland.[64] 'He would set his heäd a bit forrard', recalled one local resident interviewed by Rawnsley,

> And then he would start a bumming, and it was bum, bum, bum, stop; then bum, bum, bum reet down till t'other end, and then he'd set down and git a bit o' paper out and write a bit; and then he git up, and bum, bum, bum, and goa on bumming for long enough right down and back agean.[65]

Evidently disturbed by this strange, inhuman 'bumming and booing', the people of Westmoreland were said to the hear the sounds 'like a wild beast coming frat' rock' and that 'childer were scared fit to dëad amost'.[66] Entertaining as such accounts may be, critics have questioned their reliability. Even as they appear to confirm certain aspects of Wordsworth's perambulatory habits, Rawnsley's reminiscences may be seen to mark the beginning of what Andrew Bennett has termed 'the compositional myth of William Wordsworth'.[67] Partly a myth of the poet's own making, an idealised view of Wordsworth composing extemporaneously and out of doors has been seen as a glaring example of a pervasive and highly questionable 'ideology of Romantic composition'.[68] Angela Esterhammer summarises the recent critical trend: 'contemporary critics representing a variety of theoretical perspectives have called attention to the *constructed* quality of Romantic spontaneity'.[69] In *Revision and Romantic Authorship* (1996), Zachary Leader was among the first to dissect Romantic ideals of 'spontaneity', 'originality' and 'genius'; reflecting 'a preference for what comes naturally' and a 'concomitant devaluing of secondary processes', these ideas are seen by Leader as persisting in what he regards as the editorial 'primitivism' of Wordsworth's twentieth-century editors.[70] Michael O'Neill begins his article on Leigh Hunt with the overall assessment that 'spontaneous risings of originality were the result of much contrivance in the poetry of the Romantic period'.[71] In her seminal work *John Clare and the Place of Poetry* (2008), Mina Gorji has influentially argued that presentations of labouring poets as so many nightingales warbling their 'native woodnotes wild' have for too long obscured the degree of skill, agency and conscious craftsmanship exhibited in their writings.[72] Although these works have done much to draw attention to the studied and theatrical aspect of Romantic spontaneity, the critical emphasis on full conscious control seems at risk of propagating its own myth of authorial agency: a myth which has been criticised for assuming that writers can ever be fully conscious of the meaning of the texts they produce, and for sidelining or underplaying the reader's own role in interpreting and deriving meaning from those texts.[73] If Pinker's arguments and the testimonies of creative people are in any way to be believed, then even the most celebrated poets must inevitably struggle to fully realise or carry out their intentions – to say what they meant to say. And, similarly, even the most adroit readers must acknowledge the difficulties of fulfilling their side of the bargain – to fill in the rest. In the comically bewildered responses of the people of Westmoreland to Wordsworth's 'bumming and booing', there is hint of all that may be lost in attempting to communicate thoughts with others. And in the poet's own frequent allusions to a subvocal 'murmured' stage in composition, there is also a glimpse into the eternal human struggle to translate thoughts 'into strings of words, and vice versa'.[74] As they reflected on the pleasures and frustrations of the creative process, the writers discussed in the following chapters repeatedly referred to a language of thought that is patterned, shaped and rhythmically structured ('bum, bum, bum, stop'), but not, to adapt a phrase from Hardy, 'exactly worded' (*Tess*, p. 84).

CHAPTER 3

'Prelusive Notes'
Coleridge and the Wordsworths

> And what if all of animated nature
> Be but organic harps diversely framed,
> That tremble into thought, as o'er them sweeps
> Plastic and vast, one intellectual breeze,
> At once the Soul of each, and God of All?
> — Coleridge, 'The Eolian Harp' (1796)

Coleridge's famous question has been read to reflect his engagement with a wide range of philosophical theories (unitarianism, animal vitalism, Neoplatonism), drawn together in ways which deepen our sense of a shared origin or form of 'embryonic consciousness' connecting all forms of life and by extension all strands of human thought.[1] Coleridge's pun on that word 'tremble' perfectly captures the organic, seamless process by which a sensation, sound or feeling might *tremble* into thought, consciousness and self-awareness – an awareness which, as Coleridge swiftly indicates in the following stanza, is humbled by fear of God and recognition of its own human imperfection: 'For never guiltless may I speak of him, | The Incomprehensible!' (*Poetical Works*, I, ll. 46, 58–9). While Coleridge in 'The Eolian Harp' speculates wildly on 'the one life within us and abroad' (l. 26), crucially in the final stanza the poet shrinks back and distances himself from his own seditious musings or 'shapings of the unregenerate mind' (l. 55). Although Coleridge was in many ways more deeply engaged with larger philosophical questions surrounding birdsong, speech and poetry than either William or Dorothy Wordsworth, a deep suspicion of proto-evolutionary theory and cultural primitivism led Coleridge to recoil from those questions at critical moments throughout his literary career. Following a discussion of the political and cultural anxieties that inform Coleridge's pointed critique of his friend's views regarding the 'best part' of language, this chapter explores how Coleridge's ambivalence and anxieties are reflected in his rendering of the 'sweet jargoning' of birds in 'The Rime of the Ancyent Marinere' (*Poetical Works*, I, l. 362).[2]

While Coleridge puzzled over the philosophical questions raised in 'The Eolian Harp', Dorothy Wordsworth's close, detailed descriptions of the sounds and songs of birds are neither assimilated to nor constrained by any larger philosophical theory regarding the sentience of other creatures and our human relation to them. As well as providing both her brother and Coleridge with a rich and plentiful stock of natural sights and sounds that unquestionably enlivened the writings of both poets, Dorothy's journals also constitute a strikingly original, at once finely detailed and openly speculative approach that would become increasingly significant to both writers and scientists in the coming century. While Coleridge's writing is marked by an imagination striving to select, reconcile and harmonise all he sees and hears with larger preconceived theories and conjectures, this *a priori* method of interpretation is directly at odds with the *a posteriori* approach that characterises Dorothy's own distinctive way of thinking and writing about the natural world. Marked by radically defamiliarising similes that compare widely different and incongruous natural forms, sights and sounds, Dorothy's writing in many ways illuminates the paradox to which both her brother and Coleridge return time and again throughout their writings: ever alert to the clear and irrevocable formal differences that separate birdsong from the human art of speech, Dorothy's mode of comparison also points to underlying and surprising analogical resemblances that connote a shared and common origin.

As he responded to his sister's vivid impressions and the metaphysical arguments in which he found his friend so deeply embroiled, William Wordsworth was led into larger and politically charged discussions regarding all that may be going on inside the heads of various human and non-human others. Focusing particularly on Wordsworth's rewriting of the Lucretian myth in the Boy of Winander passage, this chapter explores how the poet at times engages with, but at others radically departs from, theories of language in late eighteenth and early nineteenth centuries. Drawing on his own experiences of walking, talking and composing with his sister, Wordsworth, throughout his writing, demonstrates his fascination with the musical origins of language and with a musical or 'murmured' subvocal language of thought. Although the poet's changing attitudes led him to recast and revise many of the views expressed in his early writings, my own approach in this chapter focuses on the continuities and tragic ironies that connect Wordsworth's early and late writings on sound, music and poetry: placing his late sonnets in the context of one of the most distressing periods in Wordsworth's life, I argue that the poet intuited modern medicine in using music and poetry to console and commune with a much-beloved, though sadly altered, sister following Dorothy's mental deterioration in the 1830s. As he reflected on the changes that he witnessed taking place in his sister, in his late sonnets Wordsworth dwells deeply on this final and tragic return to music as a form of 'divine communion'.[3]

I

While philosophers recognised significant continuities between birdsong and human speech, animal 'voices' were widely seen to lack the rational, reflective and self-conscious intelligence necessary to the production of human language. As is well known, the relationship between language and thought represents a 'persistent area of concern' in Coleridge's life and writing.[4] In a letter to William Godwin dated September 1800, Coleridge first raised the concern that would resurface repeatedly at critical moments throughout his intellectual career:

> 'Is Logic the *Essence* of Thinking?' in other words – Is *thinking* impossible without arbitrary signs? & – how far is the word 'arbitrary' a misnomer? Are not words &c parts & germinations of the Plant? And what is the Law of their Growth? – In something of this order I would endeavour to destroy the old antithesis of *Words & Things*, elevating, as it were, words into Things, and living Things too.[5]

A. C. Goodson perceives Coleridge's seemingly 'offhand question' as anticipating an almost Chomskyan notion of universal syntactic principles intrinsic to the human mind and common to all peoples throughout time and across cultures.[6] At the same time that Coleridge insists upon the common roots of all languages, however, the organic imagery implies a degree of variety, and inequality, in their growth. As Goodson further observes, a series of 'value judgments' about national languages and their speakers recur repeatedly throughout Coleridge's writings and reflect the political conflicts and biases of the age in which he wrote.[7] This essential conflict between linguistic universalism and linguistic relativism sharpened as the tensions with Wordsworth intensified. To Wordsworth's claim that he had chosen rustic subjects 'because such men hourly communicate with the best objects from which the best part of language is originally derived' (*Prose*, I, p. 124), Coleridge responded in no uncertain terms:

> It is more than probable, that many classes of the brute creation possess discriminating sounds, by which they can convey to each other notices of

such objects as concern their food, shelter, or safety. Yet we hesitate to call the aggregate of such sounds a language, otherwise than metaphorically. The best part of human language, properly so called, is derived from reflections on the acts of the mind itself. It is formed by a voluntary appropriation of fixed symbols to internal acts, to processes and results of imagination, the greater part of which have no place in the consciousness of uneducated man; though in civilised society, by imitation and passive remembrance of what they hear from their religious instructors and other superiors, the most uneducated share in the harvest which they neither sowed nor reaped.[8]

Coleridge's comments on the 'discriminating sounds' of 'the brute creation' scarcely register the deep, albeit mysterious, animal agency that he had earlier glimpsed in the 'bright, bright eyes' of nightingales ('their eyes both bright and full') ('The Nightingale', *Poetical Works*, I, l. 67). For Coleridge, such creatures categorically lack the kind of self-consciousness or awareness that Herder similarly perceived as a unique and defining human characteristic: the 'best part' of human language is derived from an ability to reflect 'on the acts of the mind itself', though the imagination is more particularly defined, in distinctly Coleridgean terms, as 'that synthetic and magical power' by which the poet 'diffuses a tone, and spirit of unity' through 'the balance or reconciliation of opposite or discordant qualities' (*Biographia Literaria*, II, ch. 14, p. 16). Returning to and revolving in his mind the central question of the 'one life within us and abroad', Coleridge here implies that 'unity' is not in the material world itself, but in the human mind that combines and reconciles its discordant elements, and ultimately seeks to discover unity with and within that world.

Although Coleridge begins by affirming a qualitative difference between the voices of animals and 'human language, properly so called', his ensuing comments on 'the consciousness of uneducated man' risk relegating the rustic to scarcely more than brute status: lacking the 'best part' of human language, the rustic's 'scanty vocabulary' is confined to 'the few things, and modes of action, requisite for his bodily conveniences' (*Biographia Literaria*, II, ch. 17, p. 53). While the 'uneducated' classes of British society may possess 'a number of confused general terms' (II, ch. 17, p. 53), those terms have mainly been derived from passive imitation of their social superiors. In further proof of this argument, Coleridge cites the 'extreme difficulty' which 'our most zealous and adroit missionaries' had experienced in finding 'words for the simplest moral and intellectual processes in the languages of uncivilised tribes' (II, ch. 17, p. 54). Although Coleridge's writing demonstrates his ongoing preoccupation with 'the one life within us and abroad', a contrary impulse seeks to demarcate clear, fixed and fundamental differences – between human beings and other animals, between civilised and uncivilised tribes, between educated and uneducated men, and, most importantly, on each and all of these grounds, between himself and Wordsworth.

In the *Biographia Literaria*, Coleridge essentially accuses Wordsworth of using the language of rustics in much the same way that poets, prophets and seers have since time immemorial used the language of birds: the poet interprets and to this extent appropriates rustic speech for his own purposes. If it is true, however, that Wordsworth speaks through and for the rustic figures presented in his poetry, then it is equally the case that Coleridge, no less than his friend, reads and represents the minds of others according to his own intellectual biases. In some particularly supercilious comments on 'the peasantry of North Wales' (*Biographia Literaria*, II, ch. 17, p. 45), Coleridge begins to resemble one of Wordsworth's 'badgering' narrators: strangers to the rustic world who persist in viewing that world through their own cultural lens.[9] Time and again in Wordsworth's poetry, the poet's own views and assumptions, however well-intentioned, are surprised and cast into doubt by the unexpected and often startling responses of the human characters encountered on the public roads and byways. In perhaps the most memorable example, a discharged soldier responds to the young poet's entreaties that he 'ask for timely furtherance and help' (*The Prelude*, IV, l. 491):

> At this reproof,
> With the same ghastly mildness in his look,
> He said, 'My trust is in the God of Heaven,
> And in the eye of him that passes me!' (IV, ll. 492–5)

In such startling moments as these, the perspective is unexpectedly reversed: it is no longer simply the poet who looks, analyses and comes to his own conclusions regarding the 'ghastly mildness' of a figure apparently resigned to the poverty of his fate, but the soldier, and the crux of Christian values that he represents, who meets and casts his own judgement upon 'the eye of him that passes me!' Challenging the assumptions of well-meaning missionaries and young idealistic poets, rustic characters in such moments abruptly take both poet and reader aback. Appearing to both acknowledge and apprehend the generalising tendencies inherent within larger philosophical theories regarding 'Man, Nature and Society', Wordsworth's speculations are continually interrupted and undermined by encounters with individuals who resist categorisation and defy expectations.

II

In *Coleridge and the Uses of Division* (1999), Seamus Perry has memorably described Coleridge as 'a man in two minds about which of two minds a man should be in'.[10] An 'intelligence keenly aspiring to the very greatest and most comprehensive kind of coherence', Coleridge's 'real, though ruinous, kind of genius' has nevertheless appeared to be characterised by division and 'double-mindedness', from the 'antithetical, self-revising texture of the notebooks' to the openly discursive nature of his 'conversation' poems.[11] Although birdsong is sometimes praised as an idealised form of communication to which the poet may only aspire, this aspiration is typically accompanied by a sudden recoil at the fear of the poet's own descent into inarticulacy, incoherence and the loss of a uniquely human consciousness. In 'The Rime of the Ancyent Marinere', Coleridge's ambivalence is centred in a single word. When 'sweet sounds' arise from the mouths of the dead crew, their voices intermingle with the 'sweet jargoning' of birds (*Poetical Works*, I, ll. 352):

> Around, around, flew each sweet sound,
> Then darted to the sun:
> Slowly the sounds came back again,
> Now mix'd, now one by one.
>
> Sometimes a dropping from the sky
> I heard the Lavrock sing;
> Sometimes all little birds that are
> How they seem'd to fill the sea and air
> With their sweet jargoning,
>
> And now 'twas like all instruments,
> Now like a lonely flute;
> And now it is an angel's song,
> That makes the heavens be mute.
>
> (*Poetical Works*, I, ll. 354–66)

Tracing its complex etymology, Robert Stark has observed the various associations surrounding the word 'jargon' which come into play in Coleridge's poem: originally derived from the old French word for birdsong *jargoun*, the word was introduced into English by Medieval writers such as Chaucer and John Gower.[12] In Gower's *Confessio Amantis* (1390), the term is used to accentuate the strange, shrill and unintelligible speech of Philomela following her rape and the violent removal of her tongue by Tereus, before her metamorphosis into a nightingale: 'Bot sche with al no word mai soune, | Bot chitre and as a brid jargoune'.[13] Mutilated and rendered incapable of sounding a single human word, the heroine may only express her suffering through the inhuman, inarticulate, though passionate and powerfully evocative music of the nightingale. As John Livingston Lowes observes in his detailed analysis of the 'genesis' of Coleridge's poem in *The Road to Xanadu* (1927), the poet certainly read Gower and is likely to have derived from him both his description of the 'sweet jargoning' of birds and his reference to the 'lavrock' (amended by Coleridge to its modern and more familiar name, 'skylark', in 1800).[14] While Philomela's tongue is violently cut out and her speech pitifully reduced to the garbled notes of the nightingale, the incantations of Medea, by contrast, demonstrate her ability to ventriloquise and translate between the various languages of birds and of men:

> Sche made many a wonder soun,
> Sometime lich unto the cock,
> Sometime unto the Laverock,
> Sometime kacleth as a Hen,
> Sometime spekth as don the men:,
> And riht so as hir jargoun strangeth
> In sondri wise hir forme changeth.
>
> (*Gower*, V, ll. 4098–104)

Through a series of surprising and incongruous rhymes (notably 'hen' and 'men'), Gower's language draws attention to how the slightest of phonetic changes to the sounds of our words can dramatically alter their sense. With that rather garbled alliteration of 'kacleth' and 'spekth', the poem hints at the ways in which the inarticulate utterances of birds may be imitated, lisped and transformed into human words. As Gower underscores in those final few lines, the power to sound those words is what makes us human: the development of language is key to the transformation of the animal into the human form. With its two contrasting myths of Philomela and Medea, Gower's poem, however, presents a profoundly ambivalent view of human linguistic progress: the loss of articulate speech may signal Philomela's descent into inarticulacy, repression and disempowerment, but it also offers Medea liberation and transcendence, an ability to communicate in the original, musical and, in this special sense, *poetic* jargon of the gods.

Unquestionably, the incantations of Medea provide a rich and powerful source for the transformations that take place in Coleridge's poem ('sometimes . . . sometimes . . . and now . . . and now'). In a classic article exploring the relationship between 'actual experience and the recounting of experience' as explored through the mariner's reverie, Raimonda Modiano noted the 'unreal' quality of the similes deployed in this passage: since 'there are no skylarks on the ocean', Modiano observes that 'the terms of this rich metaphoric exchange' appear rather derived from the 'shore world' of the mariner's auditor, the Wedding Guest.[15] In this respect, the mariner's story appears as 'a composite of his past and present, of the time of his voyage and the time of dialogue about it'.[16] Through his use of the word 'lavrock' and other archaic expressions, Coleridge further underscores the estranging power of words as historical entities: although language may have originated in musical tones and onomatopoeic expressions, phonetic shifts inevitably transform words into arbitrary signs which bear little or no resemblance to the natural sights and sounds they once stammered and lisped. While the 'sweet jargoning' of birds might in this respect appear to signal the soul's return to an original, sensual and universal language, it also connotes death, inarticulacy and the loss of a uniquely human consciousness. Whereas Medea is literally able to shift between forms and languages, Coleridge's 'supernatural' poem is more ambiguous: he deliberately leaves it unclear whether the souls of the dead have actually passed into the 'sweet jargoning' of birds, or whether the mariner, in his reverie, guilt and grief, merely mistakes and misconstrues these simple avian utterances for the voices of his departed crew. Recalling the imagery and the intellectual crisis of the 'The Eolian Harp', these sounds are compared to 'all instruments' before they subside into a more plaintive 'lonely flute': seeming to offer the mariner a momentary glimpse into the 'one life' of nature, the sounds may alternatively be read to indicate the profound *loneliness* of a human soul haplessly seeking unity with and within an irrevocably strange and incomprehensible world.

Although 'The Rime of the Ancyent Marinere' is certainly not birdsong or music, the obscurity of Coleridge's language has led many readers to feel that his poetry often subordinates the sense to the sound of his words. As Charles Lamb described the irresistible pull of the mariner's reverie, the poem 'dragged me along like Tom Piper's magic Whistle'.[17] Famously, William Hazlitt levelled a more pointed criticism at 'Kubla Khan': since 'we could repeat these lines to ourselves not the less often for not knowing the meaning of them', the poem confirmed to Hazlitt that 'Mr Coleridge can write better *nonsense* verses than any man in English'.[18] As Wordsworth and other readers early recognised, Coleridge's ballad represents a major experimentation with poetic metre and the expressive potential of sound. Loosely following the 'common metre' of the traditional ballad (iambic tetrameter followed by an iambic trimeter line), Coleridge often departs from this bass rhythm. The final iamb of that first line is replaced with a spondee which conveys our sense of the mariner's prolonging, savouring, relishing the sounds he hears ('A*round*, a*round*, flew *each sweet sound*'). Conversely, the poet often switches the stress to the first syllable of the first iamb in order to slow down the line ('*Slow*ly the sounds came back again'). Although the poem is based on the traditional ballad stanza of end rhymes (*abcb*, sometimes stretched to *abcbdb*), Coleridge complicates the pattern, notably in the second stanza (*abccb*), which further picks up on an imperfect rhyme of 'air' and 'are': the inexact echoing here perfectly captures the eery surrealism of a poem which combines supernatural visions with detailed descriptions of material, living things and which leaves the reader uncertain whether they are hearing a divine language of the heavens or the simple utterances of birds. In that crucial line, the conventional pattern of end rhymes further tempts the reader to elongate the last syllable of the birds' 'sweet jargoning'. As 'the language of birds' seems awkwardly fitted to the metre here, Coleridge deepens our sense of a hidden meaning behind these utterances: an incipient mode of communication which may seem on the very brink of breaking into words, birdsong remains a sensual, inscrutable mode of expression which we can neither fully articulate nor comprehend in our own tongue.

Although 'jargon' was closely associated with a richer, stranger and more musical form of utterance in the old English texts with which Coleridge was familiar, the responses of his critics hint at the 'conceptual transformation' which the word underwent in the eighteenth century: as Stark points out, in this period 'jargon' became more closely associated with the 'opaque', 'abstruse' and 'overly specialised' language of intellectual elites.[19] Coleridge was certainly familiar with this more modern, more derogatory sense of the word. In his marginal notes, his use of the word is colloquial, quick and biting: 'celebrated astrologers' are summarily dismissed as 'sincere believers in their own jargon'.[20] In its extensive use of archaic terms such as 'lavrock' and 'jargon', Coleridge's poetry enacts the process by which our own words may lose their meaning over time and descend into sounds unrecognisable to modern ears: as the original significance of the word 'jargon' was no longer recognised by readers such as Hazlitt, the utterances of birds may sound like nonsense not because they *are* nonsense, but because they speak a language we no longer understand. Perhaps more so than Wordsworth or any other poet of the Romantic period, Coleridge recognised the expressive potential of sound, rhythm and metre in both conveying and provoking complex emotive and psychological states beyond the ordinary bounds of human consciousness: his poems twist language into rhythms and sounds, drag their readers along against their will and drive them to repeat, relish and reiterate words musically, melodiously, without any clearer grasp of their semantic or discursive sense. Constantly stepping back from his own musings and slyly anticipating the responses of his critics, Coleridge's 'self-revising' intelligence once again shrinks back to cast a critical eye upon the philosopher's tendency to be deceived by his own jargon and to blow metaphysical 'bubbles that glitter as they rise and break | On vain Philosophy's aye-babbling spring' ('The Eolian Harp', *Poetical Works*, I, ll. 56–7).

III

'She gave me eyes, she gave me ears', wrote Wordsworth of his sister Dorothy in 'The Sparrow's Nest' (*Poems in Two Volumes*, 1807).[21] While Coleridge throughout his poetry ruminates on metaphysical theories regarding the 'one life within us and abroad', there can be little doubt that Dorothy provided her brother with an alternative way of looking, listening and responding to the natural world. No less than Coleridge, Dorothy acknowledges the human tendency to anthropomorphise or, to use her own word, to 'people' the sunbeams with human moods and emotions.[22] Ever alert to the ways in which her own imagination gives shape and colour to that which she perceives, Dorothy does not, however, present the natural world as insentient, devoid of feelings and moods of its own. Through the agentic and animating terms in which she describes the 'impatient shout' of a thrush singing in the orchard at Grasmere, the 'bemazed' expression of a young bird thrown from its perch by strong winds, and the 'very busy' activities of swallows that made their nest by her bedroom window, Dorothy imbues the natural word with an active and sympathetic, albeit elusive, animal agency (*Journals*, pp. 112, 110, 111). While Coleridge's broad, sweeping dismissal of the 'discriminating sounds' of the 'brute creation' remain difficult to reconcile with his poetic evocations of the nightingale's 'fast thick warble' ('The Nightingale', *Poetical Works*, I, l. 44), Dorothy's descriptions of birdsong are neither incorporated with nor inhibited by any larger all-encompassing theory regarding the minds of other creatures. Although Dorothy was not by any means herself a proponent of the theory of evolution, she was what Darwin might have called an 'excellent observer' (*Descent*, p. 408): her close, detailed and openly speculative musings on the 'chearful undersong' of robins in winter foreground an *a posteriori* way of thinking and writing about the natural world that would become increasingly significant in the following century (*Journals*, p. 72).

Following Pamela Woof's highly influential *Dorothy Wordsworth, Writer* (1988), critical studies have drawn attention to Dorothy's extensive, if somewhat haphazard, reading in science and natural history, Gothic literature and poetry.[23] Drawing together different ways of describing nature in both science and art, Dorothy's own writing tests their ability to fully capture the complexity of the world they seek to represent. Her early writings bear a close resemblance to White's *Natural History of Selborne*.[24] A colourful description of the holly trees 'capriciously bearing berries' in the Alfoxden Journal, for example, is immediately followed by a scientific 'Query': 'Are the male & female flowers on separate trees?' (*Journals*, p. 141). As her writing progresses, Dorothy's mode of questioning and querying becomes more idiosyncratic. Her attention turns to subtle variations of colour, temperature and weather, and our human appreciation (or lack of appreciation) of those changes: 'a perfectly Cloudless sky: N.B. is it often so?' (*Journals*, p. 94). The small and seemingly insignificant suffix '-ish' emerges as a distinctive feature of her writing, which signals her sense of the approximate nature of her own language: 'the copses green*ish*, hawthorn green' (*Journals*, p. 93). Increasingly, Dorothy develops her own particular style of mixed metaphors and similes that produce radically defamiliarising comparisons: 'the trees almost *roared*', she writes, 'and the ground seemed in motion with the multitudes of dancing leaves, which made a rustling sound distinct from that of the trees' (*Journals*, p. 143). Natural phenomena are often described with this rather disorientating sense of their strangeness and mutability, seen at different times and from different perspectives. 'A bird at the top of the crags' that was 'flying round & round' looked to Dorothy 'in thinness & transparency, shape & motion, like a moth' (*Journals*, p. 95). The crows that she watched growing 'white as silver' in the sunshine seemed 'like shapes of water passing over the green fields' (*Journals*, p. 87). With that striking simile 'like shapes of water', Dorothy hits on a central paradox to which her brother returns repeatedly throughout his writing: natural forms appear mutable, mysterious and in many ways unknowable, but also fluidly connected and derived from the same original, elemental forces.

Throughout her writing, Dorothy actively draws attention to the shaping power of the human imagination. Intermittently, she catches and draws herself back from the brink of anthropomorphism: 'that holly tree', she acknowledges, 'had a beauty about it more than its own' (*Journals*, p. 94). While she acknowledges this proclivity to project her own thoughts and emotions onto nature, Dorothy does not conform to the kind of Cartesian philosophy that reduced animals to machines devoid of reason or consciousness, or to a Coleridgean mistrust of the appearances of nature as merely the reflection of the imagination's own shapings. Nature is always in her writing a thing in itself and in its own right, however darkly glimpsed by even its most patient and excellent observers. Her writing everywhere demands sympathy for the complex and precarious lives of birds:

> I spoke of the little Birds keeping us company – & William told me that that very morning a Bird had perched upon his leg – he had been lying very still & had watched this little creature, it had come under the Bench where he was sitting & then flew up to his leg, he thoughtlessly stirred himself to look further at it & it flew onto the apple tree above him. It was a little young creature, that had just left its nest, equally unacquainted with man & unaccustomed to struggle against Storms & winds. While it was upon the apple tree the wind blew about the stiff boughs & the Bird seemed bemazed & not strong enough to strive with it. (*Journals*, p. 110)

The description recalls a similar episode in Erasmus Darwin's *Zoonomia* (1794–6), a copy of which the Wordsworths obtained in 1798.[25] In an extended discussion of animal 'instinct', Darwin argued that various species of birds possessed 'acquired' knowledge which they were able to pass down to the next generation through a form of 'artificial language'.[26] The apparent guilelessness of young birds was a case in point. 'From the difficulty of acquiring the confidence of old animals' and comparative 'ease of taming young ones', Darwin concluded that 'the fear' which 'they all conceive at the sight of mankind' appeared to be 'an acquired article of knowledge' (I, p. 158). Rather than using the example as evidence for a particular hypothesis regarding animal instinct and intelligence, Dorothy's writing expresses sympathy with a fellow creature struggling to contend, from a young age, with hostile and unpredictable forces. As Woof observes, Dorothy's journals present a 'general sense of someone alive to circumstance but at the mercy of it, and, like "Birds & Beast", grateful for "this one day's security", and never unaware that the night is stormy'.[27]

Whereas Coleridge increasingly focused on the qualitative differences between the voices of animals and 'human language, properly so called', Dorothy's own writing pays close attention to the emotional and social aspects of voice that human beings share with other animals. She recounts the story of Barbara Wilkinson's Turtle Dove, for example:

> Barbara is an old maid. She had 2 turtle Doves. One of them died the first year I think. The other bird continued to live alone in its cage for 9

years, but for one whole year it had a companion & daily visitor, a little mouse that used to come & feed with it, & the Dove would caress it, & cower over it with its wings, & make a loving noise to it. The mouse though it did not testify equal delight in the Dove's company yet it was at perfect ease. The poor mouse disappeared & the Dove was left solitary till its death. It died of a short sickness & was buried under a tree with a funeral ceremony by Barbara & her maiden & one or two others. (*Journals*, p. 60)

The story is modelled on the kind of anecdotal accounts lately popularised in natural historical works, notably the Comte de Buffon's *Natural History of Birds* (1770–83). These case studies are often presented as natural oddities, curiosities and sources of light entertainment, although this lighter style also appears to have provided scientists with opportunities to speculate, more freely and experimentally, on animal cognition. Dorothy's intimate portrayal of the dove as it appears to 'caress' the mouse, 'cower over it with its wings' and 'make a loving noise to it' is deftly counterbalanced by the comic touches by which she distances herself from sentimental interpretations (the mouse, she swiftly informs us, 'did not testify equal delight in the Dove's company'). In the distinctive handing of narrative that Lucy Newlyn perceives as characteristic of her writing, Dorothy draws parallels between the mouse, the dove and the doting maid seen performing the funeral service with just 'one or two others' at the story's close.[28] Loneliness, loving noises and grief – these are the sounds and experiences which, in her brother's words, 'prolong the endless chain | Of Joy and grief, of pleasure and of pain'.[29]

Rather than imposing human emotions and values on the animal world, Dorothy's writing may be seen to cultivate sympathy for sentient creatures equally alive and vulnerable to the workings of chance and change. On one fateful morning in the summer of 1802, she awoke to find the nest of a family of swallows in ruins:

> I looked up at my Swallow's nest & it was gone. It had fallen down. Poor little creatures they could not themselves be more distressed than I was I went upstairs to look at the Ruins. They lay in a large heap upon the window ledge; these Swallows had been ten days employed in building this nest, & it seemed to be almost finished – I had watched them early in the morning, in the day many & many a time & in the evenings when it was almost dark I had seen them sitting together side by side in their unfinished nest both morning & night. When they first came about the window they used to hang against the panes, with their white Bellies & their forked tails looking like fish, but then they fluttered & sang their own little twittering song. As soon as the nest was broad enough, a sort of ledge for them they sate both mornings & evenings, but they did not pass the night there. I watched

them one morning when William was at Eusemere, for more than an hour. Every now & then there was a feeling motion in their wings a sort of tremulousness & they sang a low song to one another. (*Journals*, p. 115)

In the low 'twittering song' of swallows and 'sort of feeling motion in their wings', Dorothy registers an expression of complex emotions and social and familial bonds. Here, as elsewhere throughout her journals, she draws implicit analogies between the tremulous lives of birds and the no less tremulous lives of human beings. Undoubtedly, Dorothy's descriptions of the swallows are coloured by her own personal emotions and worries, particularly following her brother's marriage to Mary Hutchinson and the consequent disruption caused to her domestic life. 'O beautiful place!', she wrote upon the eve of William and Mary's wedding, 'I must prepare to go – The Swallows I must leave them the well the garden the Roses all – Dear creatures!! they sang last night after I was in bed – seemed to be singing to one another, just before they settled to rest for the night. Well I must go – Farewell' (*Journals*, p. 119). With that startlingly original simile by which the swallows with their forked tails begin to look 'like fish', Dorothy encapsulates the responsive, flexible and openly speculative way in which she came to think and write about the natural world: the simile may be read to suggest that the human eye and ear are full of tricks and consequently unreliable, but it also stays open to the suggestion of deep and surprising analogical resemblances between creatures inhabiting the different worlds of sea and air. Patiently watching her swallows 'in the morning, in the day many & many a time & in the evenings', the close attention which Dorothy pays to the lives of these creatures prevents us from dismissing her reflections as merely fanciful, sentimental, anthropomorphic: however much our imaginations play over and about them, these are creatures in their own right and in their own world. As her brother finely captured this curious intermixture of imagination and careful, studied attention in his sister's writing, Dorothy's was a mind 'taught | By active Fancy or by patient Thought' (*An Evening Walk*, 1794 text, ll. 203–4).

IV

In a letter of 1832, Wordsworth famously referred to Coleridge and Dorothy as the 'two Beings' to whom his 'intellect' was 'most indebted' (*Later Years*, II, p. 536). Reflecting the subtle, though marked, points of difference between these two 'beings' or personalities, Wordsworth's language may be characterised by an incongruous mix of the general and the particular, the abstract and the concrete, the mental and the physical.[30] This intermingling may be seen to set up a contrast, but also to explore and test the boundaries between the human mind and the world from which it sprang. Unquestionably the poet's fullest and most detailed response to the Lucretian myth, Wordsworth's description of the boy of Winander draws together larger metaphysical theories with the kind of fresh, detailed descriptions of natural phenomena that characterise his sister's writings. With its vivid presentation of the poet's own imaginative development and creative processes, the passage engages with, but also, in crucial ways, marks a departure from larger philosophical arguments regarding both the origins and progress of poetry:

>   There was a Boy, ye knew him well, ye Cliffs
> And Islands of Winander! many a time
> At evening, when the stars had just begun
> To move along the edge of the hills,
> Rising or setting, would he stand alone,
> Beneath the trees, or by the glimmering Lake,
> And there, with fingers interwoven, both hands
> Press'd closely, palm to palm, and to his mouth
> Uplifted, he, as through an instrument,
> Blew mimic hootings to the silent owls
> That they might answer him.—And they would shout
> Across the watry Vale, and shout again,
> Responsive to his call, with quivering peals,
> And long halloos, and screams, and echoes loud
> Redoubled and redoubled; concourse wild
> Of mirth and jocund din! And when it chanced
> That pauses of deep silence mock'd his skill,
> Then sometimes, in that silence, while he hung
> Listening, a gentle shock of mild surprize
> Has carried far into his heart the voice
> Of mountain torrents, or the visible scene
> Would enter unawares into his mind
> With all its solemn imagery, its rocks,
> Its woods, and that uncertain Heaven, receiv'd
> Into the bosom of the steady Lake.
>   This Boy was taken from his Mates, and died
> In childhood, ere he was full ten years old.
>
> (*Prelude*, V, ll. 389–415)

As the owls answer and respond to the boy's own 'mimic hootings', Wordsworth evokes an incipient mode of communication or 'concourse wild'. 'Concourse' is not discourse, not the process of reasoning, the threading together of an argument into logical sequence; rather, it is the random and chaotic 'meeting of things' (*OED*). Following Cicero's phrase '*concursus fortuitous*', the word became closely associated with the atomic theories of Leucippus and Democritus, and later Epicurus and Lucretius. As the poet and critic Joseph Warton explained in a note to his 1750s translation of Virgil's reflections 'on the Epicurean philosophy natural and moral' in the sixth eclogue, a tradition of philosophers maintained that 'by a fortuitous concourse of these atoms, or particles of matter, the universe was formed without the assistance of a directing mind'.[31] The phrase was often used disparagingly by theologians such as Richard Bentley, whose sermons Coleridge was reading and transcribing into his notebooks in 1795–8: in his lecture 'A Confutation of Atheism' (1692), Bentley inveighed against 'that ordinary cant of illiterate and puny Atheists, the *fortuitous* or *casual concourse of atoms*, that compendious and easy dispatch of that most important and difficult affair, the formation of a world'.[32] In an emerging eighteenth-century tradition of 'philosophical' poems, the phrase is similarly used to disparage the reasoning of atheist philosophers: 'if casual Concourse did the World compose', wrote Richard Blackmore in *Creation: A Philosophical Poem* (1712), 'then any Thing might come from any Thing, | For how from Chance can constant Order spring?'[33] Although Wordsworth in his early poetry strays far from orthodox theories regarding intelligent design in the creation of the world and the formation of language, such atheistic ideas are tempered by the prayer-like position of the boy's hands 'press'd closely, palm to palm': the art of poetry is seen to derive not from a grammar of God, but from a primitive, passionate aesthetic response to the natural world.[34]

Unquestionably, the nature and origins of the human art of speech are presented in highly ambiguous terms. As J. Douglas Kneale observes, the phrase 'redoubled and redoubled' carries 'intertextual overtones of battle'; for example, Milton described the 'redoubl'd blow' of the 'Atheist crew' in *Paradise Lost* (a line to which, as Kneale points out, Wordsworth explicitly alludes in his description of the 'sceptre of the Atheist crew' in the tenth book of *The Prelude*);[35] or, alternatively, John of Gaunt's martial command in Shakespeare's *Richard II*: 'And let thy blows, doubly redoublèd | Fall like amazing thunder on the casque | Of thy adverse pernicious enemy'.[36] A similar ambiguity is evident in Wordsworth's descriptions of the birds' 'quivering peals': according to Johnson's *Dictionary of the English Language* (1755), 'peal' denoted 'a succession of loud sounds: as, of bells, thunder, cannon'.[37] Consequently, the phrase may be variously associated with the inarticulate sounds of the natural world, the ringing of church bells summoning parishioners to prayers, or a loud discharge of guns or cannon in a form of military salute – the 'peal of cannon' described in William Gilpin's *Observations, Relative Chiefly to Picturesque Beauty* (1722), whose particular focus on the mountains and lakes of Wordsworth's native Cumbria undoubtedly influenced the young poet.[38] The popular phrase 'peals of laughter' may be traced at least as far back as Addison's use of it in the *Spectator* in 1711, as the word was more generally used to denote a loud outburst or volley of sound, such as thunder or laughter.[39] In Wordsworth's poem, the phrase captures the active, though inscrutable, animal agency expressed by the birds' riotous mirth, which is further seen to be echoed in various human rituals, festivities and, more darkly, battle cries. In echoing the birds' calls, the boy's own attempt to imitate or 'redouble' their notes may also be seen to take on a combative edge in what Kneale perceives as a high-stakes 'singing contest'.[40] While voice is ambiguously associated with both conviviality and conflict, emulation and rivalry, crucially, the boy's moment of epiphany or revelation takes place in those 'pauses of deep silence' that defy emulation and frustrate the boy's best efforts.

In this sense, Wordsworth's poem appears in keeping with the inward turn that Rowland perceives as characteristic of the study of language in the eighteenth century.[41] Whatever 'skill' the boy may possess in emulating the notes of birds, the power of imitation is perceived as secondary to the silent development of the boy's inner life and being. Wordsworth might have agreed with Herder's assessment that man 'has language lying in his soul' (*Two Essays*, p. 118), but his account is distinct in certain key respects. The moment of epiphany does not arise from the kind of awareness or self-consciousness that Herder perceived as the defining trait of a uniquely human consciousness; rather, it is the loss of self-consciousness that enables the visible scene to enter the boy's mind 'unawares'. Unlike Herder's primitive man, Wordsworth's boy of Winander does not think a word or single out an object of reflection by a 'distinguishing mark' (*Two Essays*, p. 117); instead, natural sights and sounds are impressed onto him and to this extent may be seen to mark *his* inner life and being. In this respect, Wordsworth may be seen to reverse Adamic theories of language: rather than naming or marking each creature, the boy is impressed by the natural sights and sounds from which Wordsworth insisted, to Coleridge's dismay, the 'best part' of language was originally derived. In his preface to the 1815 edition of his *Poems*, Wordsworth commented:

> Guided by one of my own primary consciousnesses, I have represented a commutation and transfer of internal feelings, co-operating with external

accidents, to plant, for immortality, images of sound and sight in the celestial soil of the Imagination. The Boy, there introduced, is listening, with something of a feverish and restless anxiety, for a recurrence of the riotous sounds which he had previously excited; and, at the moment when the intenseness of his mind is beginning to remit, he is surprised into a perception of the solemn and tranquillising images which the poem describes.[42]

Although Wordsworth draws upon Coleridge's theory of the imagination, the poet is here, as Jonathan Wordsworth observed, 'on his own' and 'writing to please himself'.[43] The movement is not from within to without, but from without to within. In Coleridge's writing, the imagination is outwardly directed and inscribes its own ideas, preoccupations and acts of imagination onto the natural world: it consciously orders, selects and voluntarily appropriates 'fixed symbols to internal acts' (*Biographia Literaria*, II, ch. 17, p. 54). For Wordsworth, by contrast, the direction is inward. Ever conscious of the modifying colours of memory and association ('internal feelings' seamlessly commingle and co-operate with 'external accidents'), the resulting 'images of sound and sight' are then planted in the 'celestial soil of the Imagination'. Such a view of the imagination is in keeping with what Wordsworth elsewhere describes as the 'wise passiveness' of the contemplative mind: the boy of Winander does not actively impose his own order on 'the visible scene', but rather the scene itself *enters* his mind almost without his knowledge or full awareness.[44] In that striking and faintly oxymoronic phrase 'images of sound and sight', Wordsworth further hints at a level of consciousness or mode of thought that is preverbal, unworded: these are visual images, composed of patterns and shapes, impressions or memories of sound.

A more active response is signalled by Wordsworth's placing of the word 'hung' at the end of the line. As critics have often pointed out, the verb has 'a special virtue to Wordsworth'.[45] In the 1815 preface to his *Poems*, Wordsworth focuses in on this single word in order to explore and 'illustrate' the emergence of the faculty he denotes imagination. While a parrot hangs from its cage and a monkey hangs from a tree 'literally and actually', Wordsworth perceives a 'slight exertion' of the imagination in Shakespeare's lines from *King Lear*: 'half way up | *Hangs* one who gathers samphire' (*Wordsworth's Literary Criticism*, p. 180). For Wordsworth, what is crucial here is that the samphire-gatherer does not 'literally hang ... but, presenting to the senses something of such an appearance, the mind in its activity, for its own gratification, contemplates them as hanging' (*Wordsworth's Literary Criticism*, p. 180). In *The Prelude*, the word may be seen to trace the emergence of Wordsworth's own imaginative faculty. Reflecting on his own boyhood pursuits as a 'fell destroyer' of birds, Wordsworth painted a memorable picture of his former self: 'my shoulder all with springes hung' (I, l. 318). Later, he describes a scene that foregrounds the revelation experienced by the boy of Winander:

> Oh! when I have hung
> Above the raven's nest, by knots of grass,
> And half-inch fissures in the slippery rock
> But ill sustain'd, and almost, as it seem'd,
> Suspended by the blast which blew amain,
> Shouldering the naked crag; Oh! at that time,
> While on the perilous edge I hung alone,
> With what strange utterance did the loud dry wind
> Blow though my ears! (I, ll. 342–51)

In each of the foregoing instances, the word is used 'literally and actually': traps and springs literally *hang* from the boy's shoulder, and the boy literally *hangs* 'by half-inch fissures in the slippery rock'. But there is a slight though significant shift here: no longer taking, destroying and hanging his spoils from his shoulder, the young poet now undergoes the more perilous experience of hanging *from* natural objects – a shift that betokens a growing awareness of his own mortality and precarious position in a world of naked crags and perilous edges. In many ways, the passage foregrounds the decisive shift from the literal to the imaginative in the boy of Winander passage: the boy is not literally suspended from rock or branch, but, we are told, he 'hung | Listening'. In the heavily enjambed lines of Wordsworth's blank verse, the absence of a clear end-stopped line leaves the length of the pause open to the reader's interpretation. In his preface to the 1815 edition of his *Poems*, Wordsworth emphasised that his defiance of the rules associated with the heroic line invited a more active participation from the reader:

> Poems . . . cannot read themselves; the law of long syllable and short must not be so inflexible, – the letter of metre must not be so impassive to the spirit of versification, – as to deprive the Reader of a voluntary power to modulate, in subordination to the sense, the music of the poem; – in the same manner as his mind is left at liberty, and even summoned, to act upon its thoughts and images. (*Wordsworth's Literary Criticism*, p. 179)

In inviting the reader to read and modulate the music in their own way, Wordsworth invites the active participation of the reader – to hover, to hang their own interpretation over the verse. Following the spirit as opposed to the letter of versification, Wordsworth's blank verse, in its various and unpredictable music, further opens out an imaginative space for the reader to hang, listening, waiting and actively imagining what will follow. When Wordsworth switches the stress to the first syllable of the iambic pentameter line ('hung | *Lis*tening'), this unexpected movement is precisely what allows the reader to feel the fullest impact of the succeeding 'gentle shock of mild surprize' administered in the following line. As well as tracing the inner imaginative life of the boy, Wordsworth further seeks to encourage and bring forth – to 'summon' – a similarly imaginative and active response from the listening reader. As both the music and the sense of the poem are left open to interpretation (the 'voice of mountain torrents' may be construed in any number of ways), the poem provides a space for a subjective and imaginative response that leaves the reader's mind 'at liberty . . . to act upon its thoughts and images'. In this respect, the passage sets up a dialectic not only between thinking and expressing those thoughts in poems, but also, and equally, between reading and thinking about the words read.

To a degree which may sometimes lead readers to underestimate his investment in the 'wondrous power of words' (*The Prelude*, VII, l. 121), Wordsworth, throughout his poetry, explores psychological states and ways of thinking that stubbornly resist translation into language. Recalling Thomas Gray's musings on the lives of the obscure rustics buried in the village graveyard in 'Elegy Written in a Country Churchyard', the premature death of the boy of Winander pointedly reflects on the human reality of untapped potential and further throws into stark relief the problem formulated in 'Tintern Abbey': 'I cannot paint | What then I was' (*Lyrical Ballads*, ll. 76–7).[46] J. H. Alexander observes the significant 'number of words beginning with the prefix "under-"' employed by Wordsworth in *The Prelude*. At times, these words refer to the poet's own 'inner imaginative self, the deepest region of his subconsciousness': the 'under soul' which remained active, though 'hush'd' and 'locked up' throughout the poet's studies in Cambridge (III, ll. 539–40).[47] At others, the phrase refers to the richly imaginative lives of the poet's fellow countrymen, whatever their class background or level of education:

> Men may be found of other mold than these;
> Who are their own upholders, to themselves
> Encouragement, and energy and will,
> Expressing liveliest thoughts in lively words
> As native passion dictates. Others, too,
> There are among the walks of homely life

> Still higher, men for contemplation framed,
> Shy, and unpractis'd in the strife of phrase,
> Meek men, whose very souls perhaps would sink
> Beneath them, summon'd to such intercourse:
> Theirs is the language of the heavens, the power,
> The thought, the image, and the silent joy;
> Words are but under-agents in their souls.
>
> (*Prelude*, XII, ll. 260–72)

Wordsworth starkly criticises those who would 'read the invisible soul' according to 'the letter of the outward promise' (XII, ll. 254–5); rather than perceiving language as a painting or exact representation of the mind's inner workings, Wordsworth perceives words as 'under-agents'. Words are the instrument and auxiliary of thought, and not thought itself. And they are also the secondary power, the emissaries of a higher and inscrutable 'language of the heavens'. Alongside those 'accomplish'd', 'eloquent' and 'admired' men of parts and learning (XII, ll. 257, 258, 259), Wordsworth acknowledges the hidden, though richly imaginative, lives of men in 'homely life' who either express their thoughts in their own native phrases or, in many cases, do not express their innermost thoughts at all: shy, inward and contemplative characters – figures who might be regarded as, to quote Wordsworth's description of his brother John, 'Poet[s] in everything but words' (*Early Years*, p. 541).

Wordsworth's sense of rich, full imaginative lives that may never fully find expression might be taken as an acknowledgement of his sister's contribution to the creative process. In the 'Irregular Verses' (1829) that she composed for Jane Pollard's daughter, Julia Marshall, Dorothy reflected on her own experiences as a young woman perhaps just 'shy' of, though certainly not 'unpractis'd in the strife of phrase':

> You ask why in that jocund time
> Why did I not in jingling rhyme
> Display those pleasant guileless dreams
> That furnished still exhaustless themes?
> —I *reverenced* the Poet's skill,
> And *might have* nursed a mounting Will
> To imitate the tender Lays
> Of them who sang in Nature's praise;
> But bashfulness, a struggling shame
> A fear that elder heads might blame
> —Or something worse—a lurking pride
> Whispering my playmates would deride
> Stifled ambition, checked the aim
> If e'er by chance 'the numbers came'

> —Nay even the mild maternal smile,
> That oft-times would repress, beguile
> The over-confidence of youth,
> Even that dear smile, to own the truth,
> Was dreaded by a fond self-love;
> "Twill glance on me—and to reprove
> Or,' (sorest wrong in childhood's school)
> 'Will *point* the sting of ridicule'.⁴⁸

In this exceptionally rare instance of open reflection on all she '*might have*' been, Dorothy acknowledges that even those closest to her may have played some role in suppressing her literary ambitions: the fear of 'reproof' from the 'mild maternal smile', the deep 'reverence' that she felt for poets in general and for her brother in particular. Composed in what Dorothy lightly and self-deprecatingly refers to as 'jingling' rhyming couplets, the poem gradually matures into the kind of intricate, self-scrutinising criticism and heavily enjambed lines through which her brother had earlier sought to disentangle the 'more subtle selfishness' that at times impeded his own literary ambitions (*The Prelude*, I, l. 248). In *The Prelude*, William idealises both the moral character and poetic power of 'meek men' destined to speak the 'language of the heavens'; Dorothy, by contrast, draws attention to the complex set of social pressures exerted upon a young woman by her schoolmates, peers and, 'to own the truth', even the nearest and dearest members of her family. With bitter irony, Dorothy came to understand, in many ways more deeply than her brother, the human reality of stifled creativity.

In his deep sense of the unuttered and unutterable nature of all that goes on within a single human mind in their day-to-day experience of the world, Wordsworth's poetry has seemed to reflect what Stephen J. Land describes as a 'profound mistrust of words' as a 'necessary evil' and even to affirm that his art 'is only secondarily linguistic, that it is driven to the use of words ... in order to communicate its immaterial existence'.⁴⁹ For Bennett, such arguments are linked to a prevailing and deeply misguided 'conception of Wordsworth': the 'idea that despite what his name might suggest, his words, as words, are not worth much'.⁵⁰ Although there can be little doubt that Wordsworth recognised both the value and the downright pleasure of 'words in tuneful order' (*Prelude*, V, l. 578), he understood that value as being enhanced rather than hindered by their secondary or auxiliary role:

> Visionary power
> Attends upon the motions of the winds
> Embodied in the mystery of words.
> There darkness makes abode, and all the host

> Of shadowy things do work their changes there,
> As in a mansion like their proper home:—
> Even forms and substances are circumfus'd
> By that transparent veil with light divine;
> And through the turnings intricate of Verse
> Present themselves as objects recognis'd
> In flashes, and with a glory scarce their own. (V, ll. 619–29)

With the kind of complex circularity characteristic of his own and his sister's writing, Wordsworth appears to emphasise the apparent and irrevocable differences between words and the world they seek to represent (the terms in which we describe natural objects imbue them with 'a glory scarce their own'), at the same time that he suggests an analogical resemblance between 'the motions of the winds' and the 'mystery of the words' in which those sounds are loosely echoed. As the winds remain the only palpable sign of the invisible force that moves them, similarly words are the sign, the trace, the embodiment of a no less mysterious and intangible source: the poet's own creative energies. As they ironically exemplify the obscurity they seek to convey, the poet's words draw in the interpretative energies of the reader: as Walter Pater remarked in an 1874 essay, Wordsworth's continual suggestion that he has 'something very peculiar' to say to us, which is yet extremely 'difficult' either for him to fully convey or for us to understand, regularly prompts the reader to 'look below the surface' and actively fosters 'a habit of reading between the lines'.[51] Rather than presenting words as a painting or copy of the mind, Wordsworth's 'shadowy' language reflects both a sustained exploration and an active strengthening of the complex and mutually interdependent ways in which 'language and the human mind act and react on each other' (*Prose*, I, p. 120). Although Wordsworth's sense of words as auxiliaries or 'under-agents' has been read (perhaps rather defensively) as underestimating or even denigrating the worth of words, 'Axiologus' (the Graeco-Latin transcription of 'words-worth', as the young poet penned his own name in his first publication), throughout his writing, demonstrates a profound respect for and engagement with the immense *difficulty* of his own art: that eternal human struggle to say what we meant to say, and the endlessly creative process by which both poets and readers attempt to translate thoughts 'into strings of words, and vice versa'.[52] To acknowledge that difficulty is not to devalue the great gift of language or to humbly disparage one's own achievements as a writer, but rather to call attention to the intense struggle and heavy responsibility of that whole creative endeavour.

As the reader grapples with the shadowy semantic and discursive sense of the poet's words, their attention is drawn to how they sound (the complex alliterative, rhythmic and deep structural echoing that connects 'the motions of the winds' in some mysterious way to 'the mystery of words'). In *Wordsworth's Philosophic Song* (2006), Simon Jarvis explores how these 'turnings intricate of Verse' may help to explain why the poet's aspiration to 'philosophic Song' led him in a very different direction to that set out by Coleridge: 'I expected the Colours, Music, imaginative Life, and Passion of *Poetry*', Coleridge informed his friend, 'but the matter or arrangement of *Philosophy* – not doubting from the advantages of the Subject that the Totality of a system was not only capable of being harmonised with, but even calculated to aid, the unity (Beginning, Middle, and End) of a *Poem*' (*Collected Letters*, IV, p. 574). Rather than writing a poem in which 'philosophy gets fitted into a song' and 'all the thinking is done by philosophy and only the handiwork by verse', Wordsworth, Jarvis argues, may alternatively be read to suggest that 'the song itself, *as song*, is philosophic'.[53] According to this interpretation, to arrange words 'in tuneful order' may not mean simply to decorate or embellish with sounds and images, but rather to at once manifest and actively explore the 'different kind of thinking' that 'happens in verse': 'instead of being a sort of thoughtless ornament or reliquary for thinking, verse is itself a kind of cognition, with its own resistances and difficulties'.[54] As far as Wordsworth may have deviated from Coleridge's theodicy, ironically, his 'philosophic song' is in many ways more in keeping with his friend's earlier invocation of a musical, sensuous and in one sense more properly *philosophical* mode of utterance ciphered in the 'sweet jargoning' of birds.

At the very moment that Wordsworth draws attention to his subtle management of those 'turnings intricate of Verse', he sets up an interplay between the idea of a set metrical pattern and his own more intricate footwork: the complex set of alliterative patterns and turnings, the natural speech stress falling on the first syllable of 'intricate' which leads us to trip lightly over the stress in the fourth foot. With that characteristic tendency to switch the stress to the first syllable ('*E*ven forms and substances are circumfus'd'), Wordsworth slows down the line and evokes the gradual process by which poetic metre can pour, spread or circumfuse words with their less tangible and musical modes of signification. As Wordsworth, Coleridge and other Romantic poets expressed their disaffection with the routine predictability of the heroic line, they also, as Dennis Taylor has argued, demonstrated a growing awareness of 'the abstract nature of metrical form and the dialectic way in which it interplayed with the spoken language'.⁵⁵ At crucial moments where Wordsworth leaves his reader hanging, listening and waiting for what will come next, he draws attention to the reader's *idea* of metre, their sense of a pattern or expectation of how the line will go. Although Locke's argument that birds may be able to frame or conceptualise an idea of a tune and to use it as a 'pattern' remains a subject largely unexplored in scientific studies of animal cognition, poets have long recognised an ability to think, not in words, but in sonic patterns and shapes: a structure of sound that is different from and dialectically interplays with the poetic line.⁵⁶ As Dorothy listened attentively to the 'cheerful undersong' of redbreasts in winter (*Journals*, p. 72), she and her brother were led to reflect on their own creative practices of murmuring, whispering and composing together. With their shared sense of a deep, intimate and coeval connection between music and memory, William and Dorothy throughout their writings explore and actively play upon the associative character of music, and its consequent ability to conjure up vivid personal recollections, with their corresponding emotions and sensory impressions of particular scenes, times and places. As he at critical moments throughout his literary career actively recalls boyhood scenes with their attendant 'images of sound and sight' (*Wordsworth's Literary Criticism*, p. 190), Wordsworth's poetry offers vivid insights into a pre-verbal, musical and subvocal language of thought or 'undersong'.

V

> No noise is here, or none that hinders thought.
> The red-breast warbles still, but is content
> With slender notes and more than half suppress'd.
> Pleased with his solitude, and flitting light
> From spray to spray, where'er he rests he shakes
> From many a twig the pendent drops of ice,
> That tinkle in the wither'd leaves below.
> Stillness accompanied with sounds so soft
> Charms more than silence. Meditation may here
> Think down hours to moments.⁵⁷

In a passage which 'plainly predicts' numerous aspects of Wordsworth's own thought and writing, William Cowper, in the sixth book of *The Task* (1785), provided one of the earliest and most memorable literary representations in this period of what we would now call avian 'subsong': a quieter, more subdued and whispering song than the full summer anthem heard in the heady days of the breeding season, these 'slender notes' have throughout the centuries prompted larger philosophical questions regarding how and why birds sing – and why such things as birdsong, music or poetry should exist in a world where 'rough winter rages' (III, l. 31).[58] As Vincent Newey finely observes, 'the bird's sounds and movements mirror – indeed *are* – the rhythms of the poet's agile, quiet, poised creativity'.[59] Although the redbreast's 'more than half suppress'd' notes appear to some extent responsive and attuned to its surroundings, its soft sounds also subtly contrast with and complement the winter stillness. As Cowper at crucial moments switches the stress from the second to the first syllable of his pentameter line ('*Charms* more than silence'), the poet calls attention to the ways in which slight metrical irregularities accentuate and draw out the otherwise smooth and steady rhythms of his own blank verse. Anticipating his subsequent criticism of the 'knowledge' that may be derived from books (VI, l. 89), Cowper finds 'wisdom' in attentively studying the works of the natural world and patiently working these sensory impressions into his writing. In ways which undoubtedly appealed to the Wordsworth siblings, Cowper further presents music as an aid or stimulant to thought – a 'soothing influence' which helps the poet 'settle in soft musings' (VI, ll. 68–9).

Cowper's poem may be seen to anticipate the transformation that Adam Potkay perceives as taking place in Wordsworth's poetry. In *Wordsworth's Ethics* (2012), Potkay traces the movement by which the evangelical's 'still small voice of conscience' is transformed into the 'still, sad music of humanity' in Wordsworth's poetry; in crucial moments where the poet withdraws to listen to the singing of birds or the babbling of brooks, Potkay observes that 'something very different is happening than being guided by voices'.[60] Music 'is not, like conscience, directive: it does not tell us what to think, feel, or do'; rather, it prompts 'an affective state' akin to what Alexander Gerard described in *An Essay on Taste* (1759) as a 'pleasant disposition of soul' that 'renders us prone to every agreeable affection'.[61] In 'transforming conscience into music', Wordsworth, as Potkay argues, 'turns an ethics of obedience (thou shalt | thou shalt not) into a less structured responsiveness to the human and nonhuman other'.[62] Writing against the grain of his own strict Calvinist background, Cowper couches his defence of music as a means of engaging with and celebrating the works of a divine creator: 'and all in sight of inattentive man' (VI, l. 119). In lines which profoundly influenced Wordsworth's own reflections on the power of sound, the poet calls attention to music's unique ability to provoke a sympathetic response among its listeners:

> There is in souls a sympathy with sounds,
> And as the mind is pitch'd the ear is pleas'd
> With melting airs or martial, brisk or grave:
> Some chord in unison with what we hear
> Is touched within us, and the heart replies. (VI, ll. 1–5)

Anticipating some of the ambivalence with which Wordsworth would later reflect on those 'redoubled' screams of the owls in the boy of Winander passage, Cowper ambiguously hints at the rich potential, but also the dangers, of our human 'sympathy with sounds': such responsiveness may lead to love or war, to melting airs or martial cries. Although there can be little question that Cowper influenced Wordsworth's own ideas regarding music, sympathy and responsiveness to the other, the dark side of such sympathy is also highlighted and actively addressed in Wordsworth's poetry.

As a kind of objective correlative to the boy of Winander passage, Wordsworth describes the 'rosy babe' lisping the notes of the dissolute characters that surround him in a London theatre:

> Upon a Board,
> Whence an attendant of the Theatre
> Serv'd out refreshments, had this Child been placed
> And there he sate, environ'd with a Ring
> Of chance Spectators, chiefly dissolute men
> And shameless women; treated and caress'd,
> Ate, drank, and with the fruit and glasses play'd,
> While oaths, indecent speech, and ribaldry
> Were rife about him as are songs of birds
> In spring-time after showers. (*Prelude*, VII, ll. 383–92)

Whether born in the country or the city, in a mansion or a slum, all children are seen to possess a connate and universal 'sympathy with sounds'. While the boy of Winander blows 'mimic hootings' to the owls, the children of London's slums are no less disposed to imitate, and give back, the oaths, indecent speech and ribaldry that are as 'rife about him as are songs of birds'. In a fragmentary 'Essay on Morals' (thought to have been composed in the winter of 1798, as Wordsworth was composing the first passages of the poem that would become *The Prelude*), the poet questioned whether 'bald & naked reasonings' were capable of overcoming those habits of thought and behaviour developed from youth: 'I know no book or system of moral philosophy written with sufficient power to melt into our affections . . ., to incorporate itself with the blood & vital juices of our minds' (*Prose*, I, p. 103). With that subtle biological metaphor, Wordsworth challenges easy distinctions between the mental and the physical: mind *is* body, a muscle pulsating with 'blood & vital juices'. For Wordsworth, the well-intentioned arguments of Thomas Paine and William Godwin were incapable of melting into the affections and therefore 'powerless in regulating our judgments concerning the value of men & things' (*Prose*, I, p. 103). As he demonstrates both an awareness of and profound respect for music's unique ability to, in Rousseau's phrase, 'persuade without convincing' (*Two Essays*, p. 15), Wordsworth also acknowledged and deeply felt the poet's responsibility in actively using our human 'sympathy with sounds' to influence, shape and regulate moral judgments regarding 'the value of men & things'.

In their analysis of two key aspects of Cowper's thinking on music, Sydney and Eva Mary Grew note that the poet perceived music's power 'to stimulate memory' and thereby 'to help thought and meditation'.[63] As well as influencing Wordsworth's own reflections on the human soul's 'sympathy with sounds', Cowper also explored the associative character of music in ways that undeniably appealed to both Wordsworth and his sister:

> With easy force it opens all the cells
> Where mem'ry slept. Wherever I have heard
> A kindred melody, the scene recurs,
> And with it all its pleasures and its pains.
> Such comprehensive views the spirit takes,
> That in a few short moments I retrace
> (As in a map the voyager his course)
> The windings of my way through many years.
>
> (*The Task*, VI, ll. 11–18)

Anticipating the 'spots of time' passages that structure the narrative of *The Prelude*, Cowper here emphasises the personal and subjective associations which accompany music and sound: 'kindred' melodies vividly recall specific places, images and moments in time, and in their intimate association with personal memories, moods and experiences offer an in many ways more 'comprehensive' view of the poet's individual character and growth. These memories provide a means of not only charting or mapping an individual's character and development, but also of drawing together and reconciling both the 'pleasures' and 'pains' of lived experience. As he developed his own vivid sense of memories or 'images of sound and sight' (*Wordsworth's Literary Criticism*, p. 190), Wordsworth perceived and employed music as a means of thinking down hours to moments, as well as of exploring the nature and structure of consciousness itself – those scenes, times and places recalled by kindred melodies.

At Alfoxden with her brother and Coleridge in February 1798, Dorothy described the 'slender notes' of a redbreast in a passage which unmistakably recalls Cowper's winter walk at noon:

> A deep stillness in the thickest part of the wood, undisturbed except by the occasional dropping of the snow from the holly boughs; no other sound but that of the water, and the slender notes of the redbreast, which sang at intervals on the outskirts of the southern side of the wood. There the bright green moss was bare at the roots of the trees, and the little birds were upon it. The whole appearance of the wood was enchanting; and each tree, taken singly, was beautiful. The branches of the hollies pendent with their white burden, but still showing their bright red berries, and their glossy green leaves. (*Journals*, p. 146)

Through the rhythmic intervals and alliterative patterns of her own prose ('the bright green moss was bare'), Dorothy patiently and skilfully describes those sounds of water, dropping snow and 'slender notes' of the redbreast heard at 'intervals' from 'the southern side of the wood'. As Newlyn has finely argued in her critical biography *William and Dorothy Wordsworth: All in Each Other* (2013), Dorothy's attentiveness to the sounds of the natural world and skilful rendering of them in her own writing may in part explain her brother's observation in the 1800 preface to *Lyrical Ballads* that 'poetry ... can boast of no celestial Ichor that distinguishes her vital juices from those of prose; the same human blood circulates through the veins of them both' (*Prose*, I, p. 134).[64] With this striking biological metaphor, Wordsworth may be seen to allude to what Rousseau perceived as the shared origins or kinship of these two different media as well as to 'implicitly honour Dorothy's creative talent' and 'acknowledge the equality of their partnership in writing'.[65] Rather than using the wintry scene as a backdrop or starting point for a larger philosophical speculation regarding such things as man, nature and society, Dorothy's journals exemplify a way of noticing, describing and skilfully working those sights and sounds into her own writing that in and of itself constitutes a mode of cognition, a form of meditative thought able to think down hours to moments: 'each tree, taken singly, was beautiful'.

In *The Prelude*, Wordsworth accentuates the contrast between the sweetness of the bird's song and the 'gloom' of its surroundings:

> that single Wren
> Which one day sang so sweetly in the Nave
> Of the old Church, that, though from recent showers
> The earth was comfortless, and, touch'd by faint
> Internal breezes, sobbings of the place,
> And respirations, from the roofless walls
> The shuddering ivy dripp'd large drops, yet still,
> So sweetly 'mid the gloom the invisible Bird
> Sang to itself, that there I could have made
> My dwelling-place, and liv'd for ever there
> To hear such music.   (*Prelude*, II, ll. 125–35)

Placing this 'holy Scene' in its political and historical context (II, l. 114), Nicholas Roe points out that the ruins point to the 'reformation that has created those "roofless walls"' and suggest the larger and ongoing historical process by which any 'outworn regime' may be 'battered and broken and consigned to oblivion'.[66] While the 'mouldering Pile, with fractured Arch' are the only relics of a social order that is arbitrary and time-bound (the product of and therefore amenable to change) (II, ll. 112), the sounds of the wren singing 'so sweetly 'mid the gloom' suggest the enduring spirit, as opposed to the letter, of Christian teaching: that 'self-sufficing power of solitude' (II, ll. 78), by which the poet withdraws to listen to the bird's music as opposed to conscience or dogmatic principle. With its far more rebellious and pronounced critique of the arbitrary nature of religious dictums than anything to be found in Cowper's poetry, the passage foregrounds Wordsworth's subsequent contrast of Cambridge students dutifully rehearsing the catechism at chapel with an idealised primeval grove in which 'the Pelican | Upon the cypress spire, in lonely thought, | Might sit and sun himself' (III, ll. 452–4).

With that peculiar tendency to switch the stress from the second to the first syllable which Wordsworth shared with and possibly derived from Cowper ('the invisible Bird | *Sang* to itself'), he draws a further distinction between the spirit and 'the letter of metre' (*Wordsworth's Literary Criticism*, p. 179). With the additional stress introduced in that beautifully subtle alliterative phrase '*dripp'd large drops*', Wordsworth conveys longer, slower and heavier sounds than those heard in Cowper's more 'tinkling' verse. For Wordsworth, these slight metrical irregularities were best understood in relation to the central principle of 'similitude in dissimilitude' upon which he believed 'the pleasure received from metrical language depends' (*Prose*,

I, p. 148): such 'small, but continual and regular impulses of pleasurable surprises from the metrical arrangement' explained why 'Shakespeare's writings, in the most pathetic scenes, never act upon us, as pathetic, beyond the bounds of pleasure' (*Prose*, I, p. 146). Not simply attuned to or in harmony with its environment, Wordsworth's wren sings 'so sweetly 'mid the gloom' of a world riven by pain, hardship, loss and suffering. As the beauty of this bird's song threatens to exhaust the poet's own powers of language (the relatively conventional, stock-in-trade phrase 'so sweetly' is used twice), the poet pays recourse to the 'small, but continual and regular impulses of pleasurable surprises' of poetic metre in order to modulate and transform those 'sobbings of the place' into his own self-solacing song.

The song of 'that single wren' anticipates the poet's wider reflections on the associative character of music and consequent importance in triggering memories that can sustain the poet through long periods of loneliness 'mid the gloom' of towns and cities. At the beginning of his account of his 'Residence in London' in the seventh book of *The Prelude*, 'a little band' of redbreasts recalls the poet to his task:

> But I heard,
> After the hour of sunset yester even,
> Sitting within doors betwixt light and dark,
> A Voice that stirr'd me. 'Twas a little Band,
> A Quire of Redbreasts, gather'd somewhere near
> My threshold, Minstrels, from the distant woods
> And dells, sent in by Winter to bespeak
> For the Old Man a Welcome, to announce,
> With preparation artful and benign,
> Yea the most gentle music of the year,
> That their rough Lord had left the surly North,
> And hath begun his journey. A delight
> At this unthought-of greeting, unawares
> Smote me, a sweetness of the coming time;
> And, listening, I half whisper'd we will be,
> Ye heartsome Choristers, ye and I will be
> Brethren, and in the hearing of bleak winds
> Will chaunt together'.   (VII, ll. 20–37)

Through a series of archaisms ('Quire', 'Minstrels', 'Choristers' and 'Brethren'), Wordsworth associates and intermingles the bird's voices with human traditions of music, intimately linked with religious rituals and seasonal festivities. Introducing a rather rougher cadence than may be found in Cowper's smoother, more gentlemanly verse, the Scots dialect word 'heartsome' recalls and pays tribute to Wordsworth's northern influences (Scottish traditional ballads, as well as Scottish poets and writers such as James Hogg and Robert Burns), and points to the shared traditions, cultures and idiolects of 'border poets' who, as Wordsworth noted in a letter to the ballad collector Allan Cunningham, 'if they did not drink the water, they breathed at least the air of the two countries' (*Later Years*, I, p. 402).[67] With its particular and unique set of associations (joy, comfort and good cheer, but also intermixed with a certain degree of hearty courage and boldness), that word 'heartsome' enables Wordsworth to convey at once both the cheerfulness of the sounds and the stout *courage* of such expressions of joy when uttered 'in the hearing of bleak winds'.

With his focus on rural and rustic traditions of song, Wordsworth's poetry marks a bold, convivial and, in its own way, rather impudent departure from conventional narratives regarding the origins and progress of poetry. Although Wordsworth, like James Beattie and other forebears in this genre, draws heavily from classical mythology, these traditions are intermingled with Celtic folk songs and myths in ways which suggest continuities, affinities and cycles as opposed to linear progression. By introducing the personified figure of the 'Old Man' of winter, Wordsworth traces traditional folk characters back to their literary forebears in ancient Greek mythology, particularly the figure of Boreas seen 'scow'r[ing] the snow' elsewhere in his poetry.[68] As Wordsworth subtly interweaves these various Christian and pagan traditions, the passage evokes a sense of the historical continuities and shared concerns which connect seemingly disparate or even conflicting systems of belief. Following the sun through its 'journey' from northern to southern climes (with perhaps a glance at that famous Southerner, Rousseau, and his dismissive remarks on those supposedly harsh, grating and unpoetical languages of the north), Wordsworth suggests a shared and common origin in weathering the storms of seasonal change. As he inverts the stress at the beginning of the epiphanic line ('ye and I will be | *Bre*thren'), Wordsworth accentuates and calls attention to his remarkably free and altruistic use of this word: traditionally denoting fellow members of the Christian church (most notably in the 'dearly beloved brethren' addressed in the Common Book of Prayer), Wordsworth here radically reapplies the word in order to emphasise a more egalitarian view of human fellow-feeling and to further extend that sympathy to such creatures as a redbreast singing to itself in winter. As Wordsworth had earlier revised the Christian principle of 'The Great Chain of Being', a hierarchical structure with man placed at its summit is recast to include all forms of life that 'prolong the endless chain | Of Joy and grief, of pleasure and of pain' (*An Evening Walk*, 1794 text, ll. 205–6).

With that last archaism 'chaunt', Wordsworth suggests further affinities and continuities between the song of birds, communal singing, psalmody and other forms of 'holy rites chanted in measured round'.[69] In a later sonnet, 'On Approaching the Staub-Bach, Laterbrunne' (*Memorials of a Tour on the Continent*, 1828), Wordsworth uses the word to compare the local rituals of villagers singing at a waterfall in Switzerland with the 'chaunting' of mermaids, sirens and other mythological creatures.[70] As Wordsworth remarked in a note to this poem, the 'wild and savage air' of these 'musical Beggars' reminded him 'of religious services chanted to Streams and Fountains in Pagan Times'.[71] Quoting his friend Robert Southey's impression of the scene, Wordsworth noted that

> some half-score peasants, chiefly women and girls, assembled just out of reach of the Spring, and set up – surely, the wildest chorus that ever was heard by human ears, – a song not of articulate sounds, but in which the voice was used as a mere instrument of music, more flexible than any which art could produce, – sweet, powerful, and thrilling beyond description.[72]

As these 'savage airs' became associated with what Herder and other philosophers regarded as 'remnants from the times of the sung language' (*Two Essays*, p. 138), they also, as critical studies point out, provoked fear among 'rhetoricians, elocutionists, and critics' in the late eighteenth and early nineteenth centuries.[73] While many of his contemporaries identified 'the habit of chanting with lack of education, superstition, blind submission to the establishment, or solipsism', Wordsworth perceived the chant as crucial to understanding the musical and sensual origins of poetic language and poetry's consequent power to persuade or 'melt into our affections' (*Prose*, I, p. 104).[74] In a crucial passage in *The Excursion* (1814), Wordsworth actively uses the word to signal a bond between the natural world and the human mind: 'I, long before the blissful hour arrives, | Would chaunt, in lonely peace, the spousal verse | Of this great consummation'.[75] At once describing and enacting the peculiar '*chaunt*' that Hazlitt detected 'in the recitation both of Coleridge and Wordsworth', the poet's use of the word evidently recalled to his contemporaries the steady bass rhythm of his own iambic pentameter verse as modulated by 'small, but continual and regular impulses of pleasurable surprise' (*Prose*, I, p. 146).[76] Although Hazlitt and other readers grew suspicious of this sonorous practice as it 'acts as a spell upon the hearer, and disarms the judgment', the enchanting influence of music could be positively and proactively used to form moral habits and ways of thinking and to develop or deepen our understanding of the 'value of men & things'.[77] As well as suggesting affinities between birdsong, savage airs and the recitative aspects of his own verse, Wordsworth also calls attention to an inward, quasi-articulate or 'half whisper'd' mode of utterance. As he witnessed the mental deterioration of his sister in the 1830s, Wordsworth increasingly returned to and relied upon this subvocal and musical utterance as a form of 'divine communion' ('Oh what a Wreck!', *Last Poems*, l. 10).

VI

Singled out by Wordsworth as the 'first *Modern*' to have distinguished herself in the sonnet, Charlotte Smith unquestionably had a marked influence on Wordsworth's own experiments with the form in his late lyrics (*Later Years*, III, p. 149). Widely recognised as a major precursor to the 'sonnet revival' of the early nineteenth century, Smith's *Elegiac Sonnets* (1784) may be placed in the context of an emerging 'cult of Sensibility' which, as Paula Feldman and Daniel Robinson broadly summarise, emphasised 'feeling and mood' and sought to develop 'a poetic form ... to convey thoughts and feelings in a more natural way than poets previously had attempted'.[78] Although Smith presented her little poems as the 'simple effusions' of personal feeling, critical studies have drawn attention to the literary influences which inevitably shaped her treatment of such a highly traditional subject as the nightingale:[79]

> Borne on the warm wing of the western gale,
>   How tremulously low is heard to float
> Thro' the green budding thorns that fringe the vale,
>   The early Nightingale's prelusive note.
>
> 'Tis Hope's instinctive power that thro' the grove
>   Tells how benignant Heaven revives the earth;
> 'Tis the soft voice of young and timid Love
>   That calls these melting sounds of sweetness forth.
>
> With transport, once, sweet bird! I hail'd thy lay,
>   And bade thee welcome to our shades again,
> To charm the wandering poet's pensive way
>   And soothe the solitary lover's pain;
> But now!—such evils in my lot combine,
> As shut my languid sense—to Hope's dear voice and thine!
>   ('The Return of the Nightingale', *The Poems of Charlotte Smith*, pp. 49–50)

A series of verbal echoes recall poetic forebears and most especially Milton: the slight archaism 'lay' echoes Milton's earlier sonnet to the 'soft lay' of a bird whose 'liquid notes' offer 'fresh hope' to young lovers ('O nightingale', ll. 8, 5, 3). Smith's sonnets are not just referential, but self-referential. Smith is actively encouraging her readers to think back to two earlier sonnets addressed to the nightingale, to the 'transport' with which she 'once' greeted the bird's lay. Smith knows that she is hearing the same sounds differently. The 'melting sounds of sweetness' break down into the fragmented exclamations of the poem's final couplet. Although Smith draws attention to these essential differences between the sonnet form and the natural sights and sounds it seeks to portray, her description of the young nightingale's 'prelusive notes' suggests an underlying, and in many ways surprising, analogy: an analogy between subsong and sonnets, a young bird's bashful first tries at song and a young poet's tentative first assays. As frequently the first and the last form that a poet will try his or her hand in, the sonnet, as Smith understood, is in many ways a poem about returning: while 'ambitious young writers' may 'compose sonnets in order to act out against the tradition', the poet and critic Meg Tyler has observed a tendency among 'poets of stature' to return to this form 'at a certain age'.[80] With that peculiar tendency to 'strain ... against and toward the sonnet' that Tyler perceives as marking the career of sonneteers such as Robert Lowell, Wordsworth may be seen in his late lyrics reflecting and ruminating over the origins, nature and progress of his own poetic voice.[81]

Coleridge was quick to pick up on the irony of the sonnet as the spontaneous overflow of powerful emotion: 'now, if there be one species of poetry more difficult and artificial than another', he wrote in the preface to his collection of *Sonnets from Various Authors* (1796), 'it is an English Sonnet on the Italian model'.[82] Paradoxically, however, Wordsworth's sonnets remained for Coleridge the strongest proof of his friend's *lack* of authorial control or self-discipline – Wordsworth's inability, in other words, to sit down and write *The Recluse*. Coleridge early voiced his concern regarding the 'habit ... of writing such a multitude of small Poems' which he believed would prove 'hurtful' to his friend (*Collected Letters*, II, p. 1013). The 'multitude' of poems seemed to spill out chaotically, irrepressibly, each time Wordsworth sat down to work on *The Recluse*. For Coleridge, the Wordsworth circle and to some extent Wordsworth himself, these were sorry signs of the poet's artistic failures, compulsions, bad habits and procrastinatory activities. In the 1830s and 40s, the Wordsworth household began to lose hope as well as patience. To Dora Wordsworth's exasperation, the '100 lines' which her father composed in the spring of 1833 were composed entirely of what her mother referred to as 'tiresome small poems'.[83] 'Resolution fails', wrote Dorothy, with sadness and some reproach, though not without sympathy for the pains and frustrations to which she had borne witness throughout her brother's career (*Later Years*, II, p. 191). 'Actually he has written another *Sonnet*!' she informed her nephews in Cambridge; 'this we were not glad of', she confided, 'fearing it might be but the beginning as heretofore, of a *Batch*' (*Later Years*, II, p. 169). A highly artificial and tightly regulated form, the sonnet paradoxically remains a crucial, if surprising, vehicle through which Wordsworth and many other poets throughout the centuries have explored and ruminated on some of the most vexing questions regarding the creative process.

In a short lyric poem that he later composed for Dora, Wordsworth contrasted the 'tutored powers' of a caged parrot with the 'slender unexpected strain' of the wren ('The Contrast', *Last Poems*, ll. 19, 38). As unremarkable as this conventional contrast might at first appear, Wordsworth here draws a startlingly original analogy between the flitting of birds and the *shyness* of thought itself:

> This moss-lined shed, green, soft, and dry,
> Harbours a self-contented Wren,
> Not shunning man's abode, though shy,
> Almost as thought itself, of human ken.
>
> (*Last Poems*, ll. 29–32)

For Wordsworth, the animal is as elusive as his own thoughts – motions of the mind that take place within, and yet elude, the poet's own conscious 'ken'. In this late lyric, Wordsworth hits on a mode of metaphor that, as will be discussed in more detail in the following chapter, Clare would take to new lengths in the 'Northborough Sonnets' of the 1830s. The poet's own thoughts are figured as animals, autonomous beings, creatures that live just outside of the poet's range of vision and tantalisingly elude his conscious manipulation or control. The bird's *shyness* points to the complex and often fraught relationship between human thought and human ken, between consciousness and the kind of *self*-consciousness that risks startling the bird or scaring off the thought. Famously, Wordsworth reflects on this poetic predicament in *The Prelude*:

> The hiding-places of my power
> Seem open; I approach, and then they close;
> I see by glimpses now; when age comes on,
> May scarcely see at all, and I would give,
> While yet we may, as far as words can give,
> A substance and a life to what I feel. (XI, ll. 336–41)

While the first enjambed line seems to flow or 'open' into the next, a series of punctuation marks divide the following lines into shorter segments or units of meaning, which evoke the 'glimpses' by which the poet is able to intermittently spy into the furthest corners of consciousness. Seeming to recall Coleridge's idea of 'elevating ... words into Things, and living Things too' (*Collected Letters*, I, pp. 625–6), Wordsworth presents words as giving a 'substance' and a 'life' to 'what I feel': words are newly understood as a kind of physical embodiment, the outward expression of an inward and mysterious life – whether we understand this as the soul, the spirit, or the artist's own psyche. In this sense, words take on 'glad animal movements' all their own, physically embodying, as far as words are able, the inner imaginative life of the poet ('Tintern Abbey', *Lyrical Ballads*, l. 75).

In these late lyrics, Wordsworth frequently draws attention to the 'unexpected' workings of chance and how they interact with, but also parallel, the workings of the poet's mind. 'The law under which the processes of Fancy are carried on is as capricious as the accidents of things', wrote Wordsworth, 'and the effects are surprising, playful, ludicrous, amusing, tender, or pathetic, as the objects happen to be appositely produced or fortunately combined' (*Wordsworth's Literary Criticism*, p. 185). Recalling his sister's many references to accidents of light and shade and their effect upon the 'soft & low' singing of birds (*Journals*, p. 109), Wordsworth reflects on the mysterious forces which might inspire a bird to sing, or a poet to write:

> Hark! 'tis the Thrush, undaunted, undeprest,
> By twilight premature of cloud and rain;
> Nor does that roaring wind deaden his strain
> Who carols thinking of his Love and nest,
> And seems, as more incited, still more blest.
> Thanks; thou has snapped a fire-side Prisoner's chain,
> Exulting Warbler! eased a fretted brain,
> And in a moment charmed my cares to rest.
> Yes, I will forth, bold Bird! and front the blast,
> That we may sing together, if thou wilt,
> So loud, so clear, my Partner through life's day,
> Mute in her nest love-chosen, if not love-built
> Like thine, shall gladden, as in seasons past,
> Thrilled by loose snatches of the social lay.   (*Last Poems*, p. 326)

In the eleventh line there is a curious syntactical slippage between the thrush, the poet and the female subject. In each of the editions which

Wordsworth painstakingly oversaw in the course of his lifetime, the comma appears where we might expect a semi-colon: 'So loud, so clear; my Partner through life's day, | Mute in her nest love-chosen, if not love-built | Like thine'. Bird, poet and female subject are ambiguously linked as 'partners' in song.[84] The grammatical slip, if it is one, is nonetheless in keeping with the overall idea of song as fragmentary, intermittent and composed of many voices – 'loose snatches of the social lay'.

This sonnet is one of a small number of poems which Wordsworth composed for a complete edition of *The Sonnets of William Wordsworth* (1838).[85] These new sonnets are closely related to one of the most distressing instances in Wordsworth's personal life: Dorothy's physical deterioration following an unknown illness, and mental collapse in 1835. Against the advice of his wife and daughter, Wordsworth directly addressed the changes he had witnessed take place in a much-beloved sister:

> Oh what a Wreck! how changed in mien and speech!
> Yet—though dread Powers, that work in mystery, spin
> Entanglings of the brain; though shadows stretch
> O'er the chilled heart—reflect; far, far within
> Hers is a holy Being, freed from Sin.
> She is not what she seems, a forlorn wretch;
> But delegated Spirits comfort fetch
> To Her from heights that Reason may not win.
> Like Children, She is privileged to hold
> Divine communion; both do live and move,
> Whate'er to shallow Faith their ways unfold,
> Inly illumined by Heaven's pitying love;
> Love pitying innocence not long to last,
> In them—in Her our sins and sorrows past.
>
> (*Last Poems*, pp. 323–4)

With painful and bitter irony, Wordsworth here pays recourse to the scriptural imagery through which he had earlier imagined and understood the inner lives of such poor inarticulate things as idiot boys and birds: *'their life is hidden with God'* (*Early Years*, p. 357). The poet draws attention to his own struggle to rationally come to terms with Dorothy's transformation; the long, tortured parenthetical reference to 'entanglings of the brain' marks an uneasy and painful journey to a reasoned and compassionate stance: 'yet ... reflect'. Through the varied yet closely interwoven rhyme scheme (*ababl baabl cdcdl ee*) and intricate patterns of alliteration (notably 'speech', 'spin', 'stretch' and 'within'), the speaker reaches for the kind of sympathetic connection that cannot be achieved or won through reason alone, but through music and the power of sound. Whereas Wordsworth in his early poetry had traced the beginnings of poetry back to a childish delight in listening to and emulating the song of birds, in his late poems he is forced to confront this tragic return to 'divine communion'.

'She can talk for a time rationally enough', reported Henry Crabb Robinson, 'but she has no command of herself and has the habit of blowing with her lips very loudly and disagreeably and sometimes of uttering a strange scream, something between the noise of a turkey and a partridge but more shrill than either'; according to Robinson, the only way to 'draw' Dorothy out from this kind of episode was to ask her to recite verses, 'which she does, quite pathetically'.[86] As Newlyn sensitively observes, 'Dorothy's dementia prompted William to make therapeutic use of their lifelong habit of remembering'; seeming to 'intuitively anticipate' modern medicine, Wordsworth read poems aloud to his sister in the sickroom at Rydal Mount, in what Newlyn describes as 'invitations to revisit, or as soothing forms of shared revisitation'.[87] The relationship between music, memory and dementia remains the subject of intensive scientific investigation. As recent research has confirmed, 'musical memory is a form of implicit memory, usually hardwired into the brain unless prone to the changes in the brain which usually herald dementia': listening to music 'lights up the brain in many places, reaching the parts that others can't'.[88] Listening to familiar songs known since childhood 'lights up' emotional memories, and significantly alleviates the symptoms of dementia: it has been shown to reduce anxiety and depression, to help maintain speech and language and, in doing so, to dramatically enhance the patient's quality of life.[89] In these late 'loose snatches of the social lay', Wordsworth plays on the sonnet's joint associations with both sound and sense in order to recall the memory of his sister and 'partner' in song.

'One afternoon in 1801, my sister read to me the sonnets of Milton', Wordsworth recalled in the notes that he dictated to his friend, Isabella Fenwick; particularly 'struck on that occasion by the dignified simplicity and majestic harmony that runs through most of them', the poet 'took fire' and once more tried his hand in a form he claimed not to have attempted since boyhood.[90] As is well known, Wordsworth preferred Milton's sonnets as offering a more complex and interwoven rhyme scheme which resisted 'the neat division of the Italian sonnet through the enjambment of the octave and the sestet' and which consequently gave the effect of 'intense Unity' that the poet likened to 'an orbicular body, – a sphere – or a dew-drop' (*Later Years*, II, pp. 604–5).[91] While that slight archaism of 'social lay' may be traced back to earlier description of the nightingale by Milton, Smith and other poetic forebears, Wordsworth also recalls his sister's sensitivity to the social, familial bonds expressed in the low 'twittering song' of swallows and further picks up on his own address to Dorothy as a 'heart' alive, awake and responsive to the sounds of nature: 'their social accents never vainly hears' (*An Evening Walk*, 1794 text, l. 132). Shifting attention away from the far-famed nightingale (a stranger to the northern climes of the Wordsworths' native Cumbria), the poet recalls his sister's references to 'that Dear thrush' that the siblings heard singing in their orchard on a 'misty rainy morning' in the winter of 1802 (*Journals*, p. 71). Perhaps referring to one particular thrush that seemed to Dorothy 'to sing louder & clearer than the thrushes had sung when it was quite day' (*Journals*, p. 93), Wordsworth interweaves a series of literary allusions, verbal echoes and shared memories in what Newlyn describes as the Wordsworths' 'language of implication': since the loss of their parents and separation in childhood, both siblings actively sought to develop a shared 'language of association' which 'bonded them jointly' to each other and to 'each new place'.[92] While the grammatical slip ambiguously links bird, poet and female subject, the organic, Miltonic and closely interwoven rhyme scheme (*abba/abba/cded/ce*) invokes the musical and sonorous patterns through which Wordsworth sought to reach and comfort his sister, to ease a 'fretted' mind and recall to her memory those 'loose snatches of the social lay'.

'Hark! 'tis the Thrush, undaunted, undeprest' is immediately followed by a description of the bird's more 'subdued' note:

> 'Tis He whose yester-evening's high disdain
> Beat back the roaring storm—but how subdued
> His day-break note, a sad vicissitude!
> Does the hour's drowsy weight his glee restrain?
> Or, like the nightingale, her joyous vein
> Pleased to renounce, does this dear Thrush attune
> His voice to suit the temper of yon Moon
> Doubly depressed, setting, and in her wane?
> Rise, tardy Sun! and let the Songster prove
> (The balance trembling between night and morn
> No longer) with what ecstasy upborne
> He can pour forth his sprit. In heaven above,
> And earth below, they best can serve true gladness
> Who meet most feelingly the calls of sadness.
>
> (*Last Poems*, pp. 326–7)

Uncharacteristically, Wordsworth here comes close to following the conventional structure of the Shakespearean sonnet that he had earlier eschewed as 'merely quatrains with a couplet tacked to the end' (*Later Years*, II, p. 455). While the first eight lines are closely integrated both semantically and by the Petrarchan rhyme scheme, the two questions may be seen to divide the octet into quatrains, or smaller units of meaning, followed by a traditional 'turn' or volta in the ninth line. As well as obliquely and delicately referring to the 'sad vicissitude' that he had witnessed taking place in a much-beloved sister, Wordsworth here almost reverts into a form which seems to acknowledge or even parodically draw attention to his own more 'subdued' note. For all that the sonnet is unquestionably a highly artificial form, Wordsworth and other poets have often anxiously perceived in these little poems a tendency towards a kind of dark side of Romantic spontaneity – an inert run-though of familiar gestures and techniques, a kind of learned instinct or involuntary muscular activity of mind. For Robert Browning and other 'sonnet-refusers' (in Jospeh Phelan's jocular phrase), the form has often in this sense represented 'a kind of default mode of poetry' to which the poet might turn in his or her 'less inspired moments'.[93] With that slightly enjambed line running into the final couplet, Wordsworth in this late sonnet recalls his own former, more exalting voice before it subsides into a conventional and even rather tired couplet: 'they best can serve true gladness | Who meet most feelingly the calls of sadness'. As we shall see in the following chapter, these most vexing questions surrounding the art of poetic composition are at once reflected and actively explored in the teems and teems of little poems that John Clare composed at Northborough in the 1830s.

CHAPTER 4

'Undersong'
John Clare

'Up this green wood land ride lets softly rove', writes John Clare in 'The Nightingales Nest', '& list the nightingale' (*Middle Period*, III, ll. 1–2). Clare was a closely attentive student of the nightingale. His poems invite his readers to share in the experience of roving through woodland, creeping on hands and knees through matted thorns and nestling down to listen to the song of this famously elusive bird. The detail, accuracy and immediacy of Clare's descriptions have long been recognised and widely, if not unequivocally, praised. Early reviewers broadly acknowledged Clare's 'true and minute delineations of external nature', but in the same stroke relegated the 'Northamptonshire Peasant' as 'strictly a descriptive poet'.[1] Clare's editor, John Taylor, repeated John Keats's comment that 'the Description too much prevailed over the Sentiment' in Clare's poetry and, in his editorial remarks, increasingly drew attention to those passages in which 'the Description overlaid & stifled that which ought to be the prevailing Idea'.[2] Often compared with Coleridge, Wordsworth, Keats and other Romantic predecessors and contemporaries in this respect, the so-called 'peasant poet' has seemed, to his detractors and staunchest advocates alike, to stubbornly refuse to 'look beyond' the birds and beasts he names to any larger abstract poetic or philosophical 'Idea'.[3] As he invites his reader to 'part aside | These hazel branches' and 'stoop right cautious neath the rustling boughs' (ll. 44–6), Clare resolutely narrows his focus on the bird itself and even seems to chide the human impulse to talk over and about the nightingale's song: 'Hark there she is ... lets be hush' (l. 42).

As critical studies by Hugh Haughton, Mina Gorji and Stephanie Kuduk Weiner have underscored, however, Clare's poems are not mere copies or 'transcriptions from nature'.[4] In what has become an accepted critical approach, Haughton made the point that Clare, in writing about nightingales, was writing about poetry too:[5]

> Ive nestled down
> & watched her while she sung—& her renown
> Hath made me marvel that so famed a bird
> Should have no better dress then russet brown
> Her wings would tremble in her extacy
> & feathers stand on end as 't'were with joy
> & mouth wide open to release her heart
> Of its out sobbing songs—the happiest part
> Of summers fame she shared—for so to me
> Did happy fancies shapen her employ.   (ll. 18–27)

As he draws attention to the animal alterity of this little brown bird singing with its inhuman mouth wide open and feathers standing upon end, Clare actively calls into question what others have thought and written about nightingales. Honing in on specific details (particularly the 'russet brown' coat associated with the peasant poet's own rustic dress), Clare challenges ideas not only about nightingales but also about poetry and what constitutes the 'poetic' itself.[6] The accuracy with which Clare describes the nightingale in and of itself constitutes an informed response to mythic renderings of this bird in poetry, notably Keats's 'light-wingèd Dryad of the trees'.[7] This chapter builds on recent scholarship which has recognised both Clare's place within and contribution to the complex, manifold and 'still-evolving aesthetic of Romanticism'.[8] Although Clare often challenges poetical myths regarding the nightingale, I argue that his writing evinces a sustained and heightened awareness of how his own subjective impressions necessarily shape his responses to this bird's song. As the nightingale's 'happy' song has faded into a 'plaintive anthem' by the end of Keats's ode (ll. 5, 75), Clare shows a similar awareness of how his own 'happy fancys' transform the nightingale's 'out sobbing songs' into the 'happiest' of summer anthems: 'for so *to me* | Did happy fancies shapen her employ' (my italics).

Clare composed several prose letters and fragments on natural history, which he at one stage considered including in an unfinished 'Natural History of Helpston' under the encouragement of James Hessey, the partner of his publisher, Taylor.[9] Clare's educational background and multifarious reading in poetry, natural history and science sharpened his awareness of how birdsong has been differently interpreted by diverse schools of thought. If it is true, as critical studies have emphasised, that Clare challenges poetical misrepresentations of the nightingale's song, he is no less critical of the received terms and definitions of natural history. In his encounters with the nightingale, Clare witnessed the kind of behaviour that challenged not only poetical myths but also scientific assumptions about how and why this bird sings:

> —How subtle is the bird she started out
> & raised a plaintive note of danger nigh
> Ere we were past the brambles & now near
> Her nest she sudden stops—as choaking fear
> That might betray her home—so even now
> We'll leave it as we found it—safetys guard
> Of pathless solitudes shall keep it still
> See there shes sitting on the old oak bough
> Mute in her fears—our presence doth retard
> Her joys & doubt turns every rapture chill.   (ll. 57–66)

No mere creature of instinct, Clare's nightingale is a sentient, skilful and remarkably, to use his own word, 'subtle' bird. Traditionally, this word denoted a sly, deceptive and menacing form of animal cunning, as with Milton's famous description of the serpent as the 'subtlest beast of all the field' in *Paradise Lost* (*Complete Poems*, VI, l. 495). As Johnson's definition further shows, the word also carried connotations of an almost excessive degree of social refinement ('nice; fine; delicate; not coarse' (*Dictionary*)). Drawing on these dual associations, Clare often uses the word to unmask the brute cunning that underlies the seemingly refined speech of social superiors: the 'subtle tongue' of 'vile hypocrisy' that 'can hide a lie | In fairest speech' ('The Truth of Time', *Middle Period*, IV, ll. 1–3). In 'The Nightingales Nest', the word imbues the animal world with an active, artful and highly sensitive, if elusive, agency: Clare's nightingale is vigilantly alert and one step ahead of human intruders, ironically both more astute and more sensitive than the 'rude boys' who seek out her nest (l. 52). Clare also uses the word in another sense cited by Johnson, as referring to an immaterial thing difficult to understand ('refined; acute beyond exactness' (*Dictionary*)): the 'subtle essence' of natural mysteries, the 'blank darkness' of caverns and rocks whose secrets are 'lockt for aye in thy unspeaking mind' ('To Mystery', *Middle Period*, IV, ll. 1, 5–6). Taken aback by the nightingale's apparent foresight and skilful evasion of predators, Clare, throughout his poetry, marvels at the subtleties of a natural world that constantly surprises and outwits, and defies our assumptions and expectations. Time and again in his poetry, Clare forces his readers to acknowledge a mysterious, but nonetheless highly alert, intelligent creature anxiously defending its home: 'We'll leave it as we found it'.

In a series of natural history letters about nightingales addressed to Hessey, Clare quotes a passage from Chaucer's *Troilus and Creside* in order to 'illustrate' his own observations of this remarkably 'shoy' bird (*Natural History Prose*, p. 37):

> The new abashed nightingale
> That stinteth first when she beginneth sing
> When that she heareth any herde's tale
> Or in the hedges any white stearing
> & after siker doth her voice out ring.
> (*Natural History Prose*, p. 37)[10]

Clare's nightingales do not sing in 'full-throated ease' (Keats, 'Ode of a Nightingale', l. 10); his poetry instead offers intimate glimpses into the life of a skilful, self-aware and exceedingly 'shy' bird. Clare's fascination with the muttering of birds while learning to sing led him to reflect upon his own creative processes. By examining the deep connections between Clare's responsiveness to birdsong and the ways in which he conceived of the poetic voice, this chapter seeks to extend and redefine some of the binary terms that have framed (and continue to frame) responses to the writings of this so-called 'peasant poet': 'natural' and 'artificial', 'instinctive' and 'learned', 'spontaneous' and 'premeditated' art. Ironically, the 'naturalness' for which Clare's poetry has been praised was *learned* through patient study, continual practice and the careful honing of poetic craft. Conversely, I argue that Clare's literary development also involved unlearning a negative form of self-consciousness – the shyness which, time and again in Clare's poetry, is seen to result in silences, blocks and choking fears.

I

One summer, Clare attempted to take down the notes of a nightingale that had been singing 'constantly as it were at my very door' (*Natural History Prose*, p. 313):

> Chee chew chee chew chee
> chew—cheer cheer cheer
> chew chew chew chee
> —up cheer up cheer up
> tweet tweet tweet jug jug jug
>
> wew wew wew—chur chur
> woo it woo it tweet tweet
> tweet jug jug jug
>
> tee rew tee rew tee rew—gur
> gur—chew rit chew rit—chur-chur chur

> chur will-will will-will tweet-em
> tweet em jug jug jug jug
>
> grig grig grig chew chew
>
> wevy wit wevy wit
> wevy wit—chee-chit
> chee-chit chee chit
> weeit weeit wee
> wit cheer cheer
> cheer—pelew
> pelew pelew—
> bring a jug bring a
> jug bring a jug. (*Natural History Prose*, p. 312)

Unquestionably, the transcription represents Clare's most sustained effort to capture the sounds, rhythms and patterning of a bird's voice or 'idiom'; his technique here contrasts starkly with earlier poems in which, as Eric Robinson and Richard Fitter point out, 'doves coo and swallows twitter ... in a conventional way'.[11] As Karlin observes, however, Clare's 'accurate' transcription does nonetheless admit 'familiar words and phrases': the phrase 'cheer up', for example, is conventionally derived from distinctly human traditions of interpretation and representation; thirty years earlier, in a poem which Clare 'almost certainly knew', Coleridge had 'insisted' on much the same thing in his description of the 'merry' birds in 'The Nightingale' (*Poetical Works*, I, l. 43).[12] Like Coleridge before him, Clare frequently reverts to traditional modes of notation or 'signatures' for the nightingale's song, which date at least as far back as the Renaissance: 'sweet jug jug' and 'terue', which last phrase seems to recall Tereus of the Philomela legend. And so it goes on, to an almost maddening degree, until the criticism seems to be at risk of committing the same sins as the transcription itself – hearing things in the syllables. In this sense, neither Clare nor his reader seem able to avoid the process by which the bird's song is necessarily, in Karlin's phrase, 'overl[aid] with human meanings' when 'translated' into a human form.[13]

As an accompanying note to the transcription confirms, however, Clare was conscious of these difficulties: 'many of her notes', he writes, 'are sounds that cannot be written the alphabet having no letters that can syllable the sounds' (*Natural History Prose*, p. 312). Drawing attention to this phrase, Stephanie Kuduk Weiner has made the case that literary mimesis involves a heightened, as opposed to diminished, awareness of form.[14] Nature does not, as Matthew Arnold wrote of Wordsworth, 'take the pen out of [the poet's] hand, and write for him with her own bare, sheer, penetrating power'.[15] Rather, as Weiner observes, the act of mimesis forces the poet to confront the 'irresolvable disjuncture between words and things' and 'investigate the scope and limits' of poetic form.[16] If it is difficult to avoid the idea that Clare's nightingale is telling us to 'cheer up', is it also telling us to 'bring a jug'? Clare may be seen as self-consciously playing on and in a sense parodying his own inflected phrases in those last smiling lines. Throughout his poetry, Clare demonstrates his awareness of how the sounds of birds are reshaped and recast according to what Emily Dickinson called 'the fashion of the ear'.[17] As he writes in 'The land rail',

> Tis like a fancy every where
> A sort of living doubt
> We know tis somthing but it ne'er
> Will blab the secret out.　　(*Middle Period*, III, ll. 13–16)

The land rail calls, but never blabs or betrays its 'secret': where or what the bird is, or what it might be saying. That word 'blab' finely captures a central tension in writing about birdsong: tantalisingly close to human language in some respects, the sounds of birds have often seemed to resemble an incipient mode of communication on the verge of breaking into words and yet never *quite* doing do. Ironically, the landrail's secret can never be told or translated into a language we could understand. These sounds come from a very different kind of consciousness, an 'unknown mode of being', in Wordsworth's phrase (*Prelude*, I, l. 421).

The abiding mystery appears to have offered Clare a kind of release, or escape, from what he describes in the long poem 'Birds Nesting' as 'learnings way' (*Middle Period*, II, l. 171). In this poem, Clare dramatises the different schools of thought through which human beings have attempted to decipher the mystery. The poem begins with a description of truant schoolboys losing sight of the village spire, while their journey through 'unknown' fields becomes a kind of metaphor for human knowing itself (l. 17): 'Thus on & on they go & guess' (l. 18). But the schoolboy, the scientist and the poet each end up naming and thus imposing meaning upon the birds which they cannot understand in their own terms:

> The woodmen call them in their way
> The Willowbiters 'cause they see
> Them biting in the month of may
> The young shoots of the willow tree
> But what they are in learnings way
> Is all unknown to them or me.　　(ll. 167–72)

In 'Birds Nesting', there is no single authoritative perspective, but rather a series of different 'ways' of looking, interpreting, guessing. The abiding mystery enables Clare to challenge the authority of the learned. The willowbiters neither know nor care what they are in 'learnings way'. Their imperviousness is liberating, as it enables Clare to wriggle free from the various names and classifications imposed not only upon the bird, but also, as will be discussed in more detail later, upon himself as a so-called 'peasant poet'.

Throughout his poetry, Clare explores how the sounds of birds are differently interpreted according to not only a person's background, class or education, but also their mood or state of mind. He recognises, for example, that the 'horrible apprehe[n]sions' of villagers journeying home in the dark may have led them to mistake the 'dead thin whistling sort of sound' of the nighthawk for the signal-calls of robbers in pursuit (*Natural History Prose*, p. 35). Such fearful imaginings appear to have been a common experience and consequently to have become a relatively familiar trope in rural writing. In Hardy's *Far from the Madding Crowd* (1872), for example, the 'much afeard' Joseph Poorgrass is startled into formally addressing himself to an owl in a tree 'that happened to be crying "Whoo-whoo-whoo" (as owls do, you know)': 'Joseph Poorgrass of Weatherby, Sir!'[18] Clare incorporated this mistake into one of his village tales, 'Going to the Fair'. When a young labourer's plans to meet his new love at the fair are frustrated by a broken fence and an escaped horse, the hapless Simon hears his own fears and anxieties echoed in every bird's note:

> 'Craik' went the Land rail in the wind waved grain
> Whom idle schoolboys hearing chased in vain
> In Simons mind the noise bespoke his fate
> He thought it muttered he was all too 'late'
> 'Chewsit' the Pewit screamed in swopping wews
> 'Chuse it' said Simon I know whom to chuse
> Thus ne'er a bird could sing but Simons cares
> Shaped it to somthing of his own affairs.
> (*Middle Period*, III, ll. 291–8)

Again, Clare satirises the vanity of the human endeavour to understand the call of a bird: 'vain' not only in the sense of being unfruitful, unattainable, but also in the sense that we, like Simon, inevitably shape these sounds according to our own emotional needs and preoccupations. Returning to those familiar words and phrases which Clare admits into his transcription of the nightingale's song, we can catch his sense of human absurdity in the nightingale's insistence that we 'bring a jug bring a jug bring a jug' (*Natural History Prose*, p. 312).

Increasingly, this process of shaping became crucial to Clare's exploration of the workings of his own mind. Clare understood the importance of memory in interpreting the world which surrounded him, particularly following a painful and disorientating move from his 'old home of homes' in Helpston ('The Flitting', *Middle Period*, III, l. 1). The poems of the Northborough and asylum periods operate around a series of images which change and lose their shape within a stanza, shifting from a tangible object into a hallucinogenic figure and back again – in one of the most disturbing examples, Clare describes how the 'mountains darken into caves' in 'An Invite to Eternity'.[19] His late poems explore what happens when birdsong loses its shape, its human meaning and relevance:

> I sit me in my corner chair
> That seems to feel itself from home
> & hear bird-music here & there
> From awthorn hedge & orchard come
> I hear but all is strange & new
> —I sat on my old bench in june
> The sailing puddocks shrill 'peelew'
> Oer royce wood seemed a sweeter tune.
>
> ('The Flitting', *Middle Period*, III, ll. 17–24)

Clare's sustained and highly individualised representations of birdsong have deteriorated into 'bird-music here & there', which scattered sounds reflect the poet's own increasingly disjointed thoughts. Ironically, even the shrill, shrieking cry of the 'sailing puddock' or red kite 'seemed a sweeter tune' to the poet at his home in Royce Wood.[20] At Northborough, Clare became painfully aware of the process by which personal memories necessarily shape the song which he had so accurately transcribed: 'The nightingale is singing now | But like to me she seems at loss | For royce wood & its shielding bough' ('The Flitting', *Middle Period*, III, ll. 26–8). In poems like 'The Flitting', Clare intercepts and acknowledges that irresistible pressure of the figurative to which he realised he was not himself immune: 'But *like to me* she seems at loss' (my italics). His apparent 'passion for exactitude' may consequently be placed in the context of a larger debate regarding poetic figures and the poet's propensity to make the sounds of nature, in Coleridge's phrase, 'tell back the tale | Of his own sorrow' ('The Nightingale', *Poetical Works*, I, ll. 20–1).[21]

II

In a natural history letter about nightingales addressed to Hessey, Clare broadly distinguishes between poets who 'indulg[e] in fancys' and 'those matter of fact men the Naturalists' (*Natural History Prose*, p. 42). These remarks have been read to reflect the 'complex position' which Clare's writing occupies between natural history and poetry, between 'matters of fact and matters of poetic feeling'.[22] But the 'facts', it should be remembered, were a matter of fierce and almost constant dispute among naturalists. 'You may well exclaim "What solemn trifling"', Clare tells Hessey, in gentle mockery of that matter-of-fact individual the naturalist seen 'puzzling himself with doubts' about whether nightingales sing by day or by night, and whether their notes express joy or melancholy (*Natural History Prose*, p. 42). 'As for naturalists', Clare writes more forcibly in a later note,

> you must not let them go before your own observations for some of them are 'naturals' indeed—they often pass their own fancys off for facts & on this I shoud suppose is the reason that so many foolish lyes have been uttered respecting the nightingale. (*Natural History Prose*, p. 110)

'I have no hesitation', he declares of one such esteemed 'natural', 'in saying that Mr Pennant is a Liar' (*Natural History Prose*, p. 163). If Clare often challenges poetical misrepresentations of the nightingale, he is no less critical of the 'foolish lyes' uttered by naturalists regarding this bird's song. Like Coleridge and the Wordsworth siblings, Clare was writing at a time when it was not only poetical 'fancys' that were being brought under scrutiny; he belonged to a generation of men and women who collected, compared and vigorously disputed the 'facts' about how and why birds sing. An emerging scientific method based on direct observation, practical experience and controlled experiment would ultimately in this period undermine a key theoretical distinction between birdsong and human speech: namely that, as Clare's nemesis, Lindley Murray, confidently asserted in the opening pages of his *English Grammar*, 'men speak by art and imitation' whereas the voices of animals are 'wholly instinctive' (I, p. 23).[23]

As is well known, Clare's writing may be placed in the context of a 'rising taste' for natural history, which, as one commentator remarked, was common to both 'the man of business, as well as the philosopher'.[24] Unquestionably, one of his main points of reference is an anonymous pirated edition, *Natural History of Birds, from the Works of the Best Authors, Antient and Modern* (1815).[25] As the subtitle of this work indicates, it is largely derived from – or rather composed of – the writings of the 'best authors' on this subject: Aristotle, Pliny, Plutarch, the Comte de Buffon, Oliver Goldsmith, Thomas Bewick, Thomas Pennant and Gilbert White are each quoted at length. The conclusions of Barrington's 'Experiments and Observations on the Singing of Birds' (1773–4) are rather shamelessly plagiarised in the introduction:

> It appears, from numerous experiments, that the peculiar notes of the different species of birds are altogether acquired. The attempt of a nestling bird to sing may be fitly compared with the imperfect endeavours of a child to talk. The first assays seem not to possess the slightest rudiments of the future song; but as the bird grows older and stronger, it is not difficult to perceive what is the object of its ambition. Whilst the scholar is thus endeavouring to form his song, when he is once sure of a passage, he commonly raises his tone, which he sinks again when he is not equal to what he is attempting. What the nestling is not thoroughly master of, he hurries over; lowering his tone, as if he did not wish to be heard, and could not yet satisfy himself.... These, and other well authenticated facts, seem to prove decisively that birds have no innate notes, but that like mankind, the language of those to whose care they are committed at birth will be the language they adopt in later life.... Persons ... who have an accurate ear, and have studied the notes of different birds, can very often distinguish some that have a song mixed with that of another species.[26]

Although the anonymous author of this edition evidently perceived Barrington's conclusions as 'well authenticated facts', the introduction draws to a close by affirming the 'power' of a divine and benevolent creator who 'watches over the welfare of his creatures', 'forms' their bodies and 'regulates their instincts' (I, pp. xxxiv–v). The 'facts' about the nightingale's song were thus neither openly acknowledged nor even necessarily perceived as a challenge to the orthodox doctrine of a divinely ordained universe – or man's place within it. In this respect, Clare and others like him were writing in a pivotal though *pre*-Darwinian stage of this developing science: a growing incongruity was beginning to emerge between the overall argument and the individual case, general theory and practical experience, received wisdom and common knowledge.

In her edition of *The Natural History Prose Writings of John Clare* (1983), Margaret Grainger draws together a series of notes and fragments which Clare subtitled with the headings 'Animal Instinct', 'Instinct' and 'For "*Instinct*"' (p. 90; n. 9). Based on these headings and the 'related subject matter' of the fragments themselves, Grainger suggests that, had Clare completed his proposed 'Natural History of Helpston', he 'would probably have effected smooth transitions and put together a finished essay or letter on this subject which so obviously fascinated him' (p. 82). Grainger's remark is made in passing and in tribute to Clare's abilities as a natural historian, but it is problematic, if not misleading, to speculate on what Clare 'would have' done with what are unmistakably fragments. The set of notes and draft paragraphs neither lend themselves to 'smooth transitions' nor do they follow the linear structure implicit in those terms. The manuscripts instead include several draft passages in which Clare attempts to define 'instinct' in a broad philosophical sense:

> Instinct \in brutes/ has been admired by [*del.* some] atheists as a great [ ] of [*del.* providence] nature who laugh at the reason of human beings & account it foolish it has been set forth by as many as superior to reason & defined by others who consider it inferior as a [ ] that feels the present & has nothing to [ ] for the future – yet tho instinct may not properly be defined in words yet it seems to be a natural sympathy that comes in the world with them. (*Natural History Prose*, p. 91)

In her editorial notes, Grainger remarks that the blank spaces 'suggest that Clare is feeling his way in this quasi-philosophical passage' though 'some of the words elude him' (p. 91; n. 6). But some of the blanks may be filled in relatively easily; for example, the third may be read as follows: 'that feels the present & has nothing to [*fear*] for the future'. Read as such, the phrasing recalls a familiar distinction drawn between the human and animal mind throughout the eighteenth and early nineteenth centuries. Among the most prominent examples is the final stanza of Robert Burns's 'To a Mouse':

> Still, thou art blest, compar'd wi' *me*!
> The *present* only toucheth thee:
> But Och! I *backward* cast my e'e
>   On prospects drear!
> An' *forward*, tho' I canna *see*,
>   I *guess* an' *fear*![27]

Burns's poem abides by a relative commonplace in Enlightenment philosophy, which suggested that animals have limited powers of memory and consequently neither reflect upon past experiences nor 'fear' future harm.[28] Clare's writings on 'Animal Instinct' suggest his familiarity with both Burns's poem and the philosophical principle which underpins it. If Clare is recalling Burns, the decision to leave the word blank suggests that it is not simply a case, as Grainger infers, of the words 'eluding' him; more precisely, it suggests that Clare left out a word, a 'definition' of instinct, which he found unsatisfactory. While the word is left blank in this 'quasi-philosophical' draft, throughout his poetry and prose Clare consistently describes the fears and, in a remarkable revision of the Burnsian principle, the 'fancyd dangers' envisioned by nightingales, butterflies and other creatures (*Natural History Prose*, p. 39).

The familiar contrast between a creature that only feels the present and a human being who remembers, reflects upon and struggles to come to terms with suffering is central to a canonical set of poems about birdsong in the Romantic period. The 'unpremeditated art' of Shelley's skylark is directly contrasted with the poet's own predicament:

> We look before and after,
>   And pine for what is not:
> Our sincerest laughter
>   With some pain is fraught;
> Our sweetest songs are those that tell of saddest thought.[29]

Similarly, Keats compares his own plight to that of the nightingale:

> 'Tis not through envy of thy happy lot,
>   But, being too happy in thine happiness —
>   That thou, light-wingèd Dryad of the trees,
>   In some melodious plot
>   Of beechen green, and shadows numberless,
>   Singest of summer in full-throated ease.
>   ('Ode to a Nightingale', ll. 5–10)

In each of these poems, the bird's 'unpremeditated art' and 'full-throated ease' are contrasted with the sadder and wiser music of a reflecting human intelligence. In Coleridge's poem, too, the 'tipsy joy' of the nightingale is withheld from a human infant subjected, from the very beginnings of consciousness, to strange dreams and 'inward pain'; it is through the distinctly human power of memory and association that Hartley will grow up, not to share in the bird's joy, but to 'associate' that joy with the night ('The Nightingale', *Poetical Works*, I, ll. 86, 99–100, 108–9). One of the most pronounced differences between Clare and his Romantic predecessors and contemporaries is the noticeable absence of this conventional contrast between human wisdom and animal joy. Clare's nightingales do not sing in 'full-throated ease', but rather, like Chaucer's bird, seem to 'mutter oer their songs in fear' ('When first we hear the shy come nightingales', *Middle Period*, V, ll. 1–2).

Clare never formulated a general theory of 'animal instinct' and how it differs from 'the reason of human beings' (*Natural History Prose*, p. 91). But his writings, like Dorothy Wordsworth's journals, are suffused with close, detailed descriptions of birds and their songs. His notebooks are packed with, crammed with and even overwhelmed by innumerable examples taken from his own direct observation – or 'thousands of strong proofs', to use his own phrase (*Natural History Prose*, p. 92). They reflect that growing tension in this period between the general theory and the particular instance, the received idea and the specific example. In a fragment headed 'for instinct', Clare dwells on one particular incident in detail:

> [O]ne morning as I was crossing a common calld the north fen I saw the greatest crowd of magpies together which I had ever seen & curosity led me a long way \out of my path/ to know their business [*del.* which was the ?] they was all fighting one of their kind I was much supprisd at first but I found the bird was a tamd one & on its attempting now & then to call as it were for help the strangness of the noise for it coud talk made them flye up in a startld manner [*del.* ? ? ?] & then they woud [?poor] down agen with redoubld vengeance while some crows kept at a respectable distance \making a / croaking as it were to encourage them when I got up they se ⟨e⟩ md to fly reluctantly away & hoverd oer my head their noisey defiances. (*Natural History Prose*, pp. 93–4)

There are humorous touches of anthropomorphism, particularly in the light irony with which Clare describes the feigned 'respectability' of crows. But Clare's language is not anthropomorphic in any straightforward sense: 'sympathy', 'antipathy', 'hatred', 'fighting', 'startled', 'associate' – these are not anthropomorphic terms, unless the avian world is denied any of the social instincts and habits common to both human and non-human animals. Clare draws attention to his own necessarily subjective reading of the scene ('seemed', 'as it were'), but he also recognises that these are significant sounds, that they mean something to the 'business' of birds.

On a point which remains the subject of intensive scientific research and investigation, Clare recognised in birds a subtle, skilful and deceptive ability to mimic the notes of other species: like the bird-catcher himself, a hawklike bird is heard imitating the notes of the nightingale 'as if to decoy his prey in sight' (*Natural History Prose*, p. 238). In a well-known passage in Clare's natural history letters, two touring Londoners are heard 'lavishing praises on the beautiful song of the nightingale which', Clare notes, 'happend to be a thrush' (*Natural History Prose*, p. 37). In his reading of the passage, Haughton argues that the fault or 'mistake' lies with the Londoners: they have misheard the bird, and their mishearing reflects the pretensions and prejudices of city-dwellers who, by implication, might also mishear and misjudge Clare's poetry.[30] Yet such a reading downplays the remarkable abilities which Clare observed in this rather clever little bird:

> I noticed this summer that the little thrush that commenced singing in april sung till the middle of July & that he had got many variations from the nightingale in the last month which he did not commence with in april – indeed his song was so like that of the nightingale that it might be mistaken for it by careless observers. (*Natural History Prose*, p. 325)

Composed at roughly the same time as his transcription of the nightingale's song, it is clear that Clare's attempt to take down the notes of this bird, however imperfectly, enabled him to distinguish the 'variations' which, Clare is in no doubt, the thrush has taken directly from its far-famed rival. Clare's self-assurance in this short note – his focused attention on one particular bird as he studies its notes from April to May, the colloquial brevity and sureness of his phrasing (that emphatic '*got*' from the nightingale) – is in stark contrast with those more torturous attempts to define 'instinct in words'.

Clare's writing is suffused with close, detailed descriptions of 'the stunt & unvaried' notes of 'a young bird while learning to sing' (*Natural History Prose*, p. 47). Like the bird-catchers, Clare generally seems to have understood the '*recording*' stage as a kind of practice for the full song. As he explains this natural phenomenon in one of the many (and sadly neglected) poems that he composed for his children, 'The Birds & St Valentine', 'each bachelor bird | Who in raptures half moved on loves errands to start | Their songs muttered over to get them by heart' (*Middle Period*, III, ll. 12–14). As a bird-keeper, Clare witnessed the curious behaviour of his own pet magpie in the act of perfecting its phrases:

> [W]hen it heard a sound or word that it coud not imitate readily it woud become silent & pensive & sit ruminating on an eldern tree & muttering as it were to itself som inaudible sounds till at length it got by heart the thing it was aiming at & then it was as lively & as full of chatter as ever. (*Natural History Prose*, p. 128)

As Clare recognised, magpies and other 'talking birds' do not simply mindlessly repeat human words and phrases: they mutter and stutter, while a 'pensive' state or struggle suggests that something fundamental is going on in the production of new sounds and words. As we shall see, part of the fascination for Clare stems from a related interest in a grave disjuncture between what poets say and what or how they think, between the utterance itself and a subvocal language of thought.

Clare also comments on a comparatively neglected area of research. It was well known to bird-fanciers and bird-keepers that their subjects were inclined to 'forget' motifs in the moulting season. Training techniques were specifically developed to deal with the bullfinch's want of what was called 'firmness'; if the nine months of punishing and often cruelly restrictive training were interrupted for any reason, the birds were known to 'spoil the air, by suppressing or displacing the different parts' or even to 'forget it entirely at their first moulting'.[31] Clare observed this phenomena in the wild with evident fascination:

> When summer from the forrest starts
> Its melody with silence lies
> & like a bird from foreign parts
> It cannot sing for all it tries
> 'Cuck cuck' it cries & mocking boys
> Crie 'cuck' & still it stutters more
> Till quite forgot its own sweet voice
> It seems to know itself no more.
>
> ('Birds Nesting', *Middle Period*, II, ll. 559–66)

I previously argued that this poem is primarily concerned with different kinds of human knowing and their respective limitations – birdsong is the 'mystery' which equally eludes the schoolboy, the woodman, the scientist and the poet. But here the focus shifts to the question of self-knowledge and the inscrutable workings of the mind and memory. The 'stutter' of the cuckoo points to the unexpected and unexplained disruption of oral communication through involuntary repetitions, silences, blocks. Clare's observations of birds in the act of singing provided him with unique insights into the cognitive processes involved in the production of song and speech – insights which complicate our understanding not only of how birds sing, but also of how Clare composed.

III

Clare's sensitivity to what he regarded as the 'foolish lyes' written about nightingales derives in part from his own sense of being misheard and mischaracterised as a 'peasant poet' (*Natural History Prose*, p. 110). In *John Clare and the Place of Poetry* (2008), Gorji has observed the 'wider currency' of Milton's description of Shakespeare 'warbl[ing] his native woodnotes wild' in 'descriptions of native genius' in the late eighteenth and early nineteenth centuries.[32] As the nightingale became associated with a form of natural, spontaneous and artless expression, variations on Milton's phrase became almost proverbial in presentations of peasant-poetry. Hannah More, for example, defended the 'inexpiable poetic sins' of the milkmaid Ann Yearsley's poetry as the 'wild wood notes' of untutored yet unspoilt genius.[33] When Clare and his publishers were discussing titles for the poet's second volume, Edmund Drury (somewhat unimaginatively) suggested 'Wild Wood Notes'.[34] Whatever ideal of spontaneous song may have been attributed to poets like Yearsley and Clare, this ideal, as Gorji points out, is at risk of undermining their skill and agency as poets. In his revisionist readings of the nightingale and its song, Clare may be seen as challenging conventional ideas not only about this most poetical of birds but also about himself as a rustic singer. Gorji observes a crucial irony in Clare's frequent allusions to Milton and (through him) Shakespeare: in order to present his art as 'natural' and 'spontaneous', the peasant poet is actively placing himself in an established poetic tradition and wider literary community. In this sense, these apparently 'wild' and 'spontaneous' outpourings may be seen to represent a conscious mode of literary self-fashioning – or 'artful artlessness', as Gorji terms it.[35]

Gorji's highly influential book has proved instrumental in opening out new ways of approaching Clare as a highly self-conscious and emphatically literary poet. Although her research rightly scrutinises the terms in which poetic 'genius' was described and understood in the long nineteenth century ('natural', 'spontaneous', 'artless'), the terms of her own argument ('agency', 'craft' and 'self-consciousness') are not in themselves entirely stable. As discussed in Chapter Two, the question of authorial agency remains the subject of much dispute among literary scholars. In so far as critics have questioned the degree of conscious control that a writer possesses over the meaning of the texts they generate, the problem of agency further complicates our understanding of the craftsmanship by which the author's intentions are seen to be carried out.[36] If Clare is a 'self-conscious' poet, he is also conscious of the complexities of consciousness itself. As his biographer Jonathan Bate points out, Clare coined the term 'self-identity' in an unpublished essay of that title and, later, he coined its antonym: 'this sad non-identity'.[37] Clare is mindful of his own mind. His writing is filled with descriptions of his own psychological turns and creative processes, and it is from here that the asylum verse derives both its power and its pathos:

> Say maiden wilt thou go with me
> In this strange death of life to be
> To live in death and be the same

> Without this life, or home, or name
> At once to be, & not to be
> That was, and is not—yet to see
> Things pass like shadows—and the sky
> Above, below, around us lie.
>
> ('An Invite to Eternity', *Later Poems*, I, ll. 17–24)

A highly sophisticated, artful literariness is brought out in the allusion to Hamlet's famous question, but Clare's play on Shakespeare's phrasing in the same stroke registers an acute awareness of the complexity and contradictions of a conscious human identity: 'at once to be, & not to be'. With their rich tonal and grammatical ambiguities, Clare's late lyrics force the reader to read between the lines: while Clare's syntax in the second line could be read either to suggest the death of future life or to convey the speaker's own current death-like existence, the metre, and particularly the stress on the opening word 'say', is similarly left open to the reader's interpretation. In many ways more intensely than Wordsworth or Coleridge before him, Clare in these late poems demonstrates a profound fascination with the relationship between the mind and language, between actual lived experience and how that experience is named, represented and recounted in words.

As Clare's editor, Taylor has been roundly criticised by McKusick for projecting a misleading view of Clare as 'an ignorant Peasant Poet, thoughtlessly warbling his native woodnotes wild' in his introduction to Clare's first volume, *Poems Descriptive of Rural Life and Scenery* (1820).[38] McKusick discerns the 'marketing strategy' underpinning Taylor's introduction, in which Clare appears to have colluded, albeit dryly: 'I am not against having my humble Occupation, mean parentage, & scanty Education – or any thing of the like hinted at in your preface – Just what you think suitable so you may do'.[39] Taylor several times refers to the poet's apparent 'ignorance of grammar', although the editor's analysis of the poems themselves may give us reason to pause on a term which was hotly disputed throughout the long nineteenth century. Taylor's close familiarity with Clare's grammatical peculiarities becomes apparent in his analysis of the poems: the editor notes a particular tendency to make 'verbs of substantives' and 'verbs of adjectives', as in the line, 'Spring's pencil *pinks* thee in thy flushy stain'.[40] In using the word '*pinks*', however, Taylor insists that the poet has 'done no more than the man who first employed *crimson* as a verb' (p. xv). Although the words individually created are new and original, the process of creating them is not. Taylor insists that 'there is no innovation in such cases as these' (p. xv); it is one and the same technique or 'procedure' by which 'all languages have been formed and perfected' (p. xiv). Instead of creating an unlimited supply of new words, humankind had learned to 'abbreviate' and conjoin (p. xv). They had learned grammar, in fact. If Clare is ignorant of grammar in the prescriptive sense of eighteenth-century correctness, Taylor suggests that his language nonetheless abides by a form of what we might now call 'deep grammar': his words are formed according to 'certain laws of analogy which are inherent in the mind of man, and universally attended to in the formation of new words' (p. xv).

Taylor also touches on one of the most disputed questions in Enlightenment philology: namely, whether thought is possible without the aid of arbitrary signs. He recounts Clare's first 'poetic experience':

> He was tired one day with looking at the pictures in a volume of poems, which he thinks were Pomfret's, when his father read him one piece in the book to amuse him. The delight he felt, at hearing this read, still warms him when he thinks of the circumstance; but though he distinctly recollects the vivid pleasure which thrilled through him then, he has lost all trace of the incidents as well as of the language, nor can he find any poem of Pomfret's at all answering the faint conception he retains of it. It is possible that his chief gratification was in the harmony of the numbers, and that he had thoughts of his own floating onward with the verse very different from those which the same words would now suggest. (pp. xi–xii)

In his suggestion that Clare had 'thoughts of his own floating onward with the verse', Taylor registers a more subtle break between language and thought than Horne Tooke and other Universal Grammarians had allowed for. As discussed in Chapter Two, based on such theories, the 'lower' animals were frequently denied consciousness, while the 'vulgar' classes were deemed incapable of the higher forms of abstract thought and excluded from participation in a wider public discourse. If thought, however, is dependent on language and vice versa, why then do scientists, writers and poets experience the struggle and frustration repeatedly referred to throughout their writings? Both Wordsworth and Clare suggest that the melody came before the words, or rather that the words were hummed, muttered and gradually took shape from sound and rhythm. As Clare would later describe this subvocal stage in the creative process, '& then I hummed the words again' ('The Progress of Ryhme', *Middle Period*, III, l. 266).

As Weiner points out, Clare's account of his poetical development is not easily extracted from 'the conventions of autodidact biography'; her 'suspicion' is that such conventions play their 'part' in Clare's descriptions 'even as they reveal something important, even elemental, about Clare's craft'.[41] 'What matters', she argues, is what Clare's poems 'actually do'.[42] But Clare's autobiographical writings, like Wordsworth's and Coleridge's, contain detailed and precise descriptions of the psychological turns and processes of the mind during composition: they reflect a constant struggle to define that indefinable 'something important' or 'even elemental' about Clare's craft. That word 'mutter' resurfaces repeatedly in a consistent, focused attempt to capture a shadowy realm between an internal thought and its external expression: the 'inward stir' of the hedge sparrow's 'shadowed melody' ('The Firetails Nest', *Middle Period*, IV, ll. 7–8). Shadow suggests shape, a structure of sound, though indistinct and unuttered. Often, Clare refers to a quasi-linguistic language of the mind; in his unfinished autobiography, he describes how as a child he 'hunted curious flowers in raptures & muttered thoughts in their praise'.[43] Erin Lafford has observed Clare's 'investment' in this kind of 'subvocal register' as 'both a personalised, therapeutic mode of self-address, and a way to foster a deep poetic relationship with his natural surroundings'.[44] Clare's 'investment' is also partly political, as he affirms the existence of a universal, innate propensity for and 'right to song'. ('The Progress of Ryhme', *Middle Period*, III, l. 80).

In the previous chapter I argued that Coleridge perceived the 'scanty vocabulary' of 'uneducated man' as evidence of an equally impoverished mind (*Biographia Literaria*, II, p. 53); Wordsworth, by contrast, throughout his life affirmed the imaginative life of rustic characters surrounded by the natural scenes from which he believed the 'best part' of language was originally derived (*Prose*, I, p. 124). Clare wrestled with these larger, politically charged questions in his various, and often contradictory, reflections on 'the man of taste'.[45] In an autobiographical sketch, these tensions are deeply felt:

> I heard the cuckoos 'wandering voise' & the restless song of the Nightingale & was delighted while I pausd & mutterd its sweet jug jug as I passd its black thorn bower I often pulled my hat over my eyes to watch the rising of the lark or to see the hawk hang in the summer sky & the kite take its circles round the wood I often lingered a minute on the woodland stile to hear the wood pigeons clapping their wings among the dark oaks ... I observd all this with the same raptures as I have done since but I knew nothing of poetry it was felt & not utterd. (*Autobiographical Writings*, p. 31)

The passage is composed of extensive literary allusions, direct and indirect: the 'wandering voise' of the cuckoo echoes Wordsworth's comparison of the bird 'wandering in solitude' ('The Cuckoo at Laverna', *Sonnet Series*, ll. 98). Clare, however, insists that his initial 'raptures' existed before he knew anything of poetry or had learned to frame or express his feelings. Clare's companion on these youthful excursions, he continues, 'had never read Thompson or Cowper or Wordsworth or perhaps heard of their names'; however, the poet insists, 'nature gives every one a natural simplicity of heart to read her language' (*Autobiographical Writings*, p. 43). On the one hand, poetry gives form and shape to thoughts ('when the reader peruses real poesy he often whispers to [himself] "bless me I've felt this myself & often had such thoughts in my memory"'); on the other, innate childhood pleasures may be distorted by the 'grosser interferences of the world' which 'deaden the heart with ignorance' (*Autobiographical Writings*, p. 43). Feelings that are universal and inherent within the human mind are lost in the awakening of adult worldly concern. The poem, as Clare conceives it, is the conscious mind's recovery of an original, connate and universal *poesy*.

Clare's experience of publication further complicated his understanding of the relationship between thought and word, poesy and the poem. In a series of letters which he composed in the early 1830s, Clare reflected on this complex and prolonged process of putting his ideas down on paper. To Thomas Pringle, he wrote,

> I became a scribbler from downright pleasure in giving vent to my feelings & long & pleasing painful was my struggles to acquire a sufficient knowledge of the written language of england before I could put down my ideas on paper even so far as to understand them myself – but I mastered it in time sufficiently to be understood by others & then became an author by accident & felt astonished that the critics should notice me at all ... I shrank from myself with extacy & have never been myself since. (*Letters*, p. 571)

Clare implies that his fondness for 'scribbling' both enabled him to give 'vent' to his feelings and to 'understand' thoughts which implicitly lay dormant in his consciousness. Writing appears to have enabled Clare to articulate his innermost thoughts and feelings, but this act of cognition – of 'understanding' his own thoughts – also necessitates distance. Self-consciousness and self-knowledge lead to a form of profound alienation.

In another letter, to Henry Francis Cary in 1832, Clare reflected upon his own habits of writing in terms which go well beyond 'the conventions of autodidact biography':

> if you laugh at my ambitions I am ready to laugh with you at my own vanity for I sit sometimes & wonder <at> over the <noise> little noise I have made in the world until I think I have written nothing as yet to deserve any praise at all so the spirit of fame of living a little after life like a name on a conspic-[u]ous place urges my blood upward into unconscious melodys & striding

down my orchard & homestead I hum & sing inwardly those little madrigals & then go in & pen them down thinking them much better things then they are untill I look over them again & then the charm vanishes into the vanity that I shall do somthing better ere I die & so in spite of myself I ryhme on. (*Letters*, pp. 595–6)

Clare describes the moment of poetic inspiration as a kind of physical involuntary feeling, a rising of the blood, a pacing of the feet in time to what he terms 'unconscious melodys'. These gradually shape themselves into 'little madrigals' or part-songs; usually composed of two or more singing parts, the madrigal is often figured in pastoral poetry as an accompaniment to the murmuring of brooks and other indistinct natural sounds (*OED*).[46] Clare had earlier described the thrushes as they 'chant their m[a]drigalls' to the 'closing murmur' of day; here, he presents his own 'little madrigals' as a kind of accompaniment to the indistinct sounds and thoughts of his 'unconscious melodies'.[47] In some ways, composition appears to have offered Clare a form of self-realisation, yet the 'charm' soon vanishes, suggesting not only that the written words have lost their the capacity to please or delight their author but also that the author has lost a connection or sympathy with them. The charm is broken. Clare's agency and skill as a poet have often been underestimated, but composition, in all its complexity, is the stuff of his writing.

IV

Unquestionably, 'The Progress of Ryhme' represents Clare's most sustained exploration of the creative process in its gradual, uneasy development from infancy to maturity. Central to this endeavour is the analogy between how birds and poets practise their songs:

> A simple love a wild esteem
> As heart felt as the linnets dream
> That mutters in its sleep at night
> Some notes from extacys delight
> Thus did I dream oer joys & lie
> Muttering dream-songs of poesy.
> (*Middle Period*, III, ll. 119–24)

Clare directly compares the pensive mutterings of birds with the poet's own gradual forming of syllables and snatches of meaning, half-formed utterances, in semi-conscious states, which process disrupts the possibility of complete authorial agency and complicates our understanding of the skill set underlying birdsong, speech and poetry.

This long autobiographical poem has clear literary precursors, among them Thomson's *The Seasons* (1726–30), James Beattie's *The Minstrel* (1771–4) and Wordsworth's poems, notably the boy of Winander passage.[48] In placing himself in the tradition of Wordsworth, Beattie and Thomson, Clare is, in one sense, being 'artfully artless' here. We are confronted with the familiar irony: literary influences necessarily shape the poet's retrospective account of a life *before* he had learned to read or had any knowledge of 'poesy by books' (*Autobiographical Writings*, p. 43). Adult literacy unavoidably impinges on the recollection of a pre-literate state. Yet there persists a troubling sense in Clare's writing that his poetry was not 'crafted' in any straightforward sense. The nature of influence, as Clare conceives it in this poem, is itself complicated. He describes the early influences of natural sounds, especially birdsong, and oral folk traditions:

> In silent shame the harp was tried
> & raptures guess the tune applied
> Yet oer the songs my parents sung
> My ear in silent musings hung.   (ll. 271–4)

It is a peculiar habit of Clare's, which he shared with and possibly derived from Wordsworth, to place that word 'hung' at the end of a line. The beauty of both Clare's poem and Wordsworth's description of the boy of Winander derives from an amateurish, boyish inarticulacy arising from a profound poetic experience which at once tantalises and eludes the young poet's skill. While the placing of the word in Wordsworth's poem signals the boy's imaginative development and actively encourages the reader to hang, listening and waiting for what will come next in an unrhymed blank verse poem, Clare's strings of end-stopped rhyming couplets indicate and celebrate the endlessly generative power of rhyme: one rhyme continually suggests another, which 'hangs' or hinges on the last. As Taylor described the poet having 'thoughts of his own *floating* onwards with the verse' which his father read to him as a child, Clare describes how his ear 'hangs' over the songs of his parents in its own 'silent musings'.

Throughout the poem, Clare distinguishes between thought and form, feeling and its expression:

> —Aye birds no matter what the tune
> Or 'croak' or 'tweet'—twas natures boon
> That brought them joy—& music flung
> Its spell oer every mattin sung
> & een the sparrows chirp to me
> Was song in its felicity.   (ll. 157–62)

Clare throughout this poem distinguishes between 'feeling' and 'tune', and this distinction affirms the peasant poet's own 'right to song' (l. 80). The 'tune' is distinguished from a far broader definition of 'song', which is newly characterised by its 'felicity' – the joy of being and the most natural, appropriate or 'felicitous' expression of that joy, from the sparrow's chirp to the nightingale's virtuosity.

According to this poem, Clare's first poetic experiences were musical and non-semantic:

> No matter how the lyre was strung
> From my own heart the music sprung
> The cowboy with his oaten straw
> Although he hardly heard or saw
> No more of music then he made
> Twas sweet—& when I pluckt the blade
> Of grass upon the woodland hill
> To mock the birds with artless skill
> No music in the world beside
> Seemed half so sweet—till mine was tried.   (ll. 213–22)

Clare draws upon a familiar image of Romanticism: the eolian harp, which Coleridge, for example, used to represent 'diversely framed' instruments which differently sound one and the same 'intellectual breeze | At once the Soul of each, and God of all' ('The Eolian Harp', *Poetical Works*, I, ll. 47–8). Clare's deployment of this familiar trope asserts his own right to song. On one level, Clare recognises the 'skill' and craftsmanship which he has acquired over the cowboy and his own younger self; on the other, however, he perceives that craftsmanship as the conscious mind's recovery of an unconscious and universal poesy: '& what I felt—as now I sing' (l. 295).

As Clare describes the first stirrings of poetic feeling in the 'darksome grove' of Burghley Park (l. 194):

> [I] felt without a single skill
> That instinct that would not be still
> To think of song sublime beneath
> That heaved my bosom like my breath
> That burned & chilled & went & came
> Without or uttering or a name
> Untill the vision waked with time
> & left me itching after ryhme.   (ll. 197–204)

This moving autobiographical poem is moving precisely because it does not simply idealise a youthful poet listening in rapture to birdsong; it also records those fretful years of study, tried and failed attempts, and a form of mental anguish so intense it was almost physical. We can see a pattern emerging in these passages: indistinct sounds and physical sensations precede the 'vision' associated with what Clare later describes as 'song-pictures' (l. 336).

Clare's transcription of the nightingale's song appears in this wider context of shaping feeling into words:

> —& nightingales O I have stood
> Beside the pingle & the wood
> & oer the old oak railing hung
> To listen every note they sung
> & left boys making taws of hay
> To muse & listen half the day
> The more I listened & the more
> Each note seemed sweeter then before
> & aye so different was the strain
> She'd scarce repeat the note again
> —'Chew-chew chew-chew' & higher still
> 'Cheer-cheer cheer-cheer' more loud & shrill
> 'Cheer-up cheer-up cheer-up'—& dropt
> Low 'Tweet tweet jug jug jug' & stopt
> One moment just to drink the sound
> Her music made & then a round
> Of stranger witching notes was heard
> As if it was a stranger bird
> 'Wew-wew wew-wew chur-chur chur-chur
> 'Woo-it woo-it' could this be her
> 'Tee-rew tee-rew tee-rew tee-rew
> 'Chew-rit chew-rit'—& ever new
> 'Will-will will-will grig-grig grig-grig'
> The boy stopt sudden on the brig
> To hear the 'tweet tweet tweet' so shrill
> Then 'jug jug jug' & all was still
> A minute—when a wilder strain
> Made boys & woods to pause again
> Words were not left to hum the spell
> Could they be birds that sung so well—
> I thought & may be more then I
> That musics self had left the sky
> To cheer me with its majic strain
> & then I hummed the words again
> Till fancy pictured standing bye
> My hearts companion poesy.   (ll. 233–68)

As both Karlin and Weiner observe, Clare is not only syllabling the sounds of the nightingale; he is also 'fitting' those syllables to his own poetic line. Clare thus 'transforms the bird's song into his own lyric, altering its rhythm and phrasing, and introducing rhyme'; for both Karlin and Weiner, this transformative process is indicated in that phrase, 'and then I hummed the words again'.[49] Throughout his poetry, Clare demonstrates his fascination with this kind of quasi-linguistic form of communication: humming, muttering, seemingly on the verge of blabbing out the words and yet never quite doing so. We can think back to those terms in which Clare described how he hummed and sang inwardly those 'little madrigals' (*Letters*, pp. 595–6). Clare is thinking not only about how a bird's song may be translated into human words, but also about how the poet's own indistinct thoughts and mutterings are in this early stage of development being gradually formed into syllables and strains, stopping and starting, humming and shaping, until the poet finally pictures 'standing bye | My hearts companion poesy'.

V

Like Wordsworth, Clare, in his late poetry, increasingly turned to shorter lyrics, ballads, songs and sonnets or 'little poems', as he broadly referred to them (*Letters*, p. 82). Since the sonnet is widely regarded as one of the most artificial, constricted and tightly regulated forms in English verse, Clare's highly innovative experiments in this form have been interpreted as exemplary instances of his 'artful artlessness'.[50] Although these poems unquestionably demonstrate the development of Clare's highly original and distinctive voice, the poems themselves are about the pleasures and frustrations, the tried and failed attempts, by which he mastered the form:

> When first we hear the shy come nightingales
> They seem to mutter oer their songs in fear
> & climbing e'er so soft the spinney rails
> All stops as if no bird was any where
> The kindles bushes with the young leaves thin
> Lets curious eyes to search a long way in
> Untill impatience cannot see or hear
> The hidden music—gets but little way
> Upon the path—when up the songs begin
> Full loud a moment & then low again
> But when a day or two confirms her stay

> Boldly she sings & loud for half the day
> & soon the village brings the woodmans tale
> Of having heard the new come nightingale.
>
> (*Middle Period*, V, p. 222)

Clare's sonnet cannot be called 'original' in the eighteenth-century sense of the term. It has clear literary precursors, among them Chaucer's description of the 'new abashed nightingale', Smith's description of this bird's 'prelusive notes' and perhaps Coleridge's 'father's tale' ('The Nightingale', *Poetical Works*, I, l. 106). Clare, however, has his own 'tale' to tell. The experience of listening to the nightingale is carefully worked into the visual and sonorous effects of Clare's language: the hurried sounds evoked in the phrase 'shy come' and the onomatopoeic 'mutter', the long 'search' extended across the poetic line, the impatience suspended over two, the sudden start at the unexpected return of song 'full loud a moment & then low again'. Clare, unlike Coleridge and other poetic predecessors, is not concerned with how this bird's song has been translated into mythic narratives; rather, he tells us the 'woodman's tale' of waiting and listening for 'the new come nightingale'. Distinguishing his own approach from that of his predecessors and rivals, Clare triumphantly asserts and affirms the development of his own artistic voice: 'But when a day or two confirms her stay | Boldly she sings & loud for half the day'.

For Clare, part of the attraction appears to have derived from a disinhibiting sense of sonnets as experimental exercises or, to use his own word, 'attempts'; following the prolonged process of editing his third and final volume with Taylor and Hessey, *The Shepherd's Calendar* (1827), Clare informed his publishers in no uncertain terms:

> I have made it up in my mind to write one hundred sonnets as a set of pictures on the scenes & objects that appear in the different seasons & as I shall do it soly for amusement I shall take up wi gentle & simple as they come whatever in my eye finds any [inter]est these things are resolves not merely in the view for publication but for attempts. (*Letters*, p. 288)

Like Wordsworth, Clare found in sonnets a welcome relief from the more gruelling and mundane aspects of writing a long narrative poem (or sitting own to 'wiredraw out regular argument & then plod after it in a regular manner', as he described it to Hessey in July 1820; *Letters*, p. 80). Clare embraced the fragmentariness, or miscellaneousness, which Wordsworth similarly appears to have discovered in these little poems. And ironically, out of these 'attempts' came poems which many have come to regard as among Clare's best works:

> The happy white throat on the sweeing bough
> Swayed by the impulse of the gadding wind
> That ushers in the showers of april—now
> Singeth right joyously & now reclined
> Croucheth & clingeth to her moving seat
> To keep her hold—& till the wind for rest
> Pauses—she mutters inward melodies
> That seem her hearts rich thinkings to repeat
> & when the branch is still—her little breast
> Swells out in raptures gushing symphonies
> & then against her brown wing softly prest
> The wind comes playing an enraptured guest
> This way and that she swees—till gusts arise
> More boisterous in their play—& off she flies.
> (*Middle Period*, IV, p. 249)

This poem signals Clare's emboldened and wilful disregard for the sonnet's conventional 'argument'. He openly extols the virtues of sound over sense, sensory pleasure over rational deduction or moral resolution. He freely takes words from different historical periods and social registers: the archaic form of 'singeth', 'croucheth' and 'clingeth' contrasts with the dialect word 'swees', all of which were standardised and 'corrected' when this poem was published in Clare's fourth volume, *The Rural Muse* (1835).[51] As is not infrequently the case, the regrettable decisions of Clare's editors inadvertently serve to throw into greater relief the significance of his language: words are chosen according to their sound and mimetic aptness, as opposed to their register or social appropriateness. Like differently framed harps, these different registers nonetheless express the same essential, universal impulse of the 'gadding wind'. It all comes back to the downright pleasure and the joy of poetry. As he carefully works the sounds of the bird into his conventionally structured, but increasingly intricate and varied, rhyme scheme (*abab/cdec/dedd/ff*), Clare shows us how the sonnet's rules can facilitate this kind of linguistic play: this is not *free* play, but 'sweeing' verse that crouches and clings to a set of rules. When gusts arise too 'boisterous in their play', the sonnet is over: '—& off she flies'.

In structural terms, these are two of the most sophisticated sonnets that Clare composed. Weiner observes the importance of structure as a 'marker' of authorial control in modern criticism: nineteenth-century ideals of naturalness, spontaneity and artlessness have been supplanted by the 'fallacy of intention' or what Jonathan Culler shrewdly discerns as the 'convention of *unity*'.[52] Structural integrity has grown inseparable from what Earl R. Wasserman perceives as being 'the intention of the poem': the 'relationships, relative significances, and emphases' which make up the poem's 'grammar'.[53] The apparent lack of structure in many of Clare's sonnets has consequently been read to reflect, and to directly result from, his compositional habits – his tendency to write 'hastily and virtually without premeditation', in William D. Brewer's prognosis.[54] Such arguments are firmly refuted by poems such as 'The happy white throat on the sweeing bough' and 'When first we hear the shy come nightingales'; Clare's masterful enjambment of his lines in these poems realises the kind of 'intense Unity' which Wordsworth praised in Milton's sonnets and which he compared with 'an orbicular body, – a sphere – or a dew-drop' (*Later Years*, II, pp. 604–5). As Sara Lodge points out, Clare had evidently been studying and experimenting with metrical forms:[55]

> Styles may with fashions vary—tawdry chaste
> Have had their votaries which each fancied taste
> From Donns old homely gold whose broken feet
> Jostles the readers patience from its seat
> To Popes smooth ryhmes that regularly play
> In musics stated periods all the way
> That starts & closes starts again & times
> Its tuning gammut true as minster chimes
> From these old fashions stranger metres flow
> Half prose half verse that stagger as they go
> One line starts smooth & then for room perplext
> Elbows along & knocks against the next
> & half its neighbour where a pause marks time
> There the clause ends what follows is for ryhme.
> ('Shadows of Taste', *Middle Period*, III, ll. 79–92)

Clare is showcasing his knowledge and skills. His criticism is both highly astute and colloquially familiar, and we can see him experimenting with those characteristically Wordsworthian staggered lines, knocks and midline pauses in his description of the happy whitethroat as she 'croucheth & clingeth to her moving seat | To keep her hold' ('The happy white throat on the sweeing bough', *Middle Period*, IV, ll. 5–6).

Evidently, Clare was experimenting with these forms in the abundance of little poems that he composed at Northborough in the 1830s. Yet many of Clare's sonnets abandon, ignore or resist this kind of unity altogether.

We can only imagine what Wordsworth might have thought of a poem such as the following:

> The fire tail tells the boys when nests are nigh
> & tweets & flyes from every passer bye
> The yellow hammer never makes a noise
> But flyes in silence from the noisey boys
> The boys will come & take them every day
> & still she lays as none were taen away
> The nightingale keeps tweeting churring round
> But leaves in silence when the nest is found
> The pewet hollos chewsit as she flyes
> & flops about the shepherd where he lies
> But when her nest is found she stops her song
> & cocks [her] coppled crown & runs along
> Wrens cock their tails & chitter loud & play
> & robins hollow tut & flye away.
>
> (*Middle Period*, V, p. 247)

Sonnets like this one demonstrate an almost breathtaking disregard for the most elementary rules of poetry: there is no attempt to amend or correct the flagrant amount of repetition which Clare performs here apparently without blinking (in the most questionable example, 'away' is rhymed twice). The same words and synonymous phrases are repeated time and again within the poem itself ('noise', 'noisey'; 'silence', 'stops her song') and across the sonnets as a whole (words relating to the sounds and movements of birds abound throughout the relatively small selection of sonnets which I have discussed thus far). The structure and syntax of this sonnet are striking in their arbitrariness: grammatical clauses do not appear to be deployed in order to structure, select or compare, but rather to contain, a set number of images. To the astonishment and perturbation, the fascination and bewilderment of many of Clare's readers, these sonnets, or 'fourteen-line poems', as some have termed them, appear to embody a view of form as little more than 'a container into which a certain amount of poetry may be fitted, so many lines filling out the shape of the vessel'.[56]

As we have seen, Clare was more than capable of emulating the kind of 'intense Unity' which Wordsworth praised in Milton's sonnets; rather than being the result of Clare's 'hasty' and 'unpremeditated' mode of composition, the 'centrifugal' structure of Clare's sonnets has been read to reflect the temporal and spatial structure of the world they seek to represent.[57] For John Barrell, the 'complex manifold of impressions' presented in sonnets such as 'Emmonsails Heath in Winter' was 'something that Clare had to work for';

rejecting the kind of 'formal', 'orderly' syntax through which Clare's eighteenth-century predecessors had conventionally organised the individual parts of the landscape into a unified whole, Clare, in Barrell's reading, developed a more 'disorderly' syntax to better articulate 'the form of the place as he perceived it'.[58] Rather than imposing 'a grammar of relationships that unifies otherwise paradoxical or disparate elements', Clare's fourteen-line poems, in all their apparent arbitrariness, have been read to at once emulate and embrace what Seamus Heaney called 'the inexorable one-thing-after-anotherness' of the world.[59] What is remarkable about a sonnet such as 'The fire tail tells the boys when nests are nigh' is the lack of communication among all the noise: the lack of empathy between boys and birds, the lack of connection between couplets and the unnerving absence of explicit authorial comment or judgement upon the scene. The boys 'will' come, the yellowhammer 'still' lays and the sonnet does not progress or unfold into a reasoned or moral stance on this activity. In this context, the 'hollow tut' of Clare's robin sounds wonderfully like a parody of the closing couplet of an English sonnet; the hollowness of the sound seems to mock the futility of attempting to arrive at any moral conclusion – a conclusion which, Clare wittily implies, is only ever temporary, a momentary stoppage or resting place until the bird abruptly 'flye[s] away'.

Although Clare's sonnets have been widely recognised as refreshingly true to life in this respect, critics have seemed more reluctant to relate these poems to what was happening internally, psychologically, during what was unquestionably one of the most turbulent periods in Clare's life. That reluctance is understandable; it reflects an unwillingness to draw the kind of connections which, as Lafford's research shows, Clare's contemporaries were too quick to make between the poet's disordered speech and apparent mental 'enfeeblement'.[60] Although critics have rightly resisted speculating on the relationship between Clare's syntax and 'the symptoms of lunacy', it should not be forgotten that poets throughout the Romantic period, including both Wordsworth and Clare himself, recognised a connection between the haphazardness of the world and the 'caprice' of the human mind (*Wordsworth's Literary Criticism*, p. 185). Readers of Clare's poetry have been struck by the direct and remarkable parallel that he draws between the volition of birds and the equally 'mysterious but immediate emergence of a "sudden thought"':[61]

> The wild duck startles like a sudden thought
> & heron slow as if it might be caught
> The flopping crows on weary wing go bye

> & grey beard jackdaws noising as they flye
> The crowds of starnels wiz & hurry bye
> & darken like a cloud the evening sky
> The larks like thunder rise & suthy round
> Then drop & nestle in the stubble ground
> The wild swan hurrys high & noises loud
> With white necks peering to the evening cloud
> The weary rooks to distant woods are gone
> With length of tail the magpie winnows on
> To neighbouring trees & leaves the distant crow
> While small birds nestle in the hedge below.
> (*Middle Period*, V, pp. 269–70)

An intricate order emerges out of these seven seemingly interchangeable couplets: the 'suddenness' of the movement which marks the beginning of the sonnet gradually transitions to the small birds 'nestling' in the hedge at its close. Within this overall shift from sudden motion to a peaceful, albeit transitory, resting place, there are uneasy and unpredictable movements: if the wild duck startles like a 'sudden thought', it follows that the 'slow' heron resembles an idea which may be more easily grappled with or even 'caught', the awkward 'flopping' movements of crows pleasingly evoke an inexpert or clumsy thought process, the thunder and noise of jackdaws and starlings resemble sudden and overwhelming races of thoughts, and the abrupt 'drop' of the lark is followed by the wild swan's hurried flight into the evening clouds – an image which, in Romantic poetry, is frequently associated with the transcendent vision of the poet 'hidden | In the light of thought' (Shelley, 'To a Skylark', ll. 36–7). In his sonnets, Clare may be seen developing a highly innovative mode of metaphor which would become increasingly significant to writers in the following centuries, a mode of metaphor through which Ted Hughes would later draw comparisons between the movements of animals and the motions of his own mind, and between describing animals and 'capturing' thoughts in poems.[62] 'These winged thoughts are like birds, and will not be handled', wrote Henry David Thoreau; 'nothing was ever so unfamiliar and startling to a man as his own thoughts'.[63]

Clare's understanding of his own thought processes and poetic development were further complicated by his experiences of publication. Individual poems intended for 'The Midsummer Cushion', notably 'The Progress of Ryhme', convey a developing interest in the growth of the poet's mind. Patterns of imagery within this collection as a whole indicate a larger structural design: the structure is seasonal, moving from 'spring' poems, predominantly concerned with the 'joy' of youth, to later descriptions of autumn and winter, which very often signal a mellowed and matured adult consciousness.[64] Although these larger designs are discernible from the order of poems in manuscript, 'The Midsummer Cushion' was never completed or published in Clare's lifetime. Individual poems were selected and reset in the volume published as *The Rural Muse*. In a draft preface to this work, Clare describes the process of selecting from a larger volume:

> It is necessary that I should say somthing respecting the following poems they are selected from a great many written at different times & under very different feelings ... The Tales the longest pieces in the Vol are only a portion of what I onc(e) entended should fill a Vol but ill health under which I have long laboured interrupted my intensions & rendered m(e) encapable of compleating the others this is all I have to sa(y) for the present. (*Middle Period*, III, pp. 7–8)

Subsequent versions document Clare's uneasy relationship with prefaces, particularly with regard to the accustomed tone of a labouring poet humbly appealing to 'the kind indulgence of the public' (*Middle Period*, III, p. 8). But this early draft is characteristic in cutting straight to the point – to what Clare evidently considered vital and 'necessary' to an understanding of the volume. The 'different feelings' expressed in Clare's poems are linked to the 'different times' at which they were composed. If the autobiographical poems of 'The Midsummer Cushion' delineate the growth of the poet's mind from springtime joys to a sadder and wiser maturity, Clare's sense of his poetic development is more fragmentary here – Clare, as he described himself in a letter to his friend and patroness, Eliza Emmerson, was developing into a poet of many moods and 'many existences' (*Letters*, p. 504).

In this respect, the experience of publishing *The Rural Muse* closely allies Clare with the subject of my next chapter, Thomas Hardy. Hardy's first published volume of poetry, *Wessex Poems and Other Verses* (1898), was comprised of a series of 'miscellaneous' verses, the majority of which had never been published, though 'many were written long ago, and others partly written'.[65] In the preface to his next volume, *Poems of the Past and Present* (1901), Hardy reflected on this experience of revisiting poems written 'long ago':

> [T]hat portion which may be regarded as individual comprises a series of feelings and fancies written down in widely differing moods and circumstances, at various dates; it will probably be found, therefore, to possess little cohesion of thought or harmony of colouring. I do not greatly regret this.

> Unadjusted impressions have their value, and the road to a true philosophy of life seems to lie in humbly recording diverse readings of its phenomena as they are forced upon us by chance and change. (*Complete Poems*, p. 84)

Hardy, like Clare, had been through the process of selecting poems 'written at different times & under very different feelings'. For Hardy, the experience of collecting poems written or 'partly written' at an earlier stage of his career led to an increasingly unstable, fragmented sense of the poet's mental growth. Clare never wrote a preface so decisively setting out an alternative 'philosophy' rejecting systematic thought and linear narrative; Hardy's calm refusal to 'regret' the fractured narrative forced upon him is in marked contrast to Clare's own more troubling references to frustrations, interruptions and ill health. Out of the series of little poems which Clare composed at Northborough, however, there emerges a growing sense of both the haphazardness of the world and the turbulence of the human psyche. In his little poems, Wordsworth explored the nature of fancy 'as capricious as the accidents of things' (*Wordsworth's Literary Criticism*, p. 185); Clare's sonnets, like Hardy's lyric poetry more broadly, reflect an at once more comic and more tragic sense of the contingency of thought and world.

'There is a cruelty in all' represents Clare's darkest assessment of the disinterested workings of nature and the 'progress' of poetry:

> There is a cruelty in all
> From tyrant man to meaner things
> & nature holds inhuman thrall
> Against herself so sorrow sings
> A nightingale had built its nest
> Low in my weedy orchard hedge
> The kecks grew up to give her rest
> & safety gave its secret pledge
> That bye & bye her young should flye
> But trouble was ordained to come
> A magpie had her dwelling nigh
> & like a robber found her home
> & one by one it took away
> & murdered musics little heirs.
>
> (*Middle Period*, V, p. 62)

Clare begins by following the conventional rhyme scheme associated with the Shakespearean sonnet (*abab/cdcd/efef/gg*), although a slightly truncated metre foreshadows the death of music in the poem's unrhymed closing couplet. Music is abruptly killed off and music's 'heirs' ironically have no progenitor. The word rhymes with nothing previous. It is heir to nothing, born of nothing, seeming to brutally bring home the sense of dislocation, disharmony and 'cruelty in all'.

Clare may be seen as not only mourning the loss of the next generation, but also, in a sense, killing off history. If the nightingale has often served as a figure for poetry, the chorus of nightingales has often provided poets with a means of negotiating their relation to poetic forebears. For example, in Coleridge's 'The Nightingale':

> and far and near,
> In wood and thicket, over the wide grove,
> They answer and provoke each other's songs—
> With skirmish and capricious passagings,
> And murmurs musical and swift jug jug,
> And one low piping sound more sweet than all—
> Stirring the air with such a harmony,
> That should you close your eyes, you might almost
> Forget it was not day!
>
> (*Poetical Works*, I, ll. 56–64)

Coleridge's response to Milton and other poetic forebears, as he conceives it in this poem, is also a way of joining the chorus – of finding the individual in the universal 'one', the 'skirmish' in the 'harmony'. Dispute is endlessly creative. Conflict not only 'answers' the voices of the past but also 'provokes' the songs of the future. Clare's sense of poetic inheritance is very different. Coleridge's 'murmurs musical' contrast starkly with Clare's 'murdered music'. Conflict is unambiguously cruel in Clare's poem and harmony itself becomes a kind of brutal, pseudo-Darwinian negative – the only unity is the 'cruelty in all'. Clare's poem not only signals the loss of the next generation of singers; there is also a sense in which this poem, in its depiction of the disinterested workings of a hostile natural environment, has killed off the ideals of the past. There never was any harmony, only 'inhuman thrall'. And, Clare suggests, it ever was so. The poetic voice is newly understood as vulnerable to both external forces as well as its own internal volatility. An incoherent self in an incoherent world, the poet, as Hardy came to understand his role, must find value and purpose in 'humbly recording diverse readings' of natural phenomena as they are 'forced upon us by chance and change'.

VI

Throughout his poetry, Clare examines the uneasy process by which human feeling is formed into words. He shared this interest and this struggle with many of his Romantic predecessors, notably Wordsworth, as well as with subsequent generations of poets. Consequently, I conclude this chapter by revisiting a reading of Clare by one of his most vocal twentieth-century admirers, Seamus Heaney. In 'John Clare: A Bicentenary Lecture' (1992), Heaney praised the immediacy of Clare's descriptions and the poems in which he appears refreshingly free of what Heaney termed 'poetry-speak'.[66] In praising the 'sureness' of Clare's 'instinct' and the 'unmistakable signature' of a poetic voice which he believed was 'sounded forth most spontaneously in the scores of fourteen-line poems' which he composed at Northborough, Heaney has seemed to Gorji 'at risk of underestimating Clare's self-consciousness as a poet, and his skill and agency'.[67] But Heaney's reading of Clare may be seen to reflect his own deepening interest in the distinction between poetic 'craft' and poetic 'technique', as he earlier defined them in his seminal essay, 'Feeling into Words' (1980).[68]

The immediacy and spontaneity which Heaney praises in Clare's poetry paradoxically does not come naturally. It includes study, imitation and the careful honing of poetic 'craft', which Heaney defines as 'the skill of making' and 'what you can learn from other verse'.[69] Like Wordsworth and Clare, Heaney reaches back to the pre-conscious influences of childhood: oral traditions, schoolboy chants, familiar Ulster words and the 'lists of affixes and suffixes, and Latin roots' which he remembers hearing his mother reciting in the kitchen.[70] He fully acknowledges the shaping influence of poets whose writings speak 'something essential' to the reader and whose words become part of the 'true sounding aspects of yourself and your experience'; rather than underestimating the importance of poetic influences, Heaney outlines a complex and inscrutable process of what he terms 'in-fluence', by which the voices of others 'consciously or unconsciously' flow into the poet's own mind and experience.[71] Fluency, as Heaney conceives it, derives from this inward flow and distillation of voices. Following this process of imitation, or 'miming' the words of others, the young poet may, or may not, develop his own 'technique'; 'technique', for Heaney, does not simply involve the skilful 'management of metre, rhythm and verbal texture', but also a 'definition' of the poet's own individual 'stance toward life', the 'discovery of ways to go out of his normal cognitive bounds and raid the inarticulate: a dynamic alertness that mediates between the origins of feeling in memory and experience and the formal ploys that express these in a work of art'.[72] Drawing from Wordsworth's description of 'the hiding places of my power', Heaney defines technique as the discovery of the poet's own 'essential patterns of perception, voice and thought' and their transliteration into 'the touch and texture' of his or her writing.[73] It is his accomplishment of this 'most exacting and intuitive disciplines' that Heaney perceives in Clare's own ability 'to hit upon and hold one's true note'.[74]

For Heaney, such an endeavour involves overcoming a negative form of self-consciousness derived from a deeply rooted, internalised feeling that the language of a vernacular poet is in some way not 'literary' enough. Heaney recognises the self-consciousness of the peasant poet's 'footwork' in poems such as 'Shadows of Taste', the 'full-dress correctness' of other writings and the 'unmistakable accents' of Goldsmith, Thomson, Gray and Collins when Clare is on his 'best Augustan behaviour'.[75] It is not that Clare wrote in ignorance of a wider literary community, but that he 'wilfully and intelligently, withdrew and dug in his local heels'.[76] The 'sureness' of Clare's 'instinct' is also his 'wilful strength'.[77] Heaney does not so much suggest that Clare is without self-consciousness as that he stubbornly refused to 'think twice'; he learned not to give in to the negative form of self-consciousness which is so often seen in Clare's poetry to result in the silencing of song, both human and non-human.[78] Like that most poetical of birds, as Clare understood and described the nightingale, the poet *learns* boldness and *practises* fluency: 'But when a day or two confirms her stay | Boldly she sings & loud for half the day' ('When first we hear the shy come nightingales', *Middle Period*, V, ll. 11–12).

CHAPTER 5

'We Teach 'Em Airs That Way'
Thomas Hardy

> There was inquiry in its wistful eye,
>   And once it tried to sing;
> Of him or her who placed it there, and why,
>   No one knew anything.
> — Thomas Hardy, 'The Caged Goldfinch' (1917)

Thomas Hardy both acknowledged and respected that which 'no one knew' and can never be known about what passes in the mind of a caged goldfinch (*Complete Poems*, p. 491). The novelist and poet, however, saw no less of a difficulty in deciphering what passes through the mind of another human being – in discovering 'the link', as he phrased it in a letter to Roden Noel, 'of one form of consciousness with another' (*Collected Letters*, I, p. 262). Hardy, throughout his writing, readily accepts the limitations of a subjective human intelligence, but he no more suggests that goldfinches are without consciousness than that Tess Durbeyfield or Angel Clare, because neither can discover the 'clue to either's secret', have no thoughts or feelings of their own (*Tess*, p. 125). Hardy's engagement with both evolutionary theory and 'The New Philology' in the 1860s and 70s has been well documented, but in this chapter I place his writing in the context of the heated dispute that arose between these two disciplines regarding the relationship between language and the thinking mind.

'The word is the thought incarnate', declared Max Müller in *Lectures on the Science of Language* (1861); 'no animal thinks, and no animal speaks, except man' (I, p. 369). The absence of language in animals was widely perceived to reflect a lack of basic cognitive capacities (reason, foresight, the ability to form abstract concepts), and was, as it continues to be, covertly used to justify the widespread mistreatment of 'dumb' creatures that Hardy decried as illogical and inhumane, and 'in strictness a wrong' (*Later Years*, p. 138). Although comparative philologers sought to establish a defining set of rules common to all languages, a form of linguistic relativism persisted in interpreting the supposedly 'inferior' speech of women, savages and rustics as the sign of a no less inferior intelligence. Hardy's fiction is centrally concerned with the tragic consequences of a world in which there is both language without thought and thought without language. The chapter explores how these larger debates informed his increasingly sceptical attitude towards the dictates of novelistic realism, particularly regarding the representation of rustic speakers. While characters of all backgrounds and classes are seen to lisp and 'pipe' the church catechism with little regard for its meaning, Hardy outlines and affirms the inner, imaginative life of a milkmaid who, as the narrator describes Tess Durbeyfield's responses to the music she hears in church, 'thought, without exactly wording the thought' (*Tess*, pp. 95, 84).

In the 1890s, Hardy turned from writing novels to writing poetry, or rather he returned to the form of earlier days. For, as he reflected, 'that form of expression seems to fit my thoughts better as I grow older, as it did when I was young also' (*Collected Letters*, III, p. 43). As an archaic, musical and elliptical mode of expression, poetry, as Hardy conceived it, represented a form better 'fitted' to express both his own thoughts and the thoughts of others. In his return to poetry, Hardy perceived himself as completing the circle back to the underlying 'waves of human impulse' upon which he believed all 'deeds and words depend'.[1] In this respect, Hardy in his poetry sought to reveal an underling kinship between all races and classes of human beings, and 'the whole conscious world collectively' (*Later Years*, p. 138). In this chapter, I examine this claim with reference to a wide range of Hardy's poems about birdsong, from his most famous pieces, such as 'The Darkling Thrush' and 'The Blinded Bird', to lesser-known lyrics, such as 'The Spring Call' and 'The Puzzled Game-Birds', as well as the series of poems which he is now known to have anonymously contributed to his second wife Florence Emily Hardy's collection for children, *The Book of Baby Birds* (1912).

I

As is well known, Hardy was closely engaged in both philological and evolutionary science in the late nineteenth century. Dennis Taylor has discussed at length Hardy's interest in 'The New Philology' and the historical method inaugurated in the first edition of the *Oxford English Dictionary*, and has observed the ways in which Hardy, like Darwin, often uses the growth of languages as an analogy or metaphor for exploring evolutionary processes.[2] Darwin's influence on Hardy's writing has also been well documented, particularly with regard to the social and theological implications of evolutionary theory – the 'chronic melancholy' which, as the narrator informs us in *Tess of the D'Urbervilles*, 'is taking hold of the civilised races with the decline of a belief in a beneficent Power' (p. 118).[3] Recent studies of music in Hardy's novels and poetry have also explored questions of individual identity, free will and determinism. For example, in *Ecstatic Sound: Music and Individuality in the Work of Thomas Hardy* (2001), John Hughes argues that musical allusions in Hardy's works disrupt any sense of a coherent, stable self; characters in his novels are not so much 'personalities' as a string of vibrating chords or 'variable sensations'.[4] Mark Asquith develops Hughes's argument by placing the author's 'metaphysical' approach to music in the intellectual context of the late nineteenth century; focusing particularly on the works of Darwin, Spencer and Schopenhauer, Asquith argues that the music of wind and furze on Egdon Heath in *The Return of the Native* (1878), for example, acts as a kind of musical 'prelude' or 'chorus' which serves to remind the reader of a larger natural process or 'unconscious will' which controls the behaviour of the human characters whose 'articulations', as Hardy describes them, are 'but as another phrase of the same discourse'.[5]

In *Thomas Hardy and Animals* (2017), Anna West has placed Hardy's novels and poetry in the context of wider debates about 'animal language' in the late nineteenth century. While Müller perceived language as representing an insurmountable barrier between human beings and other animals, Darwin, as West points out, repeatedly returned to two key principles in his discussion of language: firstly, that 'the difference between humans and animals was one of *degree* and not of *kind*', and secondly, that language was not of deliberate invention but 'had been slowly and unconsciously developed by many steps'.[6] Working on the basis of these two principles, Darwin, according to West, perceived 'the emergence of language' as 'not uniquely human; other species may have developed the same prelinguistic impulse into different forms of semiotic systems, depending on coevolving biological structures shaped by environmental pressures'.[7] Overlooking the specific parallel that Darwin draws between how birds learn to sing and how children learn to speak, West perceives Hardy's depiction of talking parrots and sighing, muttering human beings as revealing areas of 'slippage' and 'uncertainty', and consequently 'subverting' straightforward distinctions between human and non-human animals.[8] In her analysis of the bullfinch scene in *Tess of the D'Urbervilles* and other episodes throughout Hardy's fiction, West concludes that Hardy's confrontation with the 'unknowable' voices of the animal world nonetheless involve 'meaningful encounters between creatures by calling upon one's empathy'.⁹ West has done much to draw attention to Hardy's engagement with these larger issues and the ethical aspect of that engagement; building on her research, this chapter places Hardy's writing in the context of an ongoing debate regarding the relationship between thought and word.

Hardy was uniquely placed in the fervid dispute arising between the science of language and the science of evolution. His friend and publisher, Leslie Stephen, contributed to the debate in his essay 'Darwin and Divinity' (*Fraser's Magazine*, 1872). Müller's 'Lectures on Mr Darwin's Philosophy of Language' swiftly followed in *Fraser's* later the same year; when Stephen republished 'Darwinism and Divinity' in *Essays on Freethinking and Plainspeaking* (1873), he inserted a direct response to 'the great philologist'.¹⁰ In turn, Stephen's remarks were incorporated into Darwin's arguments in subsequent editions of *The Descent of Man* (p. 111). It is well known that Stephen's essay was an influential source for Hardy's own growing concerns about the social implications of evolutionary theory, although the essay is more controversial and, I would argue, more significant in its attempt to overcome the 'insuperable barrier' – or 'grammatical dike', as Stephen calls it – which Müller and others had attempted to place between human and non-human animals.¹¹ Like Darwin, Stephen begins his essay by discussing the reasoning powers evident in the behaviour of animals, and carefully prepares the ground for what had become the most controversial issue pressing upon evolutionary theory:

> In fact, a dog is constantly performing rudimentary acts of reason, which can only be distinguished from our own by the fact that he cannot put them into words. He can understand a few simple words; and though he cannot articulate, he can make sounds indicative of his wants and emotions, which are to words what the embryo is to the perfect organism. He cannot, it is true, make use of such sounds as *dā*, *sthā*, or *gā*, to signify give, stand, and sing. And here, exclaims a great philologist, is the finally impassable partition wall. With all respect for his authority, I cannot imagine that the grammatical dike is destined to hold back the deluge any better than its predecessors. What is the difference between *dā* and *bow-wow*? Simply, I presume, that the one indicates and the other does not indicate a certain power of framing abstract ideas. The language will follow as a natural result when intellectual power is developed; and the use of words is merely noticeable as a symptom of the existence of the power. But we can discover the presence of intellect by other marks than the use of vocal signs. Granting that a dog cannot generalise sufficiently to say *dā*, no reasonable observer can doubt that he has a rudimentary faculty of generalisation. There is not

> a dog in England too stupid to understand vaguely the simple word *sthā*, though there is not a dog in England who is clever enough to pronounce it. But the capacity to understand is as good a proof of the presence of vocal intelligence, though in an inferior degree, as the capacity to speak. A dog frames a general concept of cats or sheep, and knows the corresponding words as well as a philologer. (pp. 81–2)

As Darwin recognised, the force of Stephen's argument resides in its holistic sense of language, which includes the capacity to 'understand' as well as to 'articulate', and the use of non-vocal as well as vocal signs. Stephen further challenges the fundamental and familiar principle, which Müller had emphasised: namely that the difference between humans and other animals resides in the latter's apparent inability to form 'abstract ideas'. Whatever the abstract nature of Müller's roots (*dā*, *sthā*, or *gā*), Stephen's own language stretches out the definition of the abstract. As Darwin would similarly argue, taking Stephen as his source, 'abstraction' includes a basic and rudimentary capacity to form a 'general concept' of an animal or species – cats or sheep. By taking these various different 'signs' of intelligence into account, Stephen is able to suggest a more complex relationship between the capacity to speak and the capacity to understand, between language and the mind, than Müller's 'monstrous' equation had allowed for. Darwin was particularly drawn to Stephen's comment upon the 'metaphysical' language of Müller, whose arguments appeared to rest upon the fact that 'because you can give two things different names, they must therefore have different natures' (*Descent*, p. 100; n. 29). As this chapter will argue, Hardy was both highly alert to and deeply critical of how 'different names' could often be used to disguise an underlying sameness in nature.

II

> You may call the whole human race a single *ego* if you like; & in that view a man's consciousness may be said to pervade the world; but nothing is gained. Each is, to all knowledge, limited to his own frame. Or with Spinoza, & the late W. K. Clifford, you may call all matter mind-stuff (a very attractive idea this, to me) but you cannot find the link (at least I can't) of one form of consciousness with another.
> (*Collected Letters*, I, p. 262)

Whereas Müller described the animal mind as a '*terra incognita*', Hardy recognised this as true of human minds also. Part of the tragedy in *Tess of the D'Urbervilles*, as throughout Hardy's novels more generally, resides in the characters each being 'limited' to their own frame: as the heroine tells her husband on their wedding night, 'it is in your own mind what you are angry at, Angel; it is not in me. O, it is not in me' (p. 231). At the same time that Hardy acknowledges the growth of human consciousness, intelligence and individual identity, he also demonstrates a growing concern for the failure of one form of consciousness to recognise, respect and empathise with another in a world where ego pervades and 'nothing is gained'.

In a letter to the Secretary of the Humanitarian League (1911), Hardy argued that the discovery of 'the common origin' of species 'logically involved a readjustment of altruistic morals by enlarging as a *necessity of rightness* the application of what has been called "The Golden Rule" beyond the area of mere mankind to that of the whole animal kingdom' (*Later Years*, p. 141). In essence, Hardy is arguing for the extension of that essential Christian tenet of 'The Golden Rule' or 'do as you would be done by' beyond 'mere' humankind to other sentient beings. The letter is characteristically muted and reserved; it rests upon a strictly logical argument, seemingly designed, by a writer keenly alert to social register, to circumvent any suggestion that his arguments were based on emotion, sentimentality or any other of the 'anthropomorphic' tendencies ridiculed by Müller and others. In each case, his argument is based upon the fact that no 'hard and fast line' may be drawn between man and animals, that there is no 'insuperable barrier': 'while man was deemed to be a creation apart from all other creations, a secondary or tertiary morality was considered good enough to practice towards the "inferior" races but no person who reasons nowadays can escape the trying conclusion that this is not maintainable' (*Later Years*, p. 142). The letter has been discussed at length, although in some ways an earlier letter of 1909 is more relevant to my purposes here.[12] While both express the same essential argument, the earlier letter more particularly relates to the question of animal 'consciousness'. In response to a reader in New York, who had written to ask the author's views on vivisection, Hardy wrote:

> The discovery of the law of evolution, which revealed that all organic creatures are of one family, shifted the centre of altruism from humanity to the whole conscious world collectively. Therefore the practice of vivisection which might have been defended while the belief ruled that men and animals are essentially different, has been left by that discovery without any logical argument in its favour . . . . [It is] in strictness a wrong, and stands precisely in the same category as would stand its practice on men themselves. (*Later Years*, p. 138)

The 'common origin' of species suggests not only physical or biological continuities, but also internal or mental continuities, particularly in the shared capacity to experience, and to suffer, pain. Recognising the ethical implications of those who argue that 'men and animals are essentially different', Hardy believed in extending the principle of the Golden Rule to 'the whole conscious world collectively'. Throughout his writing, Hardy draws attention to how the politics of 'essential difference' had been covertly used to justify not only the mistreatment and abuse of the 'lower' animals, but also slavery, war and the worst atrocities that human beings have committed against their own kind. As Hardy would later summarise the whole of his artistic effort, 'what are my books but one plea against man's inhumanity to man – to woman – and to the lower animals?'[13]

III

In 'The Profitable Reading of a Fiction' (1888), Hardy reflects on his own youthful anxieties as an aspiring novelist and recalls the 'first blush' he felt on reading the views of 'a young and ingenious, though not very profound, critic', whose views he summarises as follows:

> [N]ovels which depict life in the upper walks of society must, in the nature of things, be better reading that those which exhibit the life of any lower class, for the reason that the subjects of the former represent a higher stage of development than their less fortunate brethren. (*Personal Writings*, p. 123)

Hardy initially challenges this view by drawing attention to the fictional nature of fiction, in which the characters and their speech are necessarily drawn from and shaped by the author's own 'culture' and 'insight' (p. 124). But he also expresses a more fundamental objection to the young critic's views on 'the nature of things':

> All persons who have thoughtfully compared class with class – and the wider their experience the more pronounced their opinion – are convinced that education has as yet but little broken or modified the waves of human impulse on which deeds and words depend. So that in the portraiture of scenes in any way emotional or dramatic – the highest province of fiction – the peer and the peasant stand on much the same level . . . . In the lapse of countless ages, no doubt, improved systems of moral education will considerably and appreciably elevate even the involuntary instincts of human nature; but at present culture has only affected the surface of those lives with which it has come into contact, binding down the passions of those predisposed to turmoil as by a silken thread only, which the first ebullition suffices to break. With regard to what may be termed the minor key of

action and speech – the unemotional, every-day doings of men – social refinement operates upon character in a way which is oftener than not prejudicial to vigorous portraiture, by making the exteriors of men their screen rather than their index, as with untutored mankind. Contrasts are disguised by the crust of conventionality, picturesqueness obliterated, and a subjective system of description necessitated for the differentiation of character. In the one case the author's word has to be taken as to the nerves and muscles of his figures; in the other they can be seen as in an *écorché*. (*Personal Writings*, pp. 124–5)

Darwin argued that human languages share a common origin in a musical proto-language, comparable with birdsong, which had been developed as a means of charming the opposite sex. The theory is recalled in the use of musical metaphors which appear in this passage and, as Asquith observes, throughout Hardy's writing as a whole.[14] Whatever the linguistic peculiarities of those in the 'upper walks of society', Hardy challenges the principle that such 'exteriors', physical and verbal, indicate 'a higher stage of development' in thought or feeling. He distinguishes between what he terms the 'minor key of action and speech' and the underlying 'waves of human impulse on which deeds and words depend'. In *Tess of the D'Urbervilles*, characters of all backgrounds and classes, from the 'smockfrocked arithmeticians' of Trantridge to Angel Clare, are inclined to look for reasons, or justifications, for their 'involuntary instincts' and desires (p. 63).

Hardy's own style, however, goes further. In the concluding sentence, he appears to compare the two different styles or approaches to literature which he has been outlining in the paragraph ('in the one case ... in the other ...'). On closer inspection, however, Hardy is in fact describing one and the same thing through two different modes of expression. In either case, the 'author's word has to be taken as to the nerves and muscles of his figures', though Hardy goes on to describe this same process through the technical terminology of French art and portraiture: '*écorché*', or the treatment of an anatomical subject so as to display the 'musculature' (*OED*). It is not simply that the 'waves of human impulse' underlie the speech of both educated and uneducated humankind; Hardy's own style goes further in suggesting that one and the same 'thought', the same intellectual concept or artistic principle, may be expressed in two different languages or styles – in the academic phraseology of French portraiture or, alternatively, in the poetic language of figure and metaphor. Those who are not necessarily trained in the practices of French portraiture may nonetheless, as Hardy's own style demonstrates, express their thoughts through what Wordsworth described as the 'daring' and 'figurative' language of the ancients (*Prose*, I, p. 160). Hardy's style demonstrates that existing terms, nouns and 'things' may be extended and figuratively used to express larger abstract concepts. Such is the language of the Bible, and such is the language of Hardy's heroine in *Tess of the D'Urbervilles*; as the country girl interprets the stars, planets and unjust world in which she lives, 'they sometimes seem to be like the apples on our stubbard tree. Most of them splendid and sound – a few blighted' (p. 31).

Hardy's reviewers detected the deeper, more subversive implications of his style in *Tess of the D'Urbervilles*. While Clare has been praised for his determination to write 'locally', Hardy has often been criticised for the unwanted appearance of what one reviewer described as 'out of place' words.[15] In their response to *Tess of the D'Urbervilles* in particular, critics commonly complained that the heroine's language appeared out of place or unsuitable to a girl of her background and class. In his review of the novel, the poet and critic William Watson picked up on what he termed an 'over-academic phraseology': although Watson expressed his own personal 'wish that it were absent', his remarks are perceptive and his objections in many ways anticipate more recent (and more approving) analyses of Hardy's diction and style.[16] Watson observes that the terms appear intermittently and are therefore not adequately 'assimilated' to the novel's style as a whole, and consequently seem to draw attention to themselves.[17] Whereas Watson pointed this out as a fault in style, Peter Widdowson has since praised Hardy's 'uncompromising artificiality' as a conscious, deliberate mode of 'defamiliarization'.[18] Dennis Taylor has also placed Hardy's 'academic phraseology' in the context of Victorian philology; like Widdowson, Taylor suggests that Hardy's 'awkwardness' is deliberate and closely connected to the author's wider 'scrutiny of the class structure and its support by standardized language'.[19] Watson's review also picks up on another crucial aspect of Hardy's language. Although he remains unconvinced by the inclusion of academic phraseology in Hardy's novel, in many ways the question he raises is very similar to that posed by the author's own techniques in the text: 'are the words in *logy* and *ism* necessarily more accurate instruments of thought than simpler phrases?'[20]

Margaret Oliphant's review in *Blackwoods* is less perceptive, although her response does highlight some of the class issues ingrained in the principles of novelistic realism which she evidently perceived Hardy as challenging in *Tess of the D'Urbervilles*. Oliphant discussed the heroine's 'extraordinarily elevated and noble' character and 'pardon[ed]' the author's 'extravagance' in making 'Tess a kind of princess in this *milieu*' as symptomatic of a wider social sentimentality: 'there is scarcely a vicaress or rectoress who has not some such favourite in the parish – some girl with all the instincts of a lady, as the kind patroness will tell you'.[21] While Oliphant recognises that Tess has received a degree of education from the village school, her regard for novelistic realism leads her into a curious line of reasoning; the heroine's 'phraseology', she suggests, is indicative of Hardy's 'faith in the Sixth Standard'.[22] Oliphant remains unconvinced that a 'country girl' may be able to 'study diligently the prophecies of Ezekiel', though a later comment picks up on a significant distinction that I will be exploring in Hardy's novel.[23] It is not simply Tess's own elevated language to which Oliphant objects, but also the narrator's description or 'translation' of the heroine's interior thoughts and feelings. As Oliphant observes, the narrator's language appears able to express 'the progress of her thoughts much more articulately than she could have done herself'.[24] It was not so much his parodic undermining of educated speech that unsettled Hardy's critics as his presentation of a country girl who thinks. It was Hardy's narrative technique, with its implied suggestion that there is a form of thought without words, which appears to have posed the most subversive threat to the principles, and the politics, of novelistic 'realism'.

IV

'Can you whistle?'
'Whistle, ma'am?'
'Yes, whistle tunes.'
Tess could whistle, like most other country girls, though the accomplishment was one which she did not care to profess in genteel company. However, she blandly admitted that such was the fact.
'Then you will have to practise it every day. I had a lad who did it very well, but he has left. I want you to whistle to my bullfinches; as I cannot see them I like to hear them, and we teach 'em airs that way'.
(Hardy, *Tess*, p. 60)

When Mrs D'Urberville employs Tess to 'whistle tunes' to her bullfinches, the scene foregrounds Hardy's wider scrutiny throughout the novel of the discrepancy between style and substance, language and thought. While the human characters pipe the church catechism, lisp the pronunciation and speech patterns exacted by the Sixth Standard, and adopt the formal airs and graces of the society which surrounds them, Hardy outlines and affirms the imaginative life of a young milkmaid who, as the narrator will later describe her innermost thoughts and feelings, 'thought, without exactly wording the thought' (p. 84).

When Tess dutifully retires to practise her whistling, her first, fruitless endeavours are interrupted by the appearance of her supposed cousin, Alec D'Urberville. The 'lesson' which he subsequently gives to the heroine foregrounds her struggle to articulate her own feelings (p. 61). The young Tess, in this scene as throughout the novel as a whole, is ever vulnerable to being made to sing another's tune. Asquith has given a compelling reading of a later scene in which Tess is drawn by Angel Clare's harp music like 'a fascinated bird', which he perceives as a direct allusion to the Darwinian theory of sexual selection.[25] Yet, in the whistling scene, it is the heroine who is performing. In this subtle reversal of roles, Hardy draws attention to Tess's youth, social gaucheness and consequent vulnerability to the sexual dominance of those who seek to 'give [her] a lesson or two' (p. 61). Throughout the novel, Hardy often draws attention to Tess's lips and 'unpractised mouth' (p. 126), which, as we are told in our first meeting with the heroine, 'had hardly as yet settled into its definitive shape' (p. 15). As the heroine is taught to whistle to the tune of Alec D'Urberville and various other characters throughout the text, Hardy alerts us to the male tendency to project blame for their own misdemeanours onto their female victims. The scene foreshadows Alec's later extraordinary insistence that his victim must swear 'that you will never tempt me – by your charms or ways' (p. 311).

Since the biblical description of Babylon as 'the habitation of devils, and the hold of every foul spirit, and a cage of every unclean and hateful bird', the caged bird has been associated with moral corruption (Revelation 18:2). In Hardy's fiction, the imagery is particularly associated with the fallen woman; for example, in the description of Miss Gruchette in *The Hand of Ethelberta* (1876). While Miss Gruchette seemingly lives on Mountclere's estate to 'attend the pheasants and poultry', Ethelberta is 'puzzled' to discover that 'Miss Gruchette attends to the birds, and two servants attend to Miss Gruchette'; when the heroine presses the servant about whether 'Miss Gruchette is here to keep the fowls', she does 'not attempt to understand' the servant's response: 'Yes. But they don't keep her'.[26] In *Tess of the D'Urverbilles*, Hardy plays on another aspect of the imagery: making the bird sing emerged as a dark innuendo, and justification, for sexual violence and coercion. Among the most famous examples is Samuel Richardson's *Clarissa; Or, the History of a Young Lady* (1748), in which Lovelace uses 'the simile of a bird new caught' to 'illustrate' his theory of 'consent in struggle':

> Hast thou not observed the charming gradations by which the ensnared volatile has been brought to bear with its new condition? How, at first,

refusing all sustenance, it beats and bruises itself against the wires, till it makes its gay plumage fly about, and overspread its well-secured cage. Now it gets out its head; striking only at its beautiful shoulders: then, with difficulty, drawing back its head, it gasps for breath, and erectedly perched, with meditating eyes, first surveys, and then attempts, its wired canopy. As it gets breath, with renewed rage it beats and bruises again its pretty head and sides, bites the wires, and pecks at the fingers of its delighted tamer. Till at last, finding its efforts ineffectual, quite tired and breathless, it lays down and pants at the bottom of the cage, seeming to bemoan its cruel fate and forfeited liberty. And after a few days, its struggles to escape still diminishing, as it finds it to no purpose to attempt it, its new habitation becomes familiar; and it hops about from perch to perch, resumes its wonted cheerfulness, and every day sings a song to amuse itself, and reward its keeper ....

And now, Belford, were I to go no further, how shall I know whether this sweet bird may not be brought to sing me a fine song, and in time to be as well contented with her condition as I have brought other birds to be; some of them very shy ones?[27]

The detail with which Lovelace describes each stage of the bird's distress betrays the sadomasochistic pleasure which he takes in violence and struggle: it is Clarissa's continued resistance, and not her yielding, that seems to most delight her 'tamer'. In the comic disdain which he shows for the women he has thus ensnared ('some of them very shy ones'), Lovelace betrays his desire for both sexual and linguistic mastery. In other uses of the simile in nineteenth-century texts, the sexual associations are combined with the specific fact of the bird being made to repeat particular tunes. In Dickens's *David Copperfield* (1850), for example, Betsy Trotwood describes the effect of Mr Murdstone on that 'poor little fool' Mrs Copperfield: 'you must begin to train her, must you? begin to break her, like a poor caged bird, and wear her deluded life away, in teaching her to sing *your* notes?'[28] These various uses of the 'simile' raise questions not only of physical force, but also of manipulation and coercion; in doing so, they foreground Hardy's own examination of a heroine at once dictated to, and branded as, a fallen women over the course of her tragedy.

Much has been written on Hardy's amendments to successive editions, in which he appears to complicate Tess's feelings for Alec and by implication the issue of consent; whereas the naïve and trusting Tess of an earlier draft smiles in Alec's face 'like a child', Hardy later emphasises the 'momentary pleasure' which the heroine takes in successfully emitting 'a real round sound' so that she 'involuntarily' smiles in Alec D'Urberville's face (p. 62).²⁹ My own feeling is that these amendments reflect a sceptical response to conventional ideas of what constitutes a 'pure woman'. Hardy, I suspect, was not convinced that a woman's purity depended on the total mastery of passion, or abnegation of what he evidently perceived to be 'involuntary' sexual desires. Yet it may further be pointed out that the issue of consent relates more particularly in Hardy's novel to issues of class and of language. When Tess is compared to heroines such as Clarissa Harlowe or Mrs Copperfield, a crucial aspect of her character becomes clear: Tess's youth, class-background and 'unpractised mouth' make her especially vulnerable to manipulation and severely compromise her ability either to understand or to articulate her feelings for Alec D'Urberville.

In the allusion to Richardson, Hardy also draws attention to the formal airs which he himself is forced to assume as a novelist writing in the nineteenth century. The scene operates around the kind of literary '*dénouement*' which Hardy, in his essay on 'Candour in English Fiction' (1890), denounced as the 'fearful price' which the Victorian novelist 'has to pay for the privilege of writing in the English language'.³⁰ The scene itself follows the imagery which Hardy had earlier employed in 'Candour in English Fiction', in which he insisted that 'the crash of broken commandments is as necessary an accompaniment to the catastrophe of a tragedy as the noise of drum and cymbals to a triumphal march'; while this crash was both 'necessary' to and prevalent in the works of the Greek tragedians and the Elizabethan dramatists, Hardy observed that, in the current style or 'fashion' of the nineteenth-century novel, such a crash 'shall not be heard; or, if at all, but gently, like the roaring of Bottom – gently as any sucking dove, or as 'twere any nightingale' (*Personal Writings*, p. 129). In the heavy-handed innuendos of the whistling scene, Hardy's own political roar subdues itself, or rather reminds the reader that it is forced to subdue itself, to the whistling of a bullfinch. When Alec D'Urberville whistles 'a line of "Take, O take those lips away"', Hardy calls attention to the particular danger of this kind of sexual innuendo as it prevents the country girl from understanding the peril in which she finds herself: 'the allusion', we are told, 'was lost upon Tess' (p. 62).

Hardy further draws attention to the fact that the style which he is forced to adopt in his novel is an arbitrary and transient form or 'fashion': 'it is', he reflects, 'indeed, curious to consider what great works of the past the notions of the present day would aim to exclude from circulation, or publication, if they were issued as new fiction' (*Personal Writings*, p. 130). Whereas Müller had attempted to place language as an insuperable barrier between man and beast, Hardy describes the apparent refusal of 'English society' to accept the 'honest portrayal' of 'relations between the sexes' as a 'well-nigh insuperable bar' (*Personal Writings*, p. 128). Darwin's opponents denied man's animal origins and animal passions; Hardy implies that such a rejection, such a refusal to recognise life as a 'physiological fact', underpinned the pruderies of Victorian society, its literature and its language. In *Tess of the D'Urbervilles*, Hardy employs a language of innuendo to represent the early and fatal experiences of his heroine. Nonetheless, he transforms this partially enforced '*dénouement*' into a vehicle for probing and exploring, in the responses of the press and his own readership, the kind of psychological complexity which he had earlier touched upon in Ethelberta's paradoxical reluctance to 'attempt to understand' a situation which, as her reluctance in itself suggests, she on one level tacitly acknowledges (p. 379).

Alec D'Urberville is the first of many characters to attempt to make the heroine whistle to their tune. Throughout the novel, Hardy draws attention to the heroine's vulnerability to the Christian teachings 'lisped from infancy' (p. 104). When Tess and the maidservant present the birds to Mrs D'Urberville for inspection, she is reminded of a Confirmation 'in which Mrs D'Urberville was the bishop, the fowls the young people presented, and herself the maidservant the parson and curate of the parish bringing them up' (p. 60). This mock ceremony foreshows the 'baptismal service' which Tess later performs for the illegitimate child which she bears Alec D'Urberville. Tess imagines her infant in 'the nethermost corner of hell' and sees 'the arch-fiend tossing it with his three-pronged fork' (p. 93). Yet, as Hardy observes, with bitter irony, the young mother may only 'picture' the arch-fiend's three-pronged fork as a familiar object – 'like the one they used for heating the oven on baking days' (p. 93). At the same time that the reader feels the young mother's rising anguish, their attention is also drawn to the tragic absurdity of Tess's imaginings; the poor girl has derived these illusive fears from the many 'quaint and curious details of torment taught the young in this Christian country' (p. 93). In her distress, Tess decides to perform the ceremony herself in the hope that 'it will be just the same!' (p. 94). She sets up the washstand, the jug, and takes her position in the ceremony:

> 'SORROW, I baptize thee in the name of the Father, and of the Son, and of the Holy Ghost.'
> She sprinkled the water, and there was silence.
> 'Say "Amen," children.'
> The tiny voices piped in obedient response: 'Amen!'

'We receive this child' – and so forth – 'and do sign him with the sign of the Cross.'

Here she dipped her hand into the basin, and fervently drew an immense cross upon the baby with her forefinger, continuing with the customary sentences as to his manfully fighting against sin, the world, and the devil, and being a faithful soldier and servant unto his life's end. She duly went on with the Lord's Prayer, the children lisping it after her in a thin gnat-like wail, till, at the conclusion, raising their voices to clerk's pitch, they again piped into the silence, 'Amen!' (pp. 94–5)

Like the bullfinches, the children obediently pipe 'amen' to their sister's commands, as Tess herself duly goes on with the 'customary sentences' of Christian baptismal ritual. Hardy draws attention to the inappropriateness of the words and 'customary sentences' of the ceremony, by which an infant – a 'child's child' (p. 94) – is hailed as a 'manly' and 'faithful soldier' of the Lord. Tess's belief that her ceremony 'will be just the same' as the one conducted in church is presented as painfully naïve about the social ordinances later explained to her by the vicar. Yet, Hardy suggests that Tess's ceremony, her formal play-acting, is in one sense no different from the official ceremonies of the church. In one respect they are indeed 'just the same': the 'customary sentences' just as customary and inadequate, the maternal grief just as deep and profound. Here, as throughout his writing as a whole, Hardy draws attention to the bitter discrepancy between the spirit and the letter of Christian teaching.

Vulnerability to this kind of instilled teaching is not confined to the lower classes or to women in Hardy's novel. When Alec D'Urberville appears in his new role as a convert to evangelicalism, Tess is surprised to hear her seducer speaking 'good new words in bad old notes' (p. 306). Though Alec appears 'in earnest, unmistakably', Hardy suggests that the underlying 'passions' which had previously stirred him remain unchanged: 'the former curves of sensuousness were now modulated to lines of devotional passion' (p. 305). Alec follows the letter of Christian doctrines which he has learned from Mr Clare, the evangelist; by contrast, Tess repeats verbatim the arguments taught her by his son, 'the sceptic' (p. 322). Hardy's dialogue has been described as stilted, overly academic and farcical, and the farce of Tess and Alec's theological dispute bristles with irony and a wider satirical attack upon the arguments of those whom Hardy elsewhere describes as 'amiable theorists' (p. 104).[31] While Alec scorns Tess's 'feminine' tendency to believe her husband's words 'without the least inquiry or reasoning on your own part', his own reasoning is recognised as spurious; at the end of the conversation, he informs Tess that he has been persuaded by her husband's arguments, but Angel's scepticism is used as a justification for his own 'burning desire' for Tess (p. 323). With an 'acute memory for the letter of Angel Clare's remarks', Tess, with unwitting irony, repeats her apparent belief 'in the *Spirit* of the sermon on the mount' (p. 321). As Hardy further suggests, Angel's opinions are in themselves taken practically verbatim from theologians and philosophers; in a wry critique of a tendency towards plagiarism even among the most 'learned' authors, the narrator observes that the words which Angel's bride is now repeating 'might possibly have been paralleled in many a work of the pedigree ranging from the *Dictionnaire Philosophique* to Huxley's essays' (p. 322). Throughout the scene, Hardy pays attention not so much to the arguments themselves as to the manner in which they are repeated; Tess's dialogue breaks off, and a space is left in the manuscript where we are told 'she gave her negations' (p. 321). Tess demonstrates her 'simplicity of faith', not in her husband's words, but in Angel himself (p. 321); Alec is persuaded neither by Mr Clare's Evangelism nor his son's scepticism, but by the heroine's 'looks' (p. 317).

Arbitrary maxims are further seen as subject to change over time. Hardy emphasises throughout the novel how culture, its forms and fashions, often takes what seems to the heroine an 'unexpected direction' (p. 61). When Mrs D'Urberville asks the heroine if she can whistle, Tess is momentarily embarrassed; although 'like most other country girls' she can whistle tunes, the narrator explains that 'the accomplishment' is one that the heroine is reluctant to 'profess in genteel company' (p. 60). Tess's reluctance to own her whistling capabilities suggests that the practice has been discouraged as vulgar among country girls. The 'genteel company' among which she finds herself is itself, however, a fiction (p. 60); Mrs 'Stoke-D'Urberville' disguises her own modest origins, as a member of an insurgent self-made mercantile class (p. 39). In this respect, Hardy emphasises the common origin and faculty of speech which underlies the different forms acquired by individuals in different sections of society and, as he further emphasises, at different periods in history. When Tess finds 'her former ability to have degenerated to the production of a hollow sepulchral rush of wind through the lips' (p. 61), the description foreshadows her later visit to the 'ancestral sepulchre' of the D'Urberville vault (p. 363). Throughout her time at the poultry farm, the narrator similarly draws attention to the passing transience of human social orders and ordinances, as reflected in the buildings, fashions and styles which Hardy perceived as 'life garniture and not life' (*Personal Writings*, p. 119). Hardy describes the cottage which Mrs D'Urberville has 'indifferently turned into a fowl-house' (p. 58). On one level, the poultry farm mirrors Tess's own dilapidated state as the offspring of a 'debased' aristocratic line (p. 8); the cottage chimney is 'overrun with ivy', which lends it the 'aspect of a ruined tower' (p. 58). Although the image of the 'ruined tower' reminds the reader of Tess's own aristocratic heritage, the poultry farm also anticipates the final decline to which her family is subjected.

With playful anthropomorphism, Hardy describes the 'proprietary air' of the birds which stalk about the lower rooms of their new abode (p. 58). Hardy's anthropomorphism works both ways. The humour is not so much directed at the birds which assume a 'proprietary air' as at the absurdity, as well as the underlying tragedy, of the unhoused human creatures who, following John Durbeyfield's death, return to the place where their ancestors lie – the 'family vault' which Joan Durberyfield, with unwitting irony, recognises as 'your own freehold' (p. 362). The houseless Durbeyfield children sleep on the ground above those who lie in the vaults beneath (p. 362). Hardy describes his heroine, who 'did not read Church-Latin like a Cardinal', pausing by the inscription: 'Ostium sepulchri antiquæ familiar D'Urbmrille' (p. 363). Tess does not speak the same language as her ancestors; she is not of the same time, of the same class. The words mean little to her now. They belong to another generation, to another social order. In the churchyard, Tess is confronted with the arbitrariness and consequent tragic absurdity of human titles – for man is, as Lear finds, 'no more but such a poor, bare, fork'd animal' (*King Lear*, III.iv.107–8 (*Riverside Shakespeare*)). 'The old order changeth', her 'cousin' Alec cruelly reminds her (p. 364). And the slight archaism of his speech here underscores the essential truth: the only permanent thing in history is change. Ancient families lose their power, their lands and their titles. Words lose their meaning and their relevance in different contexts. Critics have often commented on the significance of Hardy's notebook comment: 'if you look beneath the surface of any farce you see a tragedy; and, on the contrary, if you blind yourself to the deeper issues of a tragedy you see a farce' (*Early Life*, p. 282).[32] In the churchyard, Tess perceives both the comedy and the underlying tragedy of her fate: the spoilation of the tombs reminds her of her family's social demise and what the narrator describes as the 'mockery of events' (p. 368). In a journal entry dated May 1885, following a visit to the crowded streets of the metropolis, Hardy wrote:

> This hum of the wheel – the roar of London! What is it composed of? Hurry, speech, laughter, the cries of little children. The people in this tragedy laugh, sing, smoke, toss of wines etc., make love to girls in drawing-rooms and areas; and yet are playing their parts in the tragedy just the same. Some wear jewels and feathers, some wear rags. All are caged birds; the only

difference lies in the size of the cage. This too is part of the tragedy. (*Early Life*, p. 224)

Whatever their differences in speech, mien or dress, 'the people in this tragedy' are all 'caged birds'. Their styles and manners of speech may vary from class to class, from epoch to epoch, but their words are reducible to the same bass tones – the same basic emotions, love, laughter and cries. And it is the inability to recognise and empathise with these universal human passions in others wherein the tragedy lies.

V

Hardy not only suggests that there can be words without thought, but also that there can be thought without words. Hardy's animals are animals of mind. Like his Romantic predecessors, Hardy draws attention to the dangers of anthropomorphism and the tendency to project human motives and values onto other species. The natural world is peopled by the 'phantoms and voices' of Tess's imagination, which leads her to perceive herself, standing under a 'pheasant-laden bough', as 'a figure of Guilt intruding into the haunts of Innocence' (p. 86). Hardy challenges these 'moral hobgoblins' arising from 'an arbitrary law of society which had no foundation in Nature' (pp. 85, 279). Conversely, when Tess arrives at the dairy farm, she hears her own raised spirits echoed back in the sounds of nature and particularly in the songs of birds: 'she heard a pleasant voice in every breeze, and in every bird's note seemed to lurk a joy' (p. 103). Throughout the novel, flames and elemental things each 'seem' to dance or 'jig' to the character's own 'inward tune' (p. 119). The arbitrary laws of society affect not only the way that the heroine sees herself but also the way that she is perceived by others. Clare, the 'peasant poet', was often romanticised as a 'child of nature' by his reading public; the educated characters in Hardy's novel likewise project their own ideals onto the heroine: 'What a genuine daughter of Nature that milkmaid is!' exclaims Angel Clare (p. 120). As Tess herself recognises at the end of the novel, the men in her life have consistently inscribed their own ideas onto her: as she tells Alec D'Urberville, 'O, you have torn my life all to pieces ... made me a victim, a caged bird!' (Hardy's ellipsis, p. 381). While Alec and Angel each distinguish between 'Art and Nature', Hardy's narrator underlines the fact that such terms cannot be so easily separated; as the capitalisation shows, 'Nature' is itself an abstract concept.

The natural world itself remains indifferent to the human tragedy: the 'gentle roosting birds' sleep through the first catastrophe in Tess's young life (pp. 73–4); despite her own grief, the narrator observes that 'the birds sang and the sun shone as clearly now as ever' (p. 91); when Angel returns to find that his wife has left the place of her birth, he discovers that the 'spring birds sang over their heads as if they thought there was nobody missing in particular' (p. 372). At the same time that the arbitrary laws of society are imposed upon the heroine, paradoxically, the human world also shows an underlying indifference. Tess's 'thought of the world's concern at her situation' is 'founded on an illusion':

> [S]he was not an existence, an experience, a passion, a structure of sensations, to anybody but herself. To all humankind besides Tess was only a passing thought. Even to friends she was no more than a frequently passing thought. (p. 91)

Although Hardy in such passages registers the difficulty of finding the 'link' between 'one form of consciousness and another' (*Collected Letters*, I, p. 262), the narrative emphasises that such forms of 'consciousness' nonetheless do exist in each living thing. As Angel observes,

> Tess was no insignificant creature to toy with and dismiss; but a woman living her precious life – a life which, to herself who endured or enjoyed it, possessed as great a dimension as the life of the mightiest to himself. (p. 154)

Characters such as Alec D'Urberville may attempt to 'make' Tess into a caged bird, but, at the same time, Hardy's narrative operates according to the principle that both woman and bird are real, living, suffering and, in this sense, *significant* creatures in their own right.

Hardy's writing calls attention not so much to the difference between animals and humans as their *indifference* to each other. Throughout the novel, Hardy emphasises the ability of animals to experience pain, fear and distress, as well as their propensity to exhibit more complex cognitive processes and individual personalities. Following the separation from Angel immediately after their ill-fated wedding, Tess hears 'strange noises' overhead, which she later learns are the sounds of wounded game birds abandoned after the hunt:

> Sometimes it was a palpitation, sometimes a flutter; sometimes it was a sort of gasp or gurgle. Soon she was certain that the noises came from wild creatures of some kind, the more so when, originating in the boughs overhead, they were followed by the fall of a heavy body to the ground. (p. 278)

The passage recalls the earlier scene in which the heroine had stood under the 'pheasant-laden bough', in which she 'looked upon herself as a figure of

Guilt intruding into the haunts of Innocence' (pp. 85–6). However the heroine may have pictured the birds previously, Hardy's subsequent description of them reminds the reader that these are not just symbols; they are living, palpitating things – and, in this sense, *significant* creatures. In the 'prosaic light' of the morning, Tess perceives the real and bleeding bodies of wounded animals:

> Under the trees several pheasants lay about, their rich plumage dabbled with blood; some were dead, some feebly moving their wings, some staring up at the sky, some pulsating feebly, some contorted, some stretched out – all of them writhing in agony, except the fortunate ones whose tortures had ended during the night by the inability of nature to bear more. (p. 278)

The 'poetic' is contrasted with the 'prosaic', as the figurative imagination of the heroine gives way to a consciousness of a suffering animal body; 'nature' is not capitalised, is not an abstract concept or idea, but a real, suffering, writhing body which can hardly 'bear more'. Hardy also draws a parallel between the treatment of the game pheasants and the milkmaid. The birds have been wounded by a sporting aristocracy and have been left to die among the boughs (p. 278); similarly, Tess has been pursued and wounded by Alec, abandoned by Angel Clare. However women and pheasants have been figured in the text, the emphasis is on the body, on the living, suffering thing. The connection between them resides in their treatment: a politics of difference that is routinely used to justify 'man's inhumanity to man – to woman – and to the lower animals'.[33]

As well as the capacity to suffer pain, Hardy also recognises more complex emotions in other species. When Tess presents the fowl for inspection to Mrs D'Urberville, the blind woman's touch enables her to identify each bird. Not only is she able to decipher the bird's physical health, to know 'what they had eaten, and if too little or too much'; she is also able to read the emotional state of the birds thus handled: 'Ah, this is Strut! But he is hardly so lively to-day, is he? He is alarmed at being handled by a stranger, I suppose. And Phena too – yes, they are a little frightened – aren't you, dears?' (p. 59). At the same time that Mrs D'Urberville handles and recognises each bird, the birds themselves appear 'alarmed at being handled by a stranger'; both woman and bird are able to recognise a familiar or a stranger's touch (p. 59). If Mrs D'Urberville is able to read the interior thoughts or feelings of her birds, throughout the scene Hardy similarly emphasises how the blind woman's own thoughts, though unuttered, are reflected in 'mobile' facial expressions which enact 'a vivid pantomime of the criticisms passing in her mind' (p. 59). Consistently,

Hardy draws attention to this gestural language of expression, in both human and non-human animals, which Darwin suggested is in some ways better able to 'reveal the thoughts and intentions of others more truly than do words, which may be falsified' (*Expression of the Emotions in Man and Animals*, p. 333).

The tendency to personify is counterbalanced by the heroine's own growing awareness of the varied personalities of the birds and beasts she tends. At Dairyman Crick's, we learn that 'in general the cows were milked as they presented themselves, without fancy or choice. But certain cows will show a fondness for a particular pair of hands, sometimes carrying this predilection so far as to refuse to stand at all except to their favourite, the pail of a stranger being unceremoniously kicked over' (p. 121). Like Barrington, Darwin and so many others, Hardy draws on the knowledge of the animal-trader – his or her first-hand experience of animals. The narrator assumes this professional guise with the air of one familiar with what certain cows 'will' do (a slight pun perhaps evoking the determined will of an animal life beyond human control). This professional expertise is given to the reader as a matter of course, as a well-known fact, with the appeal to common sense and practical experience which represents one of Darwin's own key modes of persuasion. The dairyman knows there is no accounting for animals, or the individual proclivities of 'certain cows' which frustrate the 'general' rule.

This passage immediately follows the narrator's previous description of Angel Clare, as he learns to recognise the individual personalities of the simple 'farm-folk' among whom he finds himself (p. 117). In contrast with 'the conventional farm-folk of his imagination', Angel becomes aware of the individual and similarly unaccountable proclivities of his companions as 'a number of varied fellow-creatures – beings of many minds, beings infinite in difference' (pp. 117–8). As Angel registers the innumerable differences between the human characters which surround him, this recognition of difference simultaneously reveals an underlying sameness; Angel sees that the 'farm-folk' are as varied as his own 'friends', paradoxically no less individual in character than their social superiors (p. 118). Hardy often emphasises the private, inward and hidden nature of individual consciousness, but the presence of an individual mind with its own peculiar moods is consistently, and purposefully, emphasised in his presentation of 'fellow-creatures'.

Throughout the novel, Hardy outlines the heroine's struggle to find 'approximate expression' for her own thoughts and feelings (p. 104). That struggle, which writers from Wordsworth to Darwin have commonly experienced, registers the break between language and thought. An adverb runs through the whole of the heroine's speech, a little word which nonetheless registers the 'approximate' nature of her own expressions and of language more generally: 'I don't quite like' (p. 47), 'I don't quite know why' (p. 46), 'I couldn't quite say' (p. 123). If Tess struggles to express her own mind and feelings, she also shows a critical awareness of the shortcomings of the language available to her. When her spirits rise at the prospect of life at Talbothay's dairy, the narrator describes how she 'tried several ballads, but found them inadequate' (p. 103). Though she discovers 'approximate expression' for her feelings in reciting 'the old *Benedicite* that she had lisped from infancy', she stops and 'murmurs' her own private doubts: 'But perhaps I don't quite know the Lord as yet' (p. 104). Tess relies on the various languages to which she has been exposed: her own 'native phrases', her 'Sixth Standard training' and the biblical texts of her childhood (p. 124). But her relative lack of education is not equivalent to a lack of thought, a lack of understanding. In 'The Profitable Reading of a Fiction', Hardy used figurative language to explain the concept of '*écorché*' (*Personal Writings*, p. 124); in *Tess of the D'Urbervilles*, he similarly demonstrates how intellectual concepts may be expressed in more 'primitive' forms – in what might be described, in Wordsworthian terms, as the 'original figurative language' of a milkmaid (*Prose*, I, p. 161).

Tess speaks in the personifying language which Hardy recognised as a 'method not unusual in imaginative prose or poetry' (*Later Years*, p. 4). When Tess expresses her fears of 'life in general', Angel is surprised by her remarks:

> 'I shouldn't have expected a young girl like you to see it so just yet. How is it you do?'
> She maintained a hesitating silence.
> 'Come, Tess, tell me in confidence.'
> She thought that he meant what were the aspects of things to her, and replied shyly–
> 'The trees have inquisitive eyes, haven't they? – that is, seem as if they had. And the river says, – "why do ye trouble me with your looks?" And you seem to see numbers of to-morrows just all in a line, the first of 'em the biggest and clearest, the others getting smaller and smaller as they stand farther away; but they all seem very fierce and cruel and as if they said, "I'm coming! Beware o' me! Beware o' me!"' (p. 124)

Tess mistakes Angel's meaning; she tells him literally 'how' she sees external things and external nature – how the 'aspects of things' seem to her. Though she has no psychological or philosophical terms available to her, the 'aspects' of things reflect what is passing in her mind, her interior moods and thoughts. The forces of nature are allegorised as a 'personality' according to an ancient tenet of poetic diction to which Hardy, as will be discussed in more detail later, increasingly turned his attention in his poetry.

In many ways, Angel and Tess speak the two languages which Hardy employed in 'The Profitable Reading of a Fiction': academic phraseology and the figurative language through which a thing, an object, may be used to express a larger abstract concept or idea. In these two characters, Hardy contrasts the two minor 'keys' of human speech; at the same time, however, in the ensuing passage he emphasises the underlying bass tone – a sameness between the ideas, thoughts and feelings of an educated man and a milkmaid:

> She was expressing in her own native phrases – assisted a little by her Sixth Standard training – feelings which might almost have been called those of the age – the ache of modernism. The perception arrested him less when he reflected that what are called advanced ideas are really in great part but the latest fashion in definition – a more accurate expression, by words in *logy* and *ism*, of sensations which men and women have vaguely grasped for centuries. (p. 124)

Critics have discussed at length the significance of 'the ache of modernism' to Hardy's novels and philosophy. Understandably, the phrase has mainly been discussed as a reference to a specifically 'modern' intellectual crisis in the years following the publication of Darwin's *Origin of Species*. While David J. de Laura has placed this phrase in the context of the increasingly strained relationship between science and theology in the late nineteenth century, such readings overlook the nuances of the complex and contradictory definition of 'modernism' that Hardy provides in this passage.[34]

As William Watson more finely intuited, the passage is in some ways less significant to Hardy's ideas about the modern world than to his ideas about language – the 'over-academic phraseology' of '*logy* and *ism*'.[35] In 'The Profitable Reading of a Fiction', Hardy suggested that manners, speech and external impressions act as a 'screen' rather than an 'index' to internal character (*Personal Writings*, p. 124); in their conversation in the garden, Tess and Angel may be seen to momentarily gain a glimpse behind the other's screen. Angel is surprised to hear a young milkmaid expressing the 'ache of modernism'; equally, Tess herself cannot understand the melancholy of her learned companion:

> Tess, on her part, could not understand why a man of clerical family and good education, and above physical want, should look upon it as a plight to

> be alive. For the unhappy pilgrim herself there was very good reason. But how could this admirable and poetic man ever have descended into the Valley of Humiliation, have felt with the man of Uz – as she herself had felt many a day and night two or three years ago – 'My soul chooseth strangling and death rather than my life. I loathe it; I would not live alway'. (pp. 124–5)

As the narrative shifts between the perspectives of Tess and Angel, Hardy on one level emphasises the differences between them: their educational backgrounds and the texts through which they make sense of the world. On another, however, their inability to understand each other is represented as partly 'prejudicial', to use Hardy's word in 'The Profitable Reading of a Fiction' (*Personal Writings*, p. 124). It is based on Angel's 'surprise' at the melancholy thoughts of a milkmaid and Tess's own inhibitions and sense of intellectual inferiority compared with 'this admirable and poetic man' (p. 124). While neither Tess nor Angel can discover 'the clue to either's secret' (p. 125), the allusion to Job emphasises an underlying sameness and continuity. Ironically, the 'ache of modernism' is in one sense nothing modern at all (p. 124).

Not only do words often fail to convey the heroine's own private thoughts, but Hardy often alludes to a subvocal language of the mind. As Wordsworth and Clare frequently refer to a 'hummed' and 'muttered' stage in composition, Hardy in this novel delineates the 'half-unconscious rhapsody' taking place within the mind of his heroine (p. 104).[36] Asquith has drawn attention to another famous passage in *Tess of the D'Urbervilles*, in which the narrator describes the heroine's responses to the music which she hears in church:

> She liked to hear the chanting – such as it was – and the old Psalms, and to join in the Morning Hymn. That innate love of melody, which she had inherited from her ballad-singing mother, gave the simplest music a power over her which could wellnigh drag her heart out of her bosom at times .... When the chants came on one of her favourites happened to be chosen among the rest – the double chant 'Langdon' – but she did not know what it was called, though she would much have liked to know. She thought, without exactly wording the thought, how strange and godlike was a composer's power, who from the grave could lead through sequences of emotion, which he alone had felt at first, a girl like her who had never heard of his name, and never would have a clue to his personality. (p. 84)

Asquith has commented upon the significance of the musical analogy in this scene, which suggests an 'innate' response that aligns the heroine's response with a Darwinian theory of common origins and music as the language of emotion; while music offers momentary relief to the young and grieving mother, Asquith notes how the whispers of gossiping parishioners return the heroine to a sense of self-consciousness, guilt and shame.[37] As Asquith shows, Hardy draws on the musical analogies employed by Darwin, Schopenhauer and other intellectuals. But it is also profoundly ironic that these 'advanced' metaphysical ideas are placed inside the mind of a milkmaid – a milkmaid who knows the tune though not the name, and who thinks 'without exactly wording the thought'.

VI

In later years, Hardy turned from writing novels to writing poetry, or rather he returned to the form of earlier days. As he explained in a letter of 1902, 'that form of expression seems to fit my thoughts better as I grow older, as it did when I was young also' (*Collected Letters*, III, p. 43). As his notebooks demonstrate, Hardy had long been developing this view of poetry as a form better 'fitted' to express human thoughts and emotions. He copied the following passage from John Addington Symonds's *Essays Speculative and Suggestive* (1890):

> The range of human thoughts & emotions greatly transcends the range of such symbols as man has invented to express them; & it becomes therefore the business of Art to use these symbols in a double way. They must be used for the direct represn. of thought & feeling; but they must also be combined by so subtle an imagination as to suggest much which there is no means of directly expressing ... In poetry of the first order, almost every word (to use a mathem. metaphor) is raised to a higher power. It continues to be an articulate sound & a logical step in the argument; but it also becomes a musical sound & a centre of emotional force. (*Literary Notebooks*, II, p. 43)

As West observes, 'poetry ties language to another system of meaning, an emotional semiotics based on sound and rhythm as much as on linguistic content'.[38] In 'poetry of the first order', the sounds of words tap into the 'centre of emotional force' that connects human beings with other animals, and with each other. In his return to poetry, Hardy perceived himself as completing the circle back to those bass tones of feeling upon which he believed all human words and actions, ancient and modern, vulgar and refined, ultimately depend.

In a note of 1892, Hardy questioned whether he might be able to 'express more fully in verse ideas and emotions which run counter to the inert crystallized opinion', though he at the same time observed that many of those 'ideas' and 'emotions' had long been familiar to poetry: for example, the 'idea' that the 'Supreme Mover or Movers, the Prime Force or Forces, must be either limited in power, unknowing, or cruel ... is obvious enough, and has been for centuries' (*Later Years*, p. 58). Later, in a note of April 1899, Hardy reflected on the ironies of human intellectual 'progress':

> [I]t would be an amusing fact if it were not one that leads to such bitter strife, that the conception of a First Cause which the theist calls 'God', and the conception of the same that the so-styled atheist calls 'no-God', are nowadays always almost exactly identical. (*Later Years*, p. 82)

In poems such as 'Nature's Questioning', 'The Mother Mourns', 'God-Forgotten' and 'The To-Be Forgotten', Hardy personifies the 'Prime Mover or Movers' as the 'god' or 'tribal gods' of Christian and pagan traditions. At the same time that intellectuals were dividing into warring schools of thought (theists, atheists and agnostics), Hardy saw a deeper irony: the inability to recognise an underlying sameness is precisely what has led to 'such bitter strife'. In this return to an archaic form, Hardy increasingly sought to reveal the kinship which exists between different, or even conflicting, ideas or conceptions of the world, to expose the shared origins of old and new words, and ultimately to create empathy for and between the 'whole conscious world collectively' (*Later Years*, p. 138).

Like Clare, Hardy has long been seen to offer a revisionist reading of Romanticism. As 'that most recalcitrant of post-Romantics', Hardy has been read against a backdrop of canonical poems which had interpreted and appropriated the bird's song for the poet's own purposes.[39] In poems such as 'The Darkling Thrush', 'Shelley's Skylark' and 'The Selfsame Song', Hardy has appeared to reject 'a romanticised songbird' in order to depict an 'actual' creature mortally vulnerable to the reality of hardship and cruelty in a post-Darwinian world.[40] Unquestionably, poems such as 'The Darkling Thrush' may be seen to represent a decisive shift away from the idealisation *of* the songbird to sympathy *with* a real, and suffering, fellow creature:

> I leant upon a coppice gate
>   When Frost was spectre-grey,
> And Winter's dregs made desolate
>   The weak'ning eye of day.
> The tangled bine-stems scored the sky
>   Like strings of broken lyres,
> And all mankind that haunted nigh
>   Had sought their household fires.

> The land's sharp features seemed to be
>   The Century's corpse outleant,
> His crypt the cloudy canopy,
>   The wind his death-lament.
> The ancient pulse of germ and birth
>   Was shrunken hard and dry,
> And every spirit upon earth
>   Seemed fervourless as I.
>
> At once a voice arose among
>   The bleak twigs overhead
> In a full-hearted evensong
>   Of joy illimited;
> An aged thrush, frail, gaunt, and small,
>   In blast-beruffled plume,
> Had chosen thus to fling his soul
>   Upon the growing gloom.
>
> So little cause for carolings
>   Of such ecstatic sound
> Was written on terrestrial things
>   Afar or nigh around,
> That I could think there trembled through
>   His happy good-night air
> Some blessed Hope, whereof he knew
>   And I was unaware.
>
>   (*Complete Poems*, p. 150)

The word 'darkling' recalls Keats's 'Ode to a Nightingale' (l. 51), and (through him) Milton's identification with 'the wakeful bird' that 'sings darkling' in *Paradise Lost* (III, ll. 38–9). For Hardy, however, this kind of poetic idealisation risks losing sight of the creature itself, 'frail, gaunt, and small'. In a subtle and poignant reworking of Shelley's description of the skylark as an 'unbodied joy' ('To a Skylark', l. 15), Hardy celebrates an actual, living bird singing in apparent defiance of its own fragile frame: 'joy illimited'.

Critics have often commented on the ambiguities of the poem's conclusion. Against those who might immediately dismiss Hardy as 'a pessimist', Merryn Williams affirmed that the novelist and poet 'had always believed that human life contained hopeful elements'; what makes the thrush sing in this poem, she argues, is that same 'invincible instinct towards self-delight' that urges the young Tess to go on living even after her 'fall' and the death of her child (*Tess*, p. 100).[41] More recently, George Levine has persuasively made the case that 'Hardy was more in love with life – and in

Darwinian ways – than most typical Darwinian readings suggest'.[42] Writing aged sixty, Hardy, like Wordsworth before him, could still be moved by that apparent 'invincible instinct towards self-delight' surviving even in the bleakest of places and the humblest of creatures: 'an aged thrush, frail, gaunt, and small'.

The ambiguities of the poem are encapsulated in its final word: 'unaware'. On one level, the word suggests that the bird represents an alternative state of being or way of 'knowing' inaccessible to the human, melancholy poet. The thrush, according to this interpretation, may be compared to the insects of 'An August Midnight' which 'know Earth-secrets' that human beings do not (*Complete Poems*, p. 146). On another, however, the word 'unaware' has a more nuanced meaning in the canonical Romantic texts from which Hardy draws so extensively throughout 'The Darkling Thrush'. For example, Wordsworth describes the epiphany of the young boy of Winander: 'the visible scene | Would enter unawares into his mind' (*The Prelude*, V, 409–10). Similarly, Coleridge's mariner utters an unpremeditated prayer as he watches the water snakes dance and leap in the shadows of the ship:

> O happy living things! no tongue
>   Their beauty might declare:
> A spring of love gushed from my heart,
>   And I bless'd them unaware:
> Sure my kind saint took pity on me,
>   And I bless'd them unaware.
>   (*Poetical Works*, I, ll. 282–7)

In these poems, the word 'unaware' does not simply mean to be unaware, to be ignorant or unthinking; more precisely, it means to do something unconsciously, inadvertently or unintentionally. In these moments where the thinking mind is temporarily suspended, the individual experiences a different kind of awareness: a heightened appreciation of the rocks, woods, trees and 'happy living things' that surround them. Ironically, then, to be 'unaware' is to be in one sense more deeply aware, more profoundly responsive to the natural world. For both Wordsworth and Coleridge, this form of awareness cannot be expressed or, more precisely, to use Coleridge's word, 'declared' in ordinary language: the 'beauty' of the water snakes can never be fully communicated or made known by any human 'tongue'. In 'The Darkling Thrush', Hardy may be seen to play on this double sense of the word: its ambiguities leave the reader uncertain as to whether the speaker is 'unaware' in the sense of being ignorant of, or more deeply attuned to, the 'blessed Hope' expressed in the bird's music.

The music of 'The Darkling Thrush' is almost unnervingly smooth, steady, regular. Hardy follows almost to the letter the common metre: alternating lines of iambic tetrameter and iambic trimeter. What makes this rhythm so unsettling is the sense of a mismatch or discrepancy between its steady, pulsating rhythm and the intellectual crisis of its speaker. While Hardy's speaker can see little harmony, unity or hope of renewal in the tangled bine-stems that 'score the sky | Like strings of broken lyres', the poem's own music seems scarcely broken at all. Quite the opposite. Almost perfectly smooth and steady, the iambic rhythms follow and affirm an abiding and deep harmony: 'Like *strings* of *bro*ken *lyres*'. Even as the speaker appears to disavow the highest ideals of Romanticism, the poem's pulsating metre evokes that 'ancient pulse of germ and birth' that Hardy's speaker, looking out across an apparently desolate winter landscape, cannot consciously perceive or reasonably discern.

Although the poem is written in common metre, Hardy departs from the traditional stanza form. Rather than stanzas of four lines (*abab*), Hardy may be seen to compound two stanzas into one: eight lines, following a set rhyme scheme of *ababcdcd*. In a sense, Hardy's innovations are far simpler and more muted than Coleridge's in 'The Ancyent Marinere', for example. Hardy's stanzas are all the same length and follow the same rhyme scheme, and are consequently far less varied than that wilder, more irregular music that characterises Coleridge's 'sweet jargoning'. Although Hardy departs from the conventional stanza form, the relative lack of metrical variety maintains a steady pulse so regular it can feel monotonous, flat, subdued – or, to use Hardy's own coinage, 'fervourless'. As Hardy invites us to drop the stress in the second foot of the stanza's closing line ('Seemed *fer*vourless as *I*'), the pulse weakens. A new Hardyan coinage, the word 'fervourless' and the idea which it denotes, underscores our sense of a post-Darwinian intellect at war with and unable to sustain its faith in the ideals of Hardy's Romantic predecessors.

Just as the pulse appears to weaken and subside, the thrush appears: 'In a full-hearted evensong | Of joy illimited'. The bird's voice thrillingly interrupts, disrupts and reinvigorates the poem's otherwise subdued rhythms. Although Hardy significantly does not accent the word, the metre might tempt us to elongate the last syllable of 'illimitèd': a curious blend of the new and the old, the word is a new coinage which nonetheless encourages the reader to follow an archaic poetic tendency to stress, elongate and accentuate. As the placing of the stress is left up to the reader, the bird's song at once signals and invites modulation, interpretation and innovation. In Wordsworth's poetry, the bird that sings 'so sweetly 'mid the gloom' leads the poet to reflect on the origins and role of aesthetic pleasure in a seemingly 'comfortless' world (*The Prelude*, II, ll. 132, 128). In Hardy's poem, the 'aged thrush' that chooses 'thus to fling his soul | Upon the growing gloom' leads to darker reflections on the apparent and indefatigable spirit of hope in a world where the poet can see 'so little cause for carolings | Of such ecstatic sound'. Although Hardy could see little 'cause' (little reason or motive for the bird's own apparent joy or indeed for human 'carolings', but also a lack of any scientific or evolutionary principle that can explain the purpose or existence of such things as birdsong, music and poetry in a cold and often hostile universe), the earth-shattering theories of Charles Darwin made this poet in many ways more deeply and profoundly moved by that 'invincible instinct towards self-delight' (*Tess*, p. 100) that he perceived surviving in even the humblest and most 'blast-beruffled' creatures. To become aware of this deep, underlying pulse and invincible instinct, poet and reader have to be able and willing to 'think' differently: not simply to read the words as 'articulate sounds' or 'logical steps' in the poem's argument, but to respond to them as 'musical sounds' and 'centres of emotional force' (*Literary Notebooks*, II, p. 43).

'The Bird-Catcher's Boy' continues the shift away from the idealisation of the songbird to sympathy with a real, sentient and, in this sense, *significant* creature. As in 'The Darkling Thrush', 'Shelley's Skylark' and 'The Selfsame Song', Hardy draws attention to the physical frailty of the little birds that 'bruise and bleed in jail':

> 'Father, I fear your trade:
> Surely it's wrong!
> Little birds limed and made
> Captive life-long.
>
> 'Larks bruise and bleed in jail,
> Trying to rise;
> Every caged nightingale
> Soon pines and dies'.   (*Complete Poems*, p. 825)

Although Hardy often challenges poetic idealisations of the bird, he also expertly parodies the practical, 'unsentimental' approach epitomised by the bird-catcher:

> 'Don't be a dolt, my boy!
> Birds must be caught;
> My lot is such employ,
> Yours to be taught.

> 'Soft shallow stuff as that
> Out from your head!
> Just learn your lessons pat,
> Then off to bed'. *(Complete Poems, p. 825)*

For Hardy, this kind of salt-of-the-earth pragmatism is no less arbitrary than the 'soft shallow stuff' of sentimentalism. With characteristic irony, he suggests that the bird-catcher is, at least in one sense, directly comparable to the birds he has made captive; both man and bird are prisoners who must accept their 'lot' and resign themselves to what society has decreed 'must be'. To his cost, the bird-catcher shows no consciousness or understanding of this deeper resemblance between himself and the birds he ensnares.

Once again returning to the Coleridgean image of the eolian harp, the boy passes the 'caged choirs' on the stairs: 'Harp-like his fingers there | Sweep on the wires' (*Complete Poems*, p. 825). The bird-catcher's boy is imbued with a kind of alternative Romantic idealism and imaginative empathy. The young idealist of the early twentieth century cannot, as Coleridge urged his contemporaries, stretch out his limbs 'beside a brook in mossy forest-dell' and surrender 'his whole spirit' to the 'the influxes | Of shapes and sounds and shifting elements' ('The Nightingale', *Poetical Works*, I, ll. 25–8); rather, the boy may only play 'harp-like' upon the wires of a cruel, inhumane and unideal world. For Hardy, the preservation of the finest ideals of Romanticism depends on this kind reckoning with, as opposed to escaping from, the reality of cruelty in a darkening world.

In a kind of poetic justice, the bird-catcher's failure to empathise leads to the loss of his son. With tragic irony, the bird-catcher, who has imprisoned birds, cannot bring himself to lock his door in the hope that his son may one day return. Freddy will never again 'flit | Soft' into the home he has abandoned. The moral is based on the principle of the Golden Rule, and the extension of that rule to include both man and bird. In the final bitter 'moral' of the poem, the sound of a 'groping touch' upon the stairs signals Freddie's death and return to the 'one life' of nature:

> That night at Durdle-Door
> Foundered a hoy,
> And the tide washed ashore
> One sailor boy. *(Complete Poems, p. 827)*

The ending resembles that of Wordsworth's 'Old Man Travelling', in which we learn the old man is walking 'many miles' to visit a son who lies dying 'there' in the hospital at Falmouth (*Lyrical Ballads*, ll. 17, 20).

Although Hardy, like Wordsworth, grounds his poem in a particular place, significantly, he does not name Freddie in the final stanza: in a potential play on Romantic concerns with unity and the 'one life', the soldier boy could be *any*one, and is in this sense all and *every*one. Writing in the aftermath of the First World War, Hardy lived to see the consequences of such a generalised, impersonal view – an appalling disregard for life, for little birds and for soldiers. In this respect, the poem reflects the humanitarian impetus of Hardy's war poems, most notably 'The Blinded Bird'.

In 'The Blinded Bird', Hardy protests the common practice of blinding bullfinches, larks and other songbirds in order to improve their singing. The practice has a long history dating back to at least the thirteenth-century Flemish tradition of *vinkensport*. 'What can we think', wrote Bechstein in eighteenth-century Germany, 'of the heart and morals of people who for a slight amusement thus enjoy the sufferings of a sensitive being that is unfortunately in their power?' (p. 136). As animal-rights arguments gradually increased over the course of the nineteenth century, the practice was banned in a number European countries: in Britain with the Wild Birds Captivity Act in 1905, and in what is now known as Belgium in 1928.[43] In Flanders and across Europe more generally, institutes for the blind led the campaign against this inhumane practice. 'We blind students of the Royal Institute for the Deaf and Dumb and Blind', reads one petition from the Brussels Royal Institute for the Deaf-Mutes and the Blind (27 December 1901),

> Painfully observing that the barbarous custom of blinding little birds, finches and linnets, still exists and is increasingly practised in our country, and considering this custom as a monstrosity of our motherland and epoch;
>
> That it perverts the character and heart of children;
> That it takes its toll on the most useful birds to agriculture;
> That there is no plausible reason which can legitimize or excuse [it];
> That its abolition, even by legal means, is desired by all right-thinking men;
> That we, the blind, have particular reasons for desiring this abolition;
>
> That better than anyone, we know the horrors of the deep and perpetual night in which children, even men, insensitively plunge these innocent and charming creatures, because, for their barbaric ears the moans and cries of distress are songs of music even more delightful than the cheerful songs of happiness.[44]

According to one Belgian finch-owner, 'the societies of animal protection' proved 'stronger than ever' after the war and 'knew how to make use of the pity which caused the sight of the innumerable war blinded in order to give shape to a new and successful attack [on] our ancient hobby'.⁴⁵ Although the particularities of the campaign and Hardy's direct involvement with it remain uncertain, it is clear that experiences during the Great War generally 'increased the public visibility of blindness and persons with visual impairment', significantly contributed to a change in the 'status of disabled people including the blind' and further 'boosted the political debates with regard to the blinding of birds'.⁴⁶ Whether or not 'The Blinded Bird' was directly inspired by the campaign led by veterans in Flanders, Hardy's poem, indeed his writing as a whole, advocates the kind of empathy which soldiers were at this time developing for little birds, finches and linnets, and other victims of human indifference.⁴⁷

'The Blinded Bird' has recently come under criticism. Though moving and well-intentioned, the poem has been seen to surrender itself to the kind of sentimental, anthropomorphising tendencies which Hardy so carefully resists elsewhere:

> So zestfully canst thou sing?
> And all this indignity,
> With God's consent, on thee!
> Blinded ere yet a-wing
> By the red-hot needle thou,
> I stand and wonder how
> So zestfully thou canst sing!
>
> Resenting not such wrong,
> Thy grievous pain forgot,
> Eternal dark thy lot,
> Groping thy whole life long;
> After that stab of fire;
> Enjailed in pitiless wire;
> Resenting not such wrong!
>
> Who hath charity? This bird.
> Who suffereth long and is kind,
> Is not provoked, though blind
> And alive ensepulchered?
> Who hopeth, endureth all things?
> Who thinketh no evil, but sings?
> Who is divine? This bird.   (*Complete Poems*, p. 446)

Karlin picks up on allusions to Milton and Corinthians in the final stanza, and suggests that the weight of poetic and scriptural traditions is at risk of 'overlaying' the bird and its song with human meanings.⁴⁸ Ironically, however, 'The Blinded Bird' was written partly in response to an article in *The Times* newspaper, 'Performing Animals: The Psychology of Pain in Man and Beast' (17 December 1913), which similarly emphasised that the objections of animal-rights activists, however well-intentioned, were necessarily 'subjective'.[49] With regard to recent protests against the treatment of caged birds and other 'performing animals', the correspondent concludes his argument in terms uncomfortably close to Karlin's own: 'humanitarians really speak for themselves, vicariously endowing the performing horses and dogs with their personal imaginations and sufferings'.

The article is part of a series of letters and commentaries appearing in the newspaper, which was following recent efforts by the RSPCA and other organisations to establish legislation restricting the practices of animal-trainers. Hardy himself contributed to this ongoing discussion when he wrote a letter to the *Times*'s editor (19 December 1913), in which he directly refuted the claims made by their correspondent.[50] The correspondent distinguishes between the immediate and predominantly physical pain experienced by animals, on the one hand, and the human capacity to remember and 'reflect' upon those experiences, on the other. In a passage which Hardy would challenge, the correspondent writes:

> The caged skylark ... experiences none of the misery of the caged man. It does not know that its liberty is hopelessly lost. It cannot relate its present position to past experience in the way in which a prisoner can and must do. The cage is merely an accidental obstruction, which may at any moment disappear. Should the bird stop struggling it does so because struggling is unpleasant, not because it is hopeless. (Anon., 'Performing Animals')

While 'an animal lives from moment to moment', the human mind struggles to comprehend the 'social or moral significance' of its suffering. The correspondent draws this familiar point of difference between the mind of an animal and that of a man, though he also falls into the accompanying tendency which Hardy was directly confronting in *Tess of the D'Urbervilles*. 'Sensitiveness to pain' not only varies between different species, but also, apparently, between different kinds of human beings: 'men are notoriously more afraid of pain than women, and preserve a much more acute recollection of it'. Although the writer duly acknowledges that 'the pain of child-birth would kill a man', women are considered better able to bear the intensity of this kind of suffering because they neither retain an 'acute recollection' of the experience nor are they tormented with philosophical speculations regarding the 'moral and social significance' of their suffering. The correspondent concludes his argument on this admittedly 'abstruse question', 'it may be stated that men are more highly imaginative than women' (Anon., 'Performing Animals').

Hardy's response is characteristically muted and pragmatic. He suggests that the correspondent has confused 'theory with practice' (Hardy, 'Performing Animals'). Ostensibly, Hardy is arguing that, in practice, animal-trainers often did not abide by the principles set down by the correspondent, though the evidence which Hardy provides implicitly challenges his larger theory of 'the psychology of pain in man and beast'. Hardy describes the 'wretched dogs' he had seen at country fairs, which

> so trembled with terror when they failed to execute the feat required of them that they could scarcely stand, and remained with eyes of misery fixed upon their master, paralysed at the knowledge of what was in store for them behind the scenes, whence their shrieks could afterwards be heard through the canvas. (Hardy, 'Performing Animals')

The evidence is based on practical experience and direct observation. Hardy describes the physical trembling of the animals, the direction of their 'eyes' fixed upon their masters, and their manifest knowledge or more particularly foreknowledge of 'what was in store for them'. While such anecdotal accounts were increasingly dismissed as anthropomorphic, Hardy emphasises that the correspondent has failed to look 'practically' and with his own eyes at what is before him; if it is true that we do not know what passes in the mind of an animal, it should be remembered that such arguments have been historically used to justify the routine mistreatment of sentient creatures whose 'shrieks' may nonetheless be heard behind the canvas.

Similarly, Hardy argues that 'the assertion that a caged skylark experiences none of the misery of caged man makes demands upon our credulity'. He refers to a common 'practice' among schoolboys':

> There is, or was when I was young, a practice among boys of putting a nearly-fledged brood of young birds, with the nest, into a cage, and hanging the cage in the tree or bush where the nest was made. The parents come regularly to feed their young ones through the bars, and there seems no reason why they should not be successfully bred; but usually the young birds die. It used to be the tradition of school-boys that the old birds poisoned their young at finding them imprisoned. However that may be, die they did. (Hardy, 'Performing Animals')

As I argued in Chapter One, this practice had often been commented on by natural historians throughout the late eighteenth and early nineteenth centuries. While Hardy recognises that the evidence is anecdotal, he slyly remarks that he can find no other 'reason' why the birds should not survive. The old 'tradition' or folktale suggests that birds lead complex social lives and do understand the concept of 'imprisonment', though Hardy rests his arguments on the grim fact: 'however that may be, die they did'. The argument is pointed though restrained, patiently worked through by a committed animal-rights advocate. And that degree of patience and commitment becomes clear when Hardy's own style is compared with that of his opponents. As discussed in Chapter One, the expertise of bird-catchers directly contributed to studies in ornithology; by the time that Hardy was writing, however, the secretary of the Cage Birds League, Henry J. Fulljames, openly denied what had been common knowledge among bird-catchers in Clare's time. As Fulljames wrote in a letter to the editor concerning 'Mr Hardy and Cage Birds' (23 December 1913), 'it is only those who allow sentiment to obscure their observation who would express such a view'.[51]

In 'The Blinded Bird', Hardy may be said to undo such arguments from the inside, to undermine them in their own terms. As the correspondent had argued that animals only experience pain from moment to moment, similarly the speaker wonders at the bird 'Resenting not such wrong, | Thy grievous pain forgot'. The bird forgets its 'grievous pain'; it neither remembers nor 'resents' such wrong. It does not reflect philosophically on the cruelty of a 'God' who appears to 'consent' to needless suffering. The speaker of Hardy's poem expresses an anger which is notably absent from the bird itself: 'So zestfully canst thou sing?' While the correspondent had claimed that the bird 'does not know that its liberty is hopelessly lost', Hardy turns round these and other arguments in the final stanza of the poem:

> Who hath charity? This bird.
> Who suffereth long and is kind,
> Is not provoked, though blind
> And alive ensepulchered?
> Who hopeth, endureth all things?
> Who thinketh no evil, but sings?
> Who is divine? This bird.

Whereas the *Times* correspondent had used the differences between animal and human psychology to justify the treatment of caged animals, Hardy turns the argument on its head: a bird, which neither remembers nor resents the suffering inflicted upon it, is in one sense more true to the Christian tenets of charity and forgiveness than a human society that shows itself 'pitiless' as wire. If the *Times* correspondent contrasted the mental powers of animals, the allusion to Corinthians emphasises that the bird, by the logic of his own argument, 'thinketh no evil'. Rather than overlaying the bird with human meanings, Hardy's poem is a scathing satire of twentieth-century society 'for all its rhetoric of morality'.

In 'The Blinded Bird', Hardy may be seen to turn such arguments back upon themselves. In other poems, however, he directly refutes them. He emphasises that the 'lower' animals share in common with human beings the same basic emotions of fear and pain, as well as the more complex cognitive processes which he observed, for example, in the trembling of dogs at country fairs. In a series of short and seemingly 'minor' poems, Hardy experimented with writing directly from the perspectives of animals. Among the most moving examples is 'The Puzzled Game-Birds':

> They are not those who used to feed us
> When we were young—they cannot be—
> These shapes that now bereave and bleed us?
> They are not those who used to feed us,—
> For would they not fair terms concede us?
> —If hearts can house such treachery
> They are not those who used to feed us
> When we were young—they cannot be!
>
> (*Complete Poems*, p. 148)

Hardy wrote a handful of such poems as triolets, one of several French romance and lyric forms which had been revived in the 1860s and 70s. In 'A Plea for Certain Exotic Forms of Verse' (*Cornhill Magazine*, 1877), for example, Edmund Gosse described the triolet as a 'tiny trill of epigrammatic melody, turning so simply on its own innocent axis'.[52] In both 'The Puzzled Game-Birds' and 'Birds at Winter Nightfall', Hardy plays on the melodic and epigrammatic qualities of the triolet, the sound and sense of the poem. If reason derives from memory, then so too does the confusion of Hardy's 'puzzled' birds.[53] The perspectives of the birds are carefully imagined: the human 'shapes' which the birds appear to recognise, but which are yet perceived from an alternative animal perspective; the repetitions which imitate not only the birds' vocal patterns and rhythms, but also evoke the kind of rudimentary powers of thought and reasoning which Darwin observed in the animal world. While the birds are imbued with such rudimentary powers, in the second section of the poem Hardy turns the poem on its axis, redirecting the criticism back at a human society which acts without rhyme or reason. Critics have observed the connection between this poem and Hardy's earlier protest against the killing of game pheasants in *Tess of the D'Urbervilles*, though it may further be pointed out that the poem directly echoes the heroine's own words on her wedding night.⁵⁴ When Angel confesses his 'eight-and-forty hours of dissipation with a stranger' in London, Tess, momentarily relieved that her own past, as Angel himself assures her, 'can hardly be more serious', jumps up 'joyfully at the hope': 'It cannot – O no it cannot! . . . No, it cannot be' (p. 225).

In poems like 'The Puzzled Game-Birds', Hardy may be seen to be wording the thoughts of animals; conversely, in other poems he satirises the minor key of human speech, drawing attention to the musical and animal origins of our words. 'The Spring Call' has often been read as a humorous play on 'The Fashion of the Ear', in Dickinson's phrase ('To Hear an Oriole Sing', *Poems*, I, l. 7). Like Dickinson's poem or E. B. White's 'A Listener's Guide to the Birds', Hardy's poem has been read as observing the 'variations in the sounds people from different regions hear in the song of the English blackbird':⁵⁵

> Down Wessex way, when spring's a-shine,
>   The blackbird's 'pret-ty de-urr!'
> In Wessex accents marked as mine
>   Is heard afar and near.
>
> He flutes it strong, as if in song
>   No Rs of feebler tone
> Than his appear in 'pretty dear',
>   Have blackbirds ever known.
>
> Yet they pipe 'prattie deerh!' I glean,
>   Beneath a Scottish sky,
> And 'pehty de-aw!' amid the treen
>   Of Middlesex or nigh.
>
> While some folk say—perhaps in play—
>   Who know the Irish isle,
> 'Tis 'purrity dare!' in treeland there
>   When songsters would beguile.
>
>   (*Complete Poems*, pp. 244–5)

The poem begins with describing how the speaker hears and interprets the bird's sounds, though the authority of this interpretation is gradually undermined by varying transcriptions in Scotland, Middlesex and Ireland. In this respect, the poem appears to delineate the process observed in recent scholarship: 'we all listen to the same bird making the same noise and represent the call in whatever way seems most natural in the phonology of our own language'.⁵⁶

Hardy appears to set up a straightforward contrast between the bird's own voice and its 'translation' in different regional dialects. Such readings, however, are complicated by the poem's closing stanzas:

> Well: I'll say what the listening birds
>   Say, hearing 'pret-ty de-urr!'—
> However strangers sound such words,
>   That's how we sound them here.
>
> Yes, in this clime at pairing time,
>   As soon as eyes can see her
> At dawn of day, the proper way,
>   To call is 'pret-ty de-urr'.   (*Complete Poems*, p. 245)

The humour depends on an underlying sameness. Whatever the differences between birdsong and human language, the poem draws to a close with a sly nod to Darwin's theory of sexual selection. In these closing stanzas, Hardy turns to a more fundamental, philosophical questioning of what constitutes 'saying'. The phonetic transcription of the bird's call as 'pretty dear' is approximate at best; the irony, however, is that in one sense the birds really are saying just that – calling to their 'pretty dears' in the mating season. Increasingly, Hardy draws parallels between birds and people. 'Pairing time' refers specifically to the mating season in the avian world, but the 'proper way' alludes to human and class-based decorums of speech. For all its insistence upon the 'proper way' of pronouncing, the English class system shows itself no more developed or refined than the tribal and ritualistic behaviours of the avian world: 'that's how we sound them here'. Although the characters in *Tess of the D'Urbervilles* differently sound their words, their speech, like all human speech, may be traced back to the same essential origin: sex and the underlying 'waves of human impulse upon which deeds and words depend' (*Personal Writings*, p. 124).

VII

Recent research has suggested Hardy's 'unproven yet almost certain' involvement in his second wife Florence Emily Dugdale Hardy's illustrated book for children, *The Book of Baby Birds* (1912).[57] In this text, prose descriptions appear alongside illustrations and poems written from the young bird's perspective. Hardy's involvement is most pronounced in the poems, which are unattributed in the text (Florence is named as the author of the descriptions and J. E. Detmold as the illustrator). Although Hardy appears to have deliberately disguised his own contributions, the approach and project as a whole suggest a more general and pervasive influence; often the prose descriptions echo the poems and vice versa, which suggests sustained collaboration. At times, the prose descriptions fall into the anthropomorphising tendencies of late eighteenth-century children's literature, in which the domesticity of birds is presented as an instructive example for human behaviour and relationships within the family.[58] The prose descriptions often idealise the 'perfect happiness' of the 'father, mother and young ones'.[59] But there are darker and more violent details which might be taken as a mark of Hardy's involvement. Certain species are capable of violence and cruelty, which is described to the child-reader in grisly detail: 'Sad to say, all the Tits are not so friendly as those we call "Long-Tailed." The largest kind of Tit has a shocking habit of driving his beak deep into the heads of other birds' (p. 12). The remark smacks of Hardy, particularly in its play on the conventional register of children's literature (it is indeed a 'shocking' habit). 'Sad to say' is repeated several times throughout the work, in both the poems and prose, until the phrase seems to become part of the book's wider examination of what human beings 'say' about birds – what we would like to say about animals which so frequently fall short of our own imposed ideals.[60]

Repeatedly, the poems draw attention to the common mischaracterisation of birdsong as happy, or melancholy, approving or 'scolding' in tone. The point is made most forcibly perhaps in 'The Whitethroat':

> If you should hear, in a stunted tree,
> An outcry made by you know not whom,
> Like someone scolding huskily,
> That's one of us, you may assume.
>
> Perhaps it is my mother dear—
> (Not scolding, I need hardly say)—
> But wild with fright to see you near
> The nest she has tended many a day!   (p. 27)

These little poems hit precisely the right balance that Hardy has been striving for throughout his poetry: the balance, that is, between anthropomorphism and anthropodenial, between, on the one hand, the tendency to *project* human characteristics onto other species and, on the other, the refusal to acknowledge that other species share various emotions and faculties in common with human beings (fear or 'fright', most especially). In 'The Whitethroat', as throughout his writing more generally, the tragedy derives from a simple misunderstanding – from the failure to recognise the whitethroat's 'scolding' voice as an expression of 'fright' at 'seeing a stranger near' (p. 28). Rather than interpreting these sounds as 'scolding' or attempting to translate them into human words, the young reader is encouraged to observe such startling signs of fear and 'marks of pleasure' among feathered creatures (p. 29).

Repeatedly, Hardy satirises the inaccuracy and 'carelessness' with which human beings have historically assigned names and 'characters' to the various figures of the avian world:

> To class us as 'Oyster-catching' birds
>   Reveals a practice that proclaims
> How carelessly the folk of words
>   Give plumed and pennoned folk their names.
>
> It's true we go hunting beside the sea,
>   And like some shell-fish fairly well;
> But none of my kindred known to me
>   Has ever pecked at an oyster-shell.
>
> And even if one of us were to state
>   That such a peck he could recall,
> It would not be quite accurate
>   To found thereon a name for all. (p. 51)

Drawing attention to the 'carelessness' with which human beings use their words, Hardy challenges the common usage of one word in particular: 'folk'. According to the *OED*, the word may refer to people in general, or to groups of people belonging to a particular religion, region, or class, or to one's relatives, blood relations or 'kinsfolk'. The poem recalls the episode in which Angel Clare is forced to reconsider 'the conventional farm-folk of his imagination' in *Tess of the D'Urbervilles* (p. 117). Ironically, the recognition of difference simultaneously reveals an underlying sameness: the 'farm-folk' are no less varied than his own class, his own family, his own 'folk'. In poems like 'The Oyster-Catcher' or 'The Spring Call', Hardy's use of the word draws attention to both the differences and the underlying kinship between 'pennoned folk' and 'the folk of words'. Hardy thus draws attention to the myth-making qualities of words and labels – the kind of 'folklore' that casts individuals as types, and that reduces a whole range of varied fellow creatures into a single character or 'name for all'.

Frequently, the language of the poems plays on its own internal contradictions; at the same time that the poems speak from the young bird's perspective, consistently the reader is reminded that the bird cannot understand human language or the accusations waged against such 'thieving' pests as the magpie: 'But we do not know what is stealing | Is it admiring and concealing?' (p. 21). If the poems often resist the human temptation to 'say' things which have no relevance to the birds themselves, elsewhere they explore what the birds themselves may be saying – the magpie's 'loud "currack" of delight', for example, when it drops a stone upon a trapped and screaming toad (p. 24). If the poems often challenge what 'people say' about birds (p. 69), elsewhere they offer an interpretation of what the sounds may mean to the birds themselves. 'Sad to say' finds its correlative in 'as much as to say' (p. 42). When a willow warbler was seen 'industriously helping to feed the hungry brood of a Redstart', the mother was seemingly 'not pleased at this attention', but would 'pounce angrily on the intruder, as much as to say she would have no stranger in her nursery' (p. 42).

Throughout *The Book of Baby Birds*, Hardy draws frequent parallels between nestling birds and human infants. In either case, the young, unpractised mind is seen to offer a fresh outlook upon the world of its parents: the long-tailed tits 'don't know' where their parents get their food from, 'but it is very good' (p. 9). The young Shetland Skua or 'Bonxies' are 'far too young to know' if any of the statements made against their kind are 'true' or 'fair':

> We are said to be hungry robber-birds,
> Taking food from our neighbours with ruthless greed:
> Whether these statements are baseless words,
> Or whether the charge is true indeed,
> We nestlings are far too young to know—
> At least, to be sure if the slur is fair;
> But when we are long-winged fliers, and go
> Far seaward, we shall be well aware. (p. 63)

Usually associated with a form of inconsequential speech or babble, the young birds in Hardy's poems offer a fresh scrutiny of the 'truth' of men's words: even grown, civilised men may sometimes speak inaccurately and 'slur' the names of others. In 'The Darkling Thrush', Hardy draws attention to different kinds of awareness; in 'The Skua', to be made 'well aware' does not simply mean that the individual has gained in knowledge, experience or understanding, but more specifically that they have grown more 'vigilant', more 'cautious', more 'on guard' against the world (*OED*). As the prose description of these birds further relates, the 'downy', 'fluffy' and even rather 'comical' chicks of the Skua will one day grow into the 'pirates' and 'highwaymen' of the seas ruthlessly 'stealing' the fish of other birds and even 'devouring' their young (pp. 63–4). For these birds, as implicitly for Hardy's own young readers, to grow more 'aware' or more acquainted with the world does not necessarily amount to moral growth or progress; experience may teach whether the word is 'true' or 'fair', but this does not necessarily mean that the next generation will act upon that knowledge.

In late poems such as 'Christmas: 1924', Hardy shows himself profoundly sceptical of any such progress in human history:

> 'Peace upon earth!' was said. We sing it,
> And pay a million priests to bring it.
> After two thousand years of mass
> We've got as far as poison-gas.
>
> (*Complete Poems*, p. 914)

Ironically, Hardy echoes Shelley's earlier insistence in *A Defence of Poetry* (1840) that 'there is no want of knowledge respecting what is wisest and best in morals, government and political economy'; what human society so tragically lacked, for Shelley, was 'the creative faculty to imagine that which we know' and 'the generous impulse to act that which we imagine'.[61] Writing almost a century later, in the interim between two world wars, Hardy lived to see the tragic consequences of such a failure to act upon that which we know to be 'wisest and best'. For Hardy, the return to poetry is an attempt to return to that same basic principle of the Golden Rule – of do as you would be done by – that each and every generation, no matter how clever, or how rich, or how religiously enlightened or technologically advanced, so catastrophically fails to live up to.

Conclusion

When the Humanitarian League wrote to Hardy requesting permission to publish three of his poems ('The Blinded Bird', 'The Puzzled Game-Birds' and 'Wagtail and Baby'), the author sent the request swiftly on to Macmillan (*Collected Letters*, V, p. 240). As its title suggests, Bertram Lloyd's *The Great Kinship: An Anthology of Humanitarian Poetry* (1921) is based on a similar principle to that which Hardy expressed in his letter to the League. The expressed intention of Lloyd's introduction and the poems selected in his anthology is to provide a general history of the representation of animals in Western literature. In his general outline of approaches to animals over a period of centuries, Lloyd observes many of the general tendencies that I have been exploring in this book. In classical literature, Lloyd observes 'a good deal of interesting speculation and observation on the position and capacity of animals', but regrets that such close observation does not amount to what he considers to be the defining principle of a humanitarian approach: 'the feeling of man's sympathetic connection or bond with the other creatures of the earth'.[1] Although Lloyd observed the biblical precept that 'a righteous man regards the life of his beast' (Proverbs 12:10), he regards the teachings of St Francis as the 'great exception' to a Christian tradition characterised by 'its stressing of the future life at the expense of the present one, its arrogant anthropocentrism, and utter lack of interest in the human creature' (pp. vi–vii). Turning to the work of the Elizabethan poets and dramatists, Lloyd also remarks on several of the tendencies observed in recent scholarship: a treatment of the animal as 'a pleasant toy' for man's own fancies and philosophical reflections (p. vii), 'charming epitaphs' and eulogies which, however well-intentioned, seem 'scarcely more than patronising in tone' (p. ix), as well as 'vague generalisations', notably regarding 'the bird's melodious lays', which Lloyd considers as being little more than 'the ordinary stock-in-trade of the poet' (p. x). In the writings of the Romantic and Victorian periods, Lloyd notes an emerging tradition of what he terms '*zoophilist*' poetry: a poetry based on 'the ever-growing and consolidating perception of the kinship of the whole animal world (including, of course, Man)' (p. xii).

For Lloyd, the poetry of the long nineteenth century at once reflected and actively contributed to a major shift in attitudes towards other species: 'mild sympathy for the ill-used animal', he writes, 'is replaced by sympathy *with* the creature, regarded as a sentient fellow-being – a sympathy betokening a wider imagination and clearer understanding' (p. xi). One of the first poems to be included within Lloyd's anthology, Cowper's 'On a Goldfinch Starved to Death in its Cage' openly condemns the practice of keeping these animals as pets; written from the goldfinch's perspective, the poem concludes by thanking its owner for its final release from the miseries of a caged existence: 'More cruelty could none express: | And I, if you had shown me less, | Had been your prisoner still' (Lloyd, p. 9). In a series of poems about birdsong in the Romantic period, the mood changes. Attention shifts to the wild bird singing in its natural habitat. Wordsworth's green linnet 'pours forth his song in gushes' from among 'the dancing leaves' (Lloyd, p. 26). Shelley's skylark is similarly at one with the elements, the beauty of its song wholly dependent upon its wild, free-flying state: 'And singing still dost soar, and soaring ever singest' (Lloyd, p. 54). In their celebration of wild songbirds, these poems do not, like Cowper, openly inveigh against the 'cruelty' of caging birds. But they do bring these animals to life. Mysterious, elusive, inscrutable and yet vividly alive. They do not ask for freedom, like Cowper's bird. They soar, they race, they sing, they defy the terms in which we seek to describe them. And in doing so they demand their freedom from human interference, however well-intentioned that may be. Rather than expressing sympathy *for* an ill-used animal, these poems go some way in asking their readers to sympathise *with* a creature that may be different, that may be alien, but which unquestionably has a life and world of its own.

In the poems included in Lloyd's anthology, a balance is being struck between the two opposing forces that I have been outlining in this book: on the one hand, anthropomorphism, or the wilful assignment of human attributes to other creatures, and, on the other, anthropodenial, defined by de Waal as 'the *a priori* rejection of shared characteristics between humans and animals' which reflects a 'pre-Darwinian antipathy to the profound similarities between human and animal behaviour'.[2] Parodying the eighteenth-century tradition of poetic elegies to household pets (established by Cowper among others), Matthew

Arnold, in 'Poor Matthias', reflects on the problem of establishing sympathy *with*, rather than simply *for*, our fellow creatures:

> Birds, companions more unknown,
> Live beside us, but alone;
> Finding not, do all they can,
> Passage from their souls to man.
> Kindness we bestow, and praise,
> Laud their plumage, greet their lays;
> Still beneath their feather'd breast,
> Stirs a history unexpress'd.
> Wishes there, and feelings strong,
> Incommunicably throng.   (Lloyd, p. 104)

Directly responding to the age-old tradition in which poets have lauded, praised and sought to emulate the song of birds, Arnold emphasises that these creatures, which live so closely alongside us, belong to a world that remains largely 'unknown' to human beings. Although these animals exist properly outside our understanding and therefore our sympathy, Arnold's poem does not present birds as mere mindless machines: 'still beneath their feather'd breast | Stirs a history unexpress'd'. This sense of a rich and complex, though hidden, animal life is evoked through the fudging of the word 'inco*mmu*nicably' in the final line. As the word's natural speech stress disrupts the metrical pattern, the slight awkwardness draws attention to the difference between the idea of metre and how the line actually sounds. An abstract idea or mental pattern, which the lines themselves may or may not follow, is key to understanding the distinction that Arnold is exploring in his poem and that I have been exploring throughout this book: the distinction, that is, not only between what an animal might think and what it is able to sing or say, but also, and by implication, between what human beings think and what they actually articulate.

Staunchly critical of the sort of misplaced 'kindness' that pet-owners unthinkingly bestow upon the feathered race, Arnold's poem asks its reader to acknowledge a deeper kind of affinity, resemblance or kinship between birds and men:

> Does it, if we miss your mind,
> Prove us so remote in kind?
> Birds! we but repeat on you
> What amongst ourselves we do.
> Somewhat more or somewhat less,
> 'Tis the same unskillfulness.
> What you feel, escapes our ken—
> Know we more our fellow-men?   (Lloyd, p. 105)

In this slight comic poem, Arnold raises one of the central questions explored in the foregoing pages: if it is true that we can never know what passes through the 'mind' of an animal, then how can we possibly 'prove', one way or the other, how that mind differs from our own? If animals appear 'remote' or inscrutable to us, are we any better at judging what passes in the minds of other members of our own species? For Arnold and so many of the writers explored in this book, the irony is that human society inflicts needless cruelty on *all* those who escape their 'ken' – whether they be other species or, indeed, other members of our own kind whose 'despairing sign' we either cannot or will not understand (Lloyd, p. 105). For Arnold, it all comes down to 'the same unskillfulness': the same blundering ineptitude, the same failure to express our own feelings and to empathise with those of others. The fact that these ideas are explored in a relatively minor and comic poem, written at a time when Arnold feared his own powers were diminishing, says something about how such 'soft sentimental stuff' has been historically sidelined, belittled and pushed to the margins of literature.

Exactly what birds feel, what their songs may or may not express, remains tantalisingly outside the reach of philosophers, scientists and poets. Increasingly throughout the long nineteenth century, however, scientists observed underlying similarities between animal minds and our own. The scientific analogy between birdsong and human speech explored in this book raises wide-ranging questions about not only the cognitive capacities of other species but also how those capacities compare with our own and in what ways. As they explored how other animals think, writers in the following century increasingly reflected on their own ways of thinking. In *To the Lighthouse* (1927), Virginia Woolf delineates the workings of Mr Ramsay's 'splendid mind':

> 'Someone had blundered,' he said again, striding off, up and down the terrace.
> But how extraordinarily his note had changed! It was like the cuckoo; "in June he gets out of tune"; as if he were trying over, tentatively seeking, some phrase for a new mood, and having only this at hand, used it, cracked though it was. But it sounded ridiculous – "Someone had blundered" – said like that, almost as a question, without any conviction, melodiously. Mrs Ramsay could not help smiling, and soon, sure enough, walking up and down, he hummed it, dropped it, fell silent.[3]

In the modernist writings anticipated by Hardy and other writers in the late nineteenth century, there emerges a growing preoccupation with exploring and representing a subvocal level of human consciousness: an ongoing struggle to hit upon 'some phrase for a new mood', a sense of a difference between what we want to say and the approximate, cracked or hackneyed expressions available, and the consequent strangeness of our own words when played back to us: 'but it sounded ridiculous!' Reflecting a post-Darwinian 'ever-growing and consolidating perception of the kinship of the whole animal world (including, of course, Man)' (Lloyd, p. xii), the analogy with birdsong raises questions not only about the sentience and artfulness of other creatures, but also about the animal-like origins and qualities of our own human arts of music, speech and poetry.

Notes

Introduction

1. The ethologist and primatologist Frans de Waal traces a deep-rooted and long-held suspicion of anthropomorphism in the scientific community in his essay 'Anthopomorphism and Anthropodenial' in *Primates and Philosophers: How Morality Evolved*, ed. by Stephen Macedo and Josiah Ober (Princeton, NJ: Princeton University Press, 2009), pp. 59–68. The long history of this concern is outlined and discussed in more detail in the following pages.
2. Daniel Karlin, *The Figure of the Singer* (Oxford: Oxford University Press, 2013), p. 59. Karlin's approach is partly informed by that of the musician and philosopher David Rothenberg in his highly influential book *Why Birds Sing* (2005). Not only do these songs 'sound out from an alien mind', but, as Rothenberg points out, the sound itself also includes rhythms, tones and unpronounceable syllables which are 'none of them too close to our systems of music or language'; *Why Birds Sing: One Man's Quest to Solve an Everyday Mystery* (London: Penguin, 2005), p. 3. If birds often sound like their names, the ornithologist and writer Jeremy Mynott observes that the name of the cuckoo sounds 'suspiciously' different in different languages: '*cuculo*' in Italian, '*kukushka*' in Russian and '*geykur*' in Faroese; *Birdscapes: Birds in Our Imagination and Experience* (Oxford: Princeton University Press, 2009), p. 161.
3. John Clare, *The Natural History Prose Writings of John Clare*, ed. by Margaret Grainger (Oxford: Oxford University Press, 1983), p. 312. Pliny the Elder, *The Historie of the World, Commonly Called, The Naturall Historie of C. Plinius Secundus*, trans. by Philemon Holland, 2 vols (London: Adam Islip, 1601), I, bk X, ch. xxix, p. 286. Although Enlightenment figures such as Joseph Addison questioned the reliability of Pliny's observations of birds and other natural phenomena, Romantic poets (notably Wordsworth and Shelley) regularly allude to Pliny and appear to have 'brought him back into favour' in their own times; see Paul Turner's Introduction to *Selections from the History of the World, Commonly Called the Natural History of C. Plinius Secundus* (Carbondale: Southern Illinois University Press, 1962), 7–17 (p. 14). Philemon

Holland's was not only the first and most popular, but also remained the only complete translation of Pliny in English until the 1850s; see J. Newsome's Introduction to *Pliny's Natural History: A Selection from Philemon Holland's Translation* (Oxford: Clarendon, 1964), xv–xxviii (p. xv).

4. Daines Barrington, 'Experiments and Observations on the Singing of Birds', *Philosophical Transactions*, vol. 63 (1773–4): 249–91 (p. 252).
5. Charles Darwin, *The Descent of Man, and Selection in Relation to Sex*, ed. by James Moore and Adrian Desmond (London: Penguin, 2004), p. 108.
6. John Clare, 'When first we hear the shy come nightingales', in *Poems of the Middle Period, 1822–37*, ed. by Eric Robinson, David Powell and P. M. S. Dawson, 5 vols. (Oxford: Clarendon, 1996–2003), V, pp. 222–3; where a sonnet or other short poem is quoted in full, I have given page numbers as opposed to line references.
7. See Rothenberg, p. 14.
8. Richard Jefferies, *Round About a Great Estate* (London: Smith, Elder, 1880), p. 30.
9. Wolfgang Amadeus Mozart, 'A Musical Joke'; the quotation is taken from the liner notes of a recording, quoted and discussed in Rothenberg, p. 189. For a full discussion of Mozart's relationship with this bird, see Lyanda Lynn Haupt, *Mozart's Starling* (London: Corsair, 2017).
10. Olivier Messiaen, quoted in Robert Sherlaw Johnson, *Messiaen* (London: Omnibus, 2008), p. 117.
11. 'Messiaen on Birds', www.youtube.com/watch?v=XRRhsX4j1Oc&t=2s, last accessed 31 August 2021.
12. Samuel Taylor Coleridge, 'The Nightingale', in *Poetical Works*, ed. by James C. C. Mays, 2 vols. [Reading Text] (Princeton, NJ: Princeton University Press, 2001), I, l. 45.
13. Karlin directly responds to Rothenberg on pp. 76, 79, 81–2.
14. pp. xvii, 60.
15. Stephanie Kuduk Weiner, *Clare's Lyric: John Clare and Three Modern Poets* (Oxford: Oxford University Press, 2014); Weiner references Rothenberg on p. 41.
16. p. 24.
17. John S. Kennedy, *The New Anthropomorphism* (Cambridge: Cambridge University Press, 1992), pp. 160–1.
18. In the 1960s the anthropologist Claude Lévi-Strauss famously described animals as 'good to think' with; *Totemism*, trans. by Rodney Needham (Boston, MA: Beacon Press, 1963), p. 89. Focusing especially on the late eighteenth and nineteenth centuries, the cultural historian Harriet Ritvo explored how human thinking about animals all too frequently expresses our own 'human concerns linked only tenuously to the natural world'; *The*

Animal Estate: The English and Other Creatures in Victorian England (Cambridge, MA: Harvard University Press, 1987), p. 3. Taking Lévi-Strauss's remarks as a point of departure, the literary critic Christine Kenyon-Jones analysed the ways in which philosophers, poets and 'human beings of all kinds' throughout the eighteenth and nineteenth centuries tended to 'conceptualise and quantify animals as a part of the human world, projecting upon them categories and values derived from human society and then serving them back as a critique or reinforcement of the human order'; *Kindred Brutes: Animals in Romantic-Period Writing* (London: Ashgate, 2001), p. 1. As subsequent studies have emphasised, any history of animals must be in truth, as Erica Fudge has more recently put it, 'a history of human attitudes towards animals'; 'A Left-Handed Blow: Writing the History of Animals', in *Representing Animals*, ed. by Nigel Rothfels (Bloomington: Indiana University Press, 2002), 3–18 (p. 6).
19. Mynott, pp. 24, 26.
20. Karlin, p. 77.
21. Particularly praising Walt Whitman's rendering of the mockingbird's notes, Karlin argues that birdsong 'is believable as a figure for poetry just in the measure that the figurative is openly acknowledged'; p. 82.
22. Mary Midgley, *Animals and Why They Matter* (Athens: Georgia University Press, 1983), p. 129.
23. Gregory Radick, *The Simian Tongue: The Long Debate about Animal Language* (Chicago: University of Chicago Press, 2007), p. 67.
24. Georges Cuvier, quoted and translated by Hans Aarsleff in *From Locke to Saussure: Essays on the Study of Language and Intellectual History* (London: Athlone, 1982), p. 37.
25. Marie-Jean Pierre Flourens, quoted and translated by Aarsleff, *From Locke to Saussure*, p. 37.
26. Max Müller, 'Lectures on Mr Darwin's Philosophy of Language, Lect. 2', *Fraser's Magazine*, vol. 7, no. 42 (1873): 659–78 (p. 661).
27. John Holmes, *Darwin's Bards: British and American Poetry in the Age of Evolution* (Edinburgh: Edinburgh University Press, 2009), p. 155.
28. George Henry Lewes, *Sea-Side Studies at Ilfracombe, Tenby, the Scilly Isles, and Jersey*, 2nd ed. (Edinburgh: Blackwood, 1860), pp. 385, 387.
29. Alexis Harley, 'Darwin's Ants: Evolutionary Theory and the Anthropomorphic Fallacy', in *Representing the Modern Animal in Culture*, ed. by Jeanne Dubino, Ziba Rashidian and Andrew Smyth (London: Palgrave, 2014), 103–18 (p. 104).
30. Thomas Nagel, 'What Is It Like to Be a Bat?', *The Philosophical Review*, vol. 83, no. 4 (1974): 435–50.
31. Ludwig Wittgenstein, *Philosophical Investigations*, trans. by Gertrude Elizabeth Margaret Anscombe, 2nd ed. (Oxford: Blackwell, 1958), p. 223.

32. Harley, p. 104.
33. Bennet G. Galef, 'The Making of a Science', in *Foundations of Animal Behaviour: Classic Papers with Commentaries*, ed. by Lynne D Houck and Lee C. Drickamer (Chicago, IL: University of Chicago Press, 1996), 5–12 (p. 9); Conwy Lloyd Morgan, *An Introduction to Comparative Psychology* (London: Walter Scott, 1894), p. 59.
34. de Waal, 'Anthropomorphism and Anthropodenial', p. 65.
35. Darwin, *The Correspondence of Charles Darwin*, ed. by Frederick H. Burkhardt et al. (Cambridge: Cambridge University Press, 1985–2006), VI, p. 514; once completed in 2022, this edition will comprise thirty volumes in total.
36. Darwin, quoted by Radick, p. 65.
37. Clifford B. Frith, *Charles Darwin's Life with Birds: His Complete Ornithology* (Oxford: Oxford University Press, 2016), p. 231.
38. Ibid.
39. Francis H. Allen, 'The Evolution of Birdsong', *Auk*, vol. 36, no. 4 (1919): 528–36 (p. 531).
40. Robert C. Berwick and Noam Chomsky, 'Foreword', in *Birdsong, Speech and Language: Exploring the Evolution of Mind and Brain*, ed. by Johan J. Bolhuis and Martin Everaert (Cambridge, MA: MIT Press, 2013), ix–xii (p. ix).
41. Aristotle, *Politics*, trans. by Lord Carnes, 2nd ed. (Chicago, IL: University of Chicago Press, 2013), 1.2.1253a.7–18.
42. Cicero, *De inventione; De optimo genere oratorum; Topica*, trans. by Harry Mortimer Hubbell (Cambridge, MA: Harvard University Press, 2014), bk I, ch. iv, pp. 12–13.
43. Nathan Bailey, Introduction to *An Universal Etymological Dictionary*, 26th ed. (Edinburgh: Neill, 1789), vii–xiv (p. vii).
44. Lindley Murray, *An English Grammar; Comprehending the Principles and Rules of Language; Illustrated by Appropriate Exercises*, new ed., 2 vols. (York: Wilson et al., 1808), I, p. 22.
45. Ludwig Noiré, *The Origin and Philosophy of Language*, 2nd revised ed. (Chicago, IL: Open Court, 1917), pp. 73–4.
46. Müller, *Lectures on the Science of Language; Delivered at the Royal Institution of Great Britain in April, May and June 1861*, 2 vols. (London: Longman, 1861), I, p. 329.
47. See Berwick and Chomsky, *Why Only Us: Language and Evolution* (Cambridge, MA: MIT Press, 2016), p. 3.
48. Modern linguists such as Berwick and Chomsky suggest that the language faculty represents a dramatic 'biological leap', which may seem irreconcilable with Darwin's essential principle of evolution by 'the shortest and slowest steps'; ibid., p. 3.

49. Ann Wierda Rowland, *Romanticism and Childhood: The Infantilization of British Literary Culture* (Cambridge: Cambridge University Press, 2012), p. 109.
50. Ibid; Johann Gottfried Herder, 'On the Education of Students in Language and Speech', quoted by Friedrich A. Kittler in *Discourse Networks: 1800–1900*, trans. by Michael Metteer, with Chris Cullins (Stanford, CA: Stanford University Press, 1990), p. 37.
51. de Waal, *Are We Smart Enough to Know How Smart Animals Are?* (London: Norton, 2016), p. 103. Also see Irene Pepperberg, *The Alex Studies: Cognitive and Communicative Abilities of Grey Parrots* (Cambridge, MA: Harvard University Press, 1999).
52. de Waal, *Are We Smart Enough?*, p. 99.
53. Rachel Mundy, *Animal Musicalities: Birds, Beasts and Evolutionary Listening* (Middletown, CT: Wesleyan University Press, 2018), p. 2.
54. For example, see Olivia Smith, *The Politics of Language: 1791–1819* (Oxford: Clarendon, 1984), Tony Crowley, *Standard English and the Politics of Language* (Urbana: University of Illinois Press, 1989), and Richard Marggraf Turley, *The Politics of Language in Romantic Literature* (London: Palgrave, 2002).
55. Thomas Hardy, *The Major of Casterbridge*, ed. by Keith Wilson (London: Penguin, 2003), p. 127.
56. Charles Darwin, *On the Origin of Species*, ed. by Gillian Beer (Oxford: Oxford University Press, 2008), p. 5.
57. Rothenberg, p. 25.
58. Thomas Hardy, *Tess of the D'Urbervilles*, ed. by Tim Dolin (London: Penguin, 2003), pp. 95, 60, 84.
59. *The Collected Letters of Thomas Hardy*, ed. by Richard Little Purdy, Michael Millgate and Keith Wilson, 8 vols. (Oxford: Clarendon, 1978–2012), III, p. 43.
60. *The Later Years of Thomas Hardy, 1892–1928* (Cambridge: Cambridge University Press, 2011), p. 138. Hardy's autobiography was dictated to and published under the name of his second wife, Florence Emily Hardy.

1 The Science of Birdsong: 1773–1871

1. Aristotle, *Historia Animalium*, trans. by A. Peck, 3 vols. (London: William Heinemann, 1965), 4.10.536b.14–20.
2. The phrase 'bird-trade' is taken from Henry Mayhew, *London Labour and the London Poor: The Condition and Earnings of Those that Will Work, Cannot Work, and Will Not Work*, 2nd enlarged ed., 4 vols. (London: Griffin, Bohn, 1861–2), II, p. 65.

3. Gilbert White, *A Natural History of Selborne*, ed. by Anne Secord (Oxford: Oxford University Press, 2013), p. 191.
4. David Rothenberg, *Why Birds Sing: One Man's Quest to Solve an Everyday Mystery* (London: Penguin, 2005), p. 19. Also see Tim Birkhead, *The Red Canary: The Story of the First Genetically Engineered Animal* (London: Bloomsbury, 2014), pp. 62–3, and Don Stap, *Birdsong: A Natural History* (Oxford: Oxford University Press, 2005), pp. 26–32. In a broadcast on BBC Radio 4 entitled *The Bird Fancyer's Delight* and aired in 2011, musician Sarah Angliss suggests that bird-fancying offered a kind of 'primordial feathered recorder in the home' a century before the invention of the phonograph and 'advent of the recorded sound' (www.bbc.co.uk/programmes/b0128pyp, last accessed 31 August 2021). *The Bird-Fancyer's Delight* was also an inspiration to William Thorpe's study of song-learning in chaffinches in the 1950s; he opened his 1954 article, 'The Process of Song-Learning in the Chaffinch', with reference to the seventeenth-century practice of bird-fancying; see William Thorpe, 'The Process of Song-Learning in the Chaffinch as Studied by Means of the Sound Spectrograph', *Nature*, vol. 173, no. 4402 (1954): 465–9 (p. 465; n. 1). Later, Thorpe discussed the manual in finer detail in 'Comments on *The Bird-Fancyer's Delight*, Together with Notes on Imitation in the Sub-song of the Chaffinch', *Ibis*, vol. 97, no. 2 (1955): 247–51.
5. Johann Matthäus Bechstein, *The Natural History of Cage Birds*, trans. by anon., new ed. (London: Groombridge, 1837), p. 24.
6. J. Macloc, *A Natural History of the Most Remarkable Quadrupeds, Birds, Fishes, Serpents, Reptiles, and Insects in the Known World*, 3rd ed. (London: Dean and Munday, 1820), pp. 178–9. Clare owned an 1820 edition of this work; see David Powell, *Catalogue of the John Clare Collection in the Northampton Public Library* (Northampton: County Borough of Northampton Public Libraries, Museum and Art Galleries Committee: 1964), p. 30; no. 292.
7. Oliver Goldsmith, *A History of the Earth and Animated Nature*, 8 vols. (London: Nourse, 1774), V, p. 328.
8. For an extended discussion of birds in eighteenth-century art, see Diana Donald, *Picturing Animals in Britain (1750–1850)* (New Haven, CT: Yale University Press, 2007), p. 23, and Lorenz Eitner, 'Cages, Prisons, and Captives in Eighteenth-Century Art', in *Images of Romanticism*, ed. by Karl Kroeber and William Walling (New Haven, CT: Yale University Press, 1978), 13–38. Moira Ferguson has examined the significance of the aviary in eighteenth-century women's writing, such as Sarah Trimmer's *Fabulous Histories; Or, the History of the Robins* (1786); as England 'teetered on the edge of chaos, if not revolution', the orchard and the aviary became 'thinly veiled' tropes through which, Ferguson argues, women writers explored the responsibilities of society towards their 'dependents'; see Moira Ferguson,

Animal Advocacy and English Women, 1770–1900 (Michigan: University of Michigan Press, 1998), pp. 10, 24. For further uses of the metaphor in eighteenth-century fiction and poetry, see Fred V. Randel, 'Coleridge and the Contentiousness of Romantic Nightingales', *Studies in Romanticism*, vol. 21, no. 1 (1982): 33–55 (esp. pp. 33–4).

9. Black was also rat- and mole-catcher to Queen Victoria at Buckingham Palace; for further details of his long and lucrative career, see Mayhew, III, pp. 11–20.
10. James Augustus Hessey, quoted in Clare, *Natural History Prose*, p. 42.
11. Richard Jefferies, *Nature Near London* (London: Chatto and Windus, 1913), p. 30.
12. Richard Rowe, *Life in the London Streets; Or, Struggles for Daily Bread* (London: Nimmo and Bain, 1881), p. 98.
13. William H. Hudson, *Birds in London* (London: Longmans, 1898), p. 198.
14. William Wordsworth, *The Thirteen-Book Prelude*, ed. by Mark L. Reed, 2 vols. (Ithaca, NY: Cornell University Press, 1991), I, bk. I, ll. 317–9. Unless otherwise indicated, all quotations from *The Prelude* are taken from the AB-Stage reading text of the 1805–6 version, printed in the first volume of this edition.
15. Thomas Hardy, 'Performing Animals: Mr Hardy's Protest', Letter to the editor, *The Times* (19 December 1913): 9.
16. Henry James Fulljames, 'Mr. Hardy and Cage Birds', Letter to the editor, *The Times* (23 December 1913): 10.
17. The phrase is taken from a newspaper article by a Flemmish bird-catcher, C. Erffelycnk, 'Lets over onze speelmuiten' (*De Vinkenier*, 1935); quoted in Pieter Verstraete, 'The Blind Finch: Expanding the Role of Disability in Heritage Studies', *Revista Pasages*, no. 1 (2015): 37–54 (p. 49).
18. David Attenborough, Introduction to Michael Bright, *Animal Language* (London: British Broadcasting Corporation, 1984), p. 7.
19. See Barrington's article 'On the Expiration of the Cornish Language', *Archaeologia*, vol. 3 (1775): 278–84.
20. According to *The Britannica Encyclopaedia*, Barrington's 'Experiments and Observations on the Singing of Birds' was 'among the most curious and ingenious of his papers'; see *The Britannica Encyclopaedia; Or, a Dictionary of the Arts, Sciences, and Miscellaneous Literature*, 6th ed., 20 vols. (Edinburgh: Constable, 1820–3), III, p. 424.
21. Comte de. Buffon, George Louis Leclerc, *Natural History of Birds*, trans. by William Smellie, 9 vols. (London: Strahan, Cadell, Murray, 1793), IV, p. 53.
22. John Wright (ed.), *Buffon's Natural History; Of the Globe, and of Man*, 4 vols. (London: Tegg, 1831), III, p. 15.
23. Erasmus Darwin, *The Temple of Nature; Or, the Origin of Society* (London: Johnson, 1803), canto 2, l. 356.

24. W. Tecumseh Fitch, 'Musical Protolanguage: Darwin's Theory of Language Evolution Revisited', in *Birdsong, Speech and Language: Exploring the Evolution of Mind and Brain*, ed. by Johan J. Bolhuis and Martin Everaert (Cambridge, MA: MIT Press, 2013), 489–504 (p. 491).
25. Fitch, 'Musical Protolanguage', p. 493.
26. For rises in pet-keeping in the eighteenth and nineteenth centuries, see Ritvo, p. 86, and David Perkins, *Romanticism and Animal Rights* (Cambridge: Cambridge University Press, 2003), esp. ch. 8.
27. Aristotle, *De Interpretatione* in *Categories and De Interpretatione*, trans. by John L. Ackrill (Oxford: Oxford University Press, 1963), 1.2.16a19–26.
28. Stephen Pinker, *The Language Instinct: The New Science of Language and Mind* (London: Penguin, 2015), p. 15.
29. Alexander von Humboldt, quoted in Fitch, 'Musical Protolanguage', p. 495.

2 The Science of Language: 1755–1873

1. Titus Lucretius Carus, *Titus Lucretius Carus. The Epicurean Philosopher; His Six Books 'De Rerum Natura'; Done into English Verse, With Notes*, trans. by Thomas Creech (Oxford: Lichfield, 1682), bk. V, p. 182. I have given the page number in accordance with this edition's own conventions.
2. Herder, 'Essay on the Origin of Language', in Jean-Jacques Rousseau and Johann Gottfried Herder, *On the Origin of Language*, trans. by John H. Moran and Alexander Gode (Chicago, IL: University of Chicago Press, 1966), 85–177 (p. 136); hereafter, *Two Essays*. W. Tecumseh Fitch outlines modern approaches to the theory of 'musical proto-language' in *The Evolution of Language* (Cambridge: Cambridge University Press, 2012), pp. 465–507.
3. Pinker, p. 53.
4. Jean-Jacques Rousseau, *A Discourse on Inequality*, trans. by Maurice Cranston (London: Penguin, 1984), p. 93.
5. Rousseau, 'Essay on the Origin of Languages', in *Two Essays*, 5–83 (p. 12).
6. Rousseau, quoted by Cranston in the Introduction to *A Discourse on Inequality*, 9–54 (p. 28).
7. Jean Starobinski, *Blessings in Disguise; Or, the Morality of Evil* (Cambridge, MA: Harvard University Press, 1993), pp. 119–20.
8. Rousseau, quoted in Starobinski, p. 127.
9. Rousseau, quoted in Starobinski, p. 155.
10. Starobinski, p. 155.
11. Adam Smith, Letter to the *Edinburgh Review* (1756), in *Essays on Philosophical Subjects: The Glasgow Edition of the Works and Correspondence of Adam Smith* (Oxford: Oxford University Press, 1967–1983), III, pp. 242–56.

12. James Burnett Lord Monboddo, *Of the Origin and Progress of Language*, 6 vols., 2nd ed. (Edinburgh: Balfour, 1774–92), I, p. 289.
13. According to James Boswell's account, Johnson responded with characteristically pointed ridicule to the speculative theories of his contemporaries: 'Rousseau *knows* he is talking nonsense, and laughs at the world for staring at him . . . . Why, Sir, a man who talks nonsense so well, must know that he is talking nonsense. But I am *afraid* (chuckling and laughing) Monboddo does not *know* he is talking nonsense'; see Boswell, *The Life of Samuel Johnson; Together with the Journal of a Tour to the Hebrides*, 10 vols (London: Murray, 1835), III, p. 74.
14. Monboddo, Letter to James Harris (1772), rpt. in William Angus Knight, *Lord Monboddo and Some of His Contemporaries* (London: Murray, 1900), p. 73.
15. Olivia Smith, p. 26.
16. James Burnett Lord Monboddo, Preface to *An Account of a Savage Girl, Caught Wild in the Woods of Champagne*, translated from the French of Madame Hecquet (Edinburgh: Kincaid and Bell, 1768), iii–xviii (pp. iv–v).
17. Charles Dickens, *Little Dorrit*, ed. by Stephen Wall and Helen Small (London: Penguin, 2003), p. 500.
18. Richard W. Serjeantson, 'The Passions and Animal Language, 1540–1700', *Journal of the History of Ideas*, vol. 62, no. 3 (2001): 425–44 (p. 427).
19. Hans Aarsleff, *The Study of Language in England, 1780–1860* (London: Athlone, 1983), pp. 14–15.
20. Rowland, p. 113.
21. pp. 113–4.
22. p. 123.
23. Johann Gottfried Herder, 'Fragments on Recent German Literature', in *Philosophical Writings*, trans. and ed. by Michael N. Forster (Cambridge: Cambridge University Press, 2002), 33–64 (p. 61).
24. Herder, quoted by Kittler, pp. 37–8.
25. Ibid.
26. James Harris, *Hermes; Or, a Philosophical Inquiry concerning Universal Grammar* (London: Woodfall, 1751), p. 11.
27. Olivia Smith, p. 3.
28. p. 22.
29. p. 3.
30. p. 27.
31. pp. 26–7.
32. Leonora Nattrass, 'John Clare and William Cobbett: The Personal and the Political', in *The Independent Spirit: John Clare and the Self-Taught Tradition*, ed. by John Goodridge (Helpston: John Clare Society and Margaret Grainger Memorial Trust, 1994), 44–54 (esp. pp. 45, 48).

33. Olivia Smith, p. vii.
34. William Cobbett, *A Grammar of the English Language, in a Series of Letters; Intended for the Use of Schools and of Young Persons in General; But, More Especially, for the Use of Soldiers, Sailors, Apprentices and Plough-Boys* (Cambridge: Cambridge University Press, 2014), p. 15.
35. Aarsleff, *The Study of Language,* p. 229.
36. Dugald Stewart, quoted by Aarsleff, *The Study of Language*, p. 107.
37. p. 127; also see Crowley, p. 14, and Turley, p. 130.
38. Herbert Spencer, 'The Origin and Function of Music', in *Essays: Scientific, Political and Speculative*, 3 vols. (London: Williams and Norgate, 1891), II, 400–51 (p. 404).
39. Charles Darwin, *The Expression of the Emotions in Man and Animals*, ed. by Joe Cain and Sharon Messenger (London: Penguin, 2009), p. 86.
40. Max Müller, 'Lectures on Mr Darwin's Philosophy of Language, Lect. 3', *Fraser's Magazine*, vol. 8, no. 43 (1873): 1–24 (p. 12).
41. Darwin Papers, Off-print Collection, no. R240; cited in Radick, p. 41.
42. John Muir, quoted in Mary Colwell, *John Muir: The Scotsman who Saved America's Wild Places* (Oxford: Lion Hudson, 2014), p. 66.
43. William Dwight Whitney, *Oriental and Linguistic Studies: The Veda; The Avesta; The Science of Language* (New York: Scribner, 1873), p. 297.
44. Radick, p. 43.
45. John Locke, *An Essay concerning Human Understanding*, ed. by Roger Woolhouse (London: Penguin, 1997), bk. II, ch. x, pp. 151–2.
46. de Waal, *Are We Smart Enough?* p. 101.
47. Robert Yerkes, *Almost Human* (New York: Century, 1925), p. 120.
48. de Waal, *Are We Smart Enough?* p. 65.
49. p. 113.
50. Pepperberg, p. 327.
51. de Waal, *Are We Smart Enough?* pp. 112, 102.
52. Pinker, p. 55.
53. p. 54.
54. p. 56. Pinker is alluding to Bertrand Russel's comment that 'a dog cannot relate his autobiography; however eloquently he may bark, he cannot tell you that his parents were honest though poor'; see 'The Uses of Language' in *The Basic Writings of Bertrand Russel*, ed. by Robert E. Egner and Lester E. Dennon (London: Routledge, 1961), 131–6 (p. 133).
55. Pinker, p. 55.
56. p. 79.
57. Ibid.
58. pp. 76–7.
59. p. 55.

60. p. 79.
61. p. 68.
62. Ibid.
63. Pinker, p. 69; Albert Einstein, testimonial recorded in Jacques Hadamard, *The Mathematician's Mind: The Psychology of Invention in the Mathematical Field* (Princeton, NJ: Princeton University Press, 1945), pp. 141–3.
64. Hardwicke D. Rawnsley, *Reminiscences of Wordsworth among the Peasantry of Westmoreland* (London: Dillon's University Bookshop, 1969), p. 40.
65. p. 18.
66. pp. 13, 31.
67. Andrew Bennett, *Wordsworth Writing* (Cambridge: Cambridge University Press, 2007), p. 23.
68. p. 48.
69. Angela Esterhammer, 'Spontaneity, Immediacy and Improvisation in Romantic Poetry', in *A Companion to Romantic Poetry*, ed. by Charles Mahoney (London: Wiley, 2010), 321–36 (p. 321).
70. Zachary Leader, *Revision and Romantic Authorship* (Oxford: Clarendon, 1996), p. 1.
71. Michael O'Neill, '"Even Now While I Write": Leigh Hunt and Romantic Spontaneity', in *Leigh Hunt: Life, Poetics, Politics*, ed. by Nicholas Roe (London: Routledge, 2003), 135–55 (p. 135).
72. Mina Gorji, *John Clare and the Place of Poetry* (Liverpool: Liverpool University Press, 2008), pp. 29–30; the phrase is from Milton's 'L'Allegro' in *The Complete Poems*, ed. by John Leonard (London: Penguin, 1998), l. 134.
73. In the 1940s, the critic William K. Wimsatt and Philosopher Monroe C. Beardsley argued that 'the design or intention of the author is neither available nor desirable as a standard of judging the success of a work of literary art'; see 'The Intentional Fallacy', *The Sewanee Review*, vol. 54, no. 3 (1946): 468–88 (p. 468). For a full discussion of the long debate regarding authorial intention, see John Farrell, *Varieties of Authorial Intention* (London: Palgrave, 2017).
74. Pinker, p. 80.

3 'Prelusive Notes': Coleridge and the Wordsworths

1. Catherine Packham, *Eighteenth-Century Vitalism: Bodies, Culture, Politics* (London: Palgrave, 2012), p. 1; for a general introduction to the various and conflicting philosophical influences drawn uneasily together in Coleridge's poem, see Paul Magnuson, 'The "Conversation" Poems', in *The Cambridge Companion to Coleridge*, ed. by Lucy Newlyn (Cambridge: Cambridge University Press, 2002), 32–44.

2. William Wordsworth, 1800 Preface to *Lyrical Ballads* in *The Prose Works of William Wordsworth*, ed. by Warwick J. B. Owen and Jane Worthington Smyser, 3 vols. (Oxford: Oxford University Press, 1974), I, 118–60 (p. 124).
3. William Wordsworth, 'Oh what a Wreck! How changed in mien and speech!' in *Last Poems, 1821–1850*, ed. by Jared R. Curtis, Apryl Lea Denny-Ferris and Jillian Heydt-Stevenson (Ithaca, NY: Cornell University Press, 1999), l. 10.
4. James C. McKusick, *Coleridge's Philosophy of Language* (New Haven, CT: Yale University Press, 1956), p. 1.
5. Samuel Taylor Coleridge, *The Collected Letters of Samuel Taylor Coleridge*, ed. by Earl Leslie Griggs, 6 vols. (Oxford: Clarendon, 1956–71), I, pp. 625–6.
6. Alfred C. Goodson, Introduction to *Coleridge's Writings; On Language* (London: Palgrave, 1998), pp. 10–11; also see Alan Richardson, *British Romanticism and the Science of the Mind* (Cambridge: Cambridge University Press, 2001), p. 154.
7. Goodson, p. 12.
8. Samuel Taylor Coleridge, *Biographia Literaria*, ed. by James Engell and Walter Jackson Bate, 2 vols. (Princeton, NJ: Princeton University Press, 1983), II, ch. 17, pp. 53–4.
9. Scott McEathron, 'Wordsworth and Coleridge, *Lyrical Ballads*', in *A Companion to Romanticism*, ed. by Duncan Wu (Oxford: Blackwell, 1999), 144–54 (p. 147).
10. Seamus Perry, *Coleridge and the Uses of Division* (Oxford: Oxford University Press, 1999), p. 2.
11. pp. 2–3, 6.
12. Robert Stark, *Ezra Pound's Early Verse and Lyric Tradition: A Jargoner's Apprenticeship* (Edinburgh: Edinburgh University Press, 2012), p. 15. Chaucer uses the word to convey the amorous chatter of the besotted elderly knight, January, in 'The Merchant's Tale': 'he was al coltish, ful of ragerye | And ful of jargon as a flekked pye'; *The Canterbury Tales*, ed. by Arthur C. Cawley (London: Everyman, 1992), ll. 1847–8.
13. John Gower, *Confessio Amantis* in *The Complete Works of John Gower*, ed. by George C. Macaulay, 4 vols. (Oxford: Clarendon, 1899–1902), II, bk. V, ll. 5699–700.
14. John Livingston Lowes, *The Road to Xanadu: A Study in the Ways of the Imagination* (Boston: Houghton Mifflin, 1955), p. 561.
15. Raimonda Modiano, 'Words and "Languageless" Meanings: Limits of Expression in *The Rime of the Ancient Mariner*', *Modern Language Quarterly*, vol. 38, no. 1 (1977): 40–61 (pp. 41, 51).
16. p. 51.

17. Charles Lamb and Mary Anne Lamb, *The Letters of Charles and Mary Anne Lamb*, ed. by Edwin W. Marrs, Jr., 3 vols. (Ithaca, NY: Cornell University Press, 1975–8), I, p. 266.
18. William Hazlitt, Review of *Christabel; Kubla Khan, a Vision; The Pains of Sleep* in the *Examiner* (1816), rpt. in Donald Reiman, *The Romantics Reviewed: Part A – The Lake Poets*, 2 vols. (New York: Garland, 1972), II, p. 531.
19. Stark, p. 18.
20. Samuel Taylor Coleridge, *Coleridge's Miscellaneous Criticism*, ed. by Thomas Middleton Raysor (Cambridge, MA: Harvard University Press, 1936), p. 337.
21. William Wordsworth, 'The Sparrows Nest', in *Poems in Two Volumes, and Other Poems, 1800–1807* (Ithaca, NY: Cornell University Press, 1983), l. 17.
22. Dorothy Wordsworth, *The Grasmere and Alfoxden Journals*, ed. by Pamela Woof (Oxford: Oxford University Press, 2002), p. 141.
23. Pamela Woof was the first to explore in detail Dorothy's literary influences and development in *Dorothy Wordsworth, Writer* (Grasmere: The Wordsworth Trust, 1988). Mary Ellen Bellanca has since linked Dorothy's journals to 'a variety of discourse communities that were ... increasingly important in British print culture at the turn of the nineteenth century. Her journals', she argues, 'share characteristics with published natural history writing and topographical works; with poetry, science primers, and other books by women interested in botany; and with other nature diaries'; *Daybooks of Discovery: Nature Diaries in Britain, 1770–1870* (Charlottesville: University of Virginia Press, 2007), p. 109.
24. In 1833, Wordsworth wrote on Dorothy's behalf to request the most recent edition of White's *Natural History of Selborne*, 'which she has long wished to possess'; *Letters of William and Dorothy Wordsworth: The Later Years*, ed. by Ernest de Sélincourt and Alan G. Hill, 2nd rev. ed., 4 vols. (Oxford: Clarendon, 1978–88), II, p. 622. From Gilbert White, declared Jonathan Bate in *Romantic Ecology* (1991), it is only 'a short step' to 'the journals of Dorothy Wordsworth'; *Romantic Ecology*, 2nd ed. (London: Routledge, 2013), p. 38. For a full discussion of Dorothy's avid reading and re-reading of White's *Natural History* and its pervasive influence on her own writing, see Dewey W. Hall, 'Naturalists' Interpretations: Daffodils, Swallows and a Floating Island', in *Romantic Ecocriticism: Origins and Legacies*, ed. by Dewey W. Hall (London: Lexington, 2016), 43–60.
25. In February 1798, William implored his publisher Joseph Cottle to send him the recently published two-volume edition of Darwin's *Zoonomia* 'by the first carrier'; *The Letters of William and Dorothy Wordsworth: The Early Years*, ed. by Ernest de Sélincourt and Chester L. Shaver, 2nd rev. ed. (Oxford: Oxford University Press, 1967), pp. 198–9. By mid-March, Dorothy reported that the requested volumes had 'already completely answered the purpose for which

William wrote for them' (*Early Years*, pp. 214–15). Wordsworth's purpose in requesting Darwin's work has been interpreted in a number of ways. James H. Averill argues that Darwin's case studies provided much of the material for Wordsworth's poems about madness and depression in *Lyrical Ballads*, notably 'The Idiot Boy', 'The Last of the Flock' and 'The Thorn'; see James Averill, *Wordsworth and the Poetry of Human Suffering* (Ithaca, NY: Cornell University Press, 1980), esp. pp. 153–8; also see Averill's essay on 'Wordsworth and "Natural Science": The Poetry of 1798', *The Journal of English and Germanic Philology*, vol. 77, no. 2 (1978): 232–46. Others, such as Richard Matlak, have analysed the 'profounder impact of *Zoonomia* on Wordsworth's biological study of life' and most especially his understanding of the connections between 'physiology and psychology'; see Richard Matlak, 'Wordsworth's Reading of *Zoonomia* in Early Spring', *The Wordsworth Circle*, vol. 21, no. 2 (1990): 76–81 (p. 76). For more recent analyses of Darwin's influence on Wordsworth's developing ideas about 'mind and body', see Gavin Budge, *Romanticism, Medicine and the Natural Supernatural* (London: Palgrave, 2012), pp. 48–76. From each of these accounts, it may be surmised that Darwin's *Zoonomia* played a vital role in shaping Wordsworth's developing ideas about mind and consciousness in both human and non-human animals.
26. Erasmus Darwin, *Zoonomia; Or, the Laws of Organic Life*, 2 vols. (London: Johnson, 1794–6), I, pp. 154, 158.
27. Woof, pp. 18–19.
28. As Newlyn emphasises, Dorothy is doing far more than 'telling things merely as they happened'; Lucy Newlyn, *William and Dorothy Wordsworth: All in Each Other* (Oxford: Oxford University Press, 2013), p. 170.
29. William Wordsworth, *An Evening Walk*, ed. by James Averill (Ithaca, NY: Cornell University Press, 1984), 1794 text, ll. 205–6.
30. Noting this peculiarity, John Jones observed that Wordsworth 'had something new to say about mental and physical' in *The Egotistical Sublime: A History of Wordsworth's Imagination* (Westport, CT: Greenwood Press, 1978), p. 24. For a detailed discussion of Wordsworth's use of metaphor, see Keith Hinchliffe, 'Wordsworth and the Kinds of Metaphor', *Studies in Romanticism*, vol. 23, no. 1 (1984): 81–100.
31. Joseph Warton, Eclogue VII 'On the Epicurean Philosophy Natural and Moral', in *The Works of Virgil, in Latin and English*, 4 vols. (London: Dodsley, 1753), I, l. 44, n. 77.
32. Richard Bentley, 'A Confutation of Atheism, From the Origin and Frame of the World', in *Sermons Preached at Boyle's Lecture; Remarks Upon a Discourse of Free Thinking* (London: MacPherson, 1838), sermon VII, pt. ii, 146–72 (p. 147). For Coleridge's remarks on and transcriptions from Bentley, see

Samuel Taylor Coleridge, *Shorter Works and Fragments*, ed. by H. J. Jackson and James Robert de Jager Jackson, 2 vols. (London: Routledge, 1995), I, pp. 29, 34–5.

33. Richard Blackmore, *Creation: A Philosophical Poem* (London: Buckley and Tonson, 1712), bk. III, ll. 163–66.
34. Such passages may help to explain why Wordsworth's poetry, following the publication of Darwin's *On the Origin of Species* in the mid-nineteenth century, gained additional importance as 'an intellectual resource for those who resisted the materialistic implications of a theory that seemed to deprive nature of all moral and religious significance'; see Robert M. Ryan, *Charles Darwin and the Church of Wordsworth* (Oxford: Oxford University Press, 2016), p. 13.
35. The lines from *Paradise Lost* and *The Prelude* are quoted and discussed in J. Douglas Kneale, *Romantic Aversions: Aftermaths of Classicism in Wordsworth and Coleridge* (Quebec: McGill-Queen's University Press, 1999), p. 24.
36. Kneale, *Romantic Aversions*, p. 24; William Shakespeare, *Richard II*, in *The Riverside Shakespeare*, ed. by Gwynne Blakemore Evans et al., 2nd ed. (Boston, MA: Houghton Mifflin, 1997), Act I, sc. iii, ll. 80–2.
37. Samuel Johnson, *A Dictionary of the English Language*, 2 vols. (London: Offor, Allason, et al., 1824).
38. William Gilpin, *Observations, Relative Chiefly to Picturesque Beauty, Made in the Year 1772, on Several Parts of England, Particularly the Mountains and Lakes of Cumberland, and Westmoreland*, 2 vols. (London: Blamire, 1788), I, p. 52. For Gilpin's influence on Wordsworth, see James A. W. Heffernan, 'Wordsworth and Landscape', in *The Oxford Handbook of William Wordsworth*, ed. by Richard Gravil and Daniel Robinson (Oxford: Oxford University Press, 2015), 614–28 (p. 614).
39. Joseph Addison, *Spectator* (21st April 1711), vol. 3, no. 45, https://bit.ly/3vTbDhk, last accessed 31 August 2021.
40. Kneale, p. 24.
41. Rowland, p. 115.
42. William Wordsworth, 'Preface of 1815', in *Wordsworth's Literary Criticism*, ed. by W. J. B. Owen (London: Routledge, 1974), 175–91 (p. 190; n. 29).
43. Jonathan Wordsworth, *Ancestral Voices: Fifty Books from the Romantic Period*, new ed. (Poole: Woodstock Books, 1996), p. 153.
44. Wordsworth, 'Expostulation and Reply', in *'Lyrical Ballads', and Other Poems, 1797–1800*, ed. by James Butler and Karen Green (Ithaca, NY: Cornell University Press, 1992), l. 24.
45. Robert Rehder, *Wordsworth and the Beginnings of Modern Poetry* (London: Routledge, 1981), p. 105. Paul de Man observes the crucial significance of the word to Wordsworth's developing ideas regarding the imagination in 'Time and History in Wordsworth', *Diacritics*, vol. 17, no. 4 (1987): 4–17 (pp. 7–8).

46. Wallace Jackson and Paul Yoder have analysed in detail verbal allusions to Gray in the boy of Winander passage and Wordsworth's poetry more broadly; 'Wordsworth Reimagines Thomas Gray: Notations on Begetting a Kindred Spirit', *Criticism*, vol. 31, no. 3 (1989): 287–300. Henry Weinfield has further argued that Gray's elegy 'had an enormous influence on Wordsworth, that he frequently tried to evade' in *The Blank-Verse Tradition from Shakespeare to Milton* (Cambridge: Cambridge University Press, 2012), p. 113. Also see Weinfield's *The Poet without a Name: Gray's Elegy and the Problem of History* (Carbondale: Southern Illinois University Press, 1991), pp. 164–94.
47. John H. Alexander, *Reading Wordsworth* (London: Routledge, 1987), p. 56.
48. Dorothy Wordsworth, 'Irregular Verses', in *Dorothy Wordsworth*, ed. by Susan M. Levin (London: Longman, 2009), ll. 56–77.
49. Stephen K. Land, 'The Silent Poet: An Aspect of Wordsworth's Semantic Theory', *University of Toronto Quarterly*, vol. 42, no. 2 (1973): 157–69 (p. 163).
50. Bennett, *Wordsworth Writing*, p. 2.
51. Walter Pater, 'Wordsworth', in *Appreciations, with an Essay on Style* (London: Macmillan, 1889), 37–63 (p. 40).
52. Bennett, *Wordsworth Writing*, p. 1; Pinker, p. 80.
53. Simon Jarvis, *Wordsworth's Philosophic Song* (Cambridge: Cambridge University Press, 2006), pp. 3–4.
54. p. 4.
55. Dennis Taylor, *Hardy's Metres and Victorian Prosody* (Oxford: Clarendon, 1988), pp. 5, 15–16.
56. Under the mentorship of William Thorpe, the American ethologist and zoosemiotician Peter Marler pioneered scientific studies of avian 'song syntax' or 'phonological syntax' as distinct from 'lexical syntax'; as Marler further reflects, 'generally speaking, the sequences are not meaningfully distinct, in the referential sense. Semantically, each winter wren song means the same thing. The variety is introduced, not to enrich meaning, but to create diversity for its own sake, to alleviate boredom in singer and listener, perhaps with individual differences serving to impress the listener with the singer's virtuosity'; Peter Marler, 'Animal Communication and Human Language', in *The Origin and Diversification of Language*, ed. by Nina G. Jablonski, Leslie C. Aiello and Nancy Gee (San Francisco: California Academy of Sciences, 1998), 1–20 (pp. 11–12).
57. William Cowper, 'The Task', in *The Poems of William Cowper*, ed. by John D. Baird and Charles Ryskamp, 3 vols. (Oxford: Clarendon, 1980–95), II, bk. 6, ll. 76–85.
58. Vincent Newey, 'Cowper Prospects: Self, Nature and Society', in *Romanticism and Religion from Cowper to Wallace Stevens*, ed. by Gavin Hopps and Jane Stabler (London: Routledge, 2006), 41–56 (p. 45).
59. p. 44.

60. Adam Potkay, *Wordsworth's Ethics* (Baltimore: John Hopkins University Press, 2012), p. 90. Potkay traces some of the eighteenth-century precursors to Wordsworth's use of music in his article 'Ear and Eye: Counteracting Senses in Loco-Descriptive Poetry', in *A Companion to Romantic Poetry*, ed. by Charles Mahoney (London: Wiley, 2010), 176–94.
61. Potkay, *Wordsworth's Ethics*, pp. 90–1; also see Alexander Gerard, *An Essay on Taste* (London: Millar, 1759), p. 64.
62. Potkay, *Wordsworth's Ethics*, p. 101.
63. Sydney Grew and Eva Mary Grew, 'William Cowper: His Acceptance and Rejection of Music', *Music & Letters*, vol. 13, no. 1 (1932): 31–41 (pp. 34–5).
64. Newlyn, *All in Each Other*, p. 149.
65. pp. 149–50.
66. Nicholas Roe, *Wordsworth and Coleridge: The Radical Years*, 2nd ed. (Oxford: Oxford University Press, 2018), p. 280.
67. For Wordsworth's engagement with Scottish literary and folk traditions and their role in his creative development (particularly following his tour of Scotland with Dorothy in 1803), see Fiona Stafford's chapter on 'Inhabited Solitudes: Wordsworth in Scotland, 1803', in *Scotland, Ireland and the Romantic Aesthetic*, ed. by David Duff and Catherine Jones (Lewisberg, PA: Buckness University Press, 2007), 93–113.
68. William Wordsworth, 'On the Disinterment of the Remains of the Duke of D'enghein', in *The Poems of William Wordsworth: Collected Reading Texts from the Cornell Wordsworth*, ed. by Jared Curtis, 3 vols. (Penrith: Humanities Ebooks, 2011), III, l. 93.
69. William Wordsworth, *Descriptive Sketches*, ed. by Eric Birdsall (Ithaca, NY: Cornell University Press, 1984), 1836 version, l. 58.
70. William Wordsworth, 'On Approaching the Staub-Bach, Lauterbrunnen', in *Sonnet Series and Itinerary Poems, 1820–1845*, ed. by Geoffrey Jackson (Ithaca, NY: Cornell University Press, 2004), ll. 2, 8.
71. See Wordsworth's notes to the poem in *The Poems of William Wordsworth*, new ed. (London: Moxon, 1849), p. 542.
72. Ibid.
73. Joshua King, 'Broken Promises and Blind Pleasures in Wordsworth's "The Idiot Boy"', *CEA Critic*, vol. 73, no. 3 (2011): 48–68 (p. 57). Also see Lucy Newlyn's chapter on 'Reading Aloud' in *Reading, Writing and Romanticism: The Anxiety of Reception* (Oxford: Oxford University Press, 2000), 333–60.
74. King, p. 57.
75. William Wordsworth, *The Excursion*, ed. by Sally Bushell, James Butler and Michael C. Jaye (Ithaca, NY: Cornell University Press, 2007), Preface, ll. 56–8.
76. William Hazlitt, 'My First Acquaintance with Poets', in *Selected Writings*, ed. by Jon Cook (Oxford: Oxford University Press, 2009), 211–29 (p. 225).

77. Ibid.
78. Paula A. Feldman and Daniel Robinson, Introduction to *A Century of Sonnets: The Romantic-Era Revival, 1750–1850*, ed. by Paula A. Feldman and Daniel Robinson (Oxford: Oxford University Press, 1999), 3–19 (p. 10).
79. Charlotte Smith, Dedication to William Hayley Esquire, in *The Poems of Charlotte Smith*, ed. by Stuart Curran (Oxford: Oxford University Press, 1993), p. 2. Although Stuart Curran recognises Smith's 'singular achievement' in freeing 'established poetic discourse from its reliance on polished couplets, formal diction, and public utterances', he rightly scrutinises the 'pretence' to naturalness in such a highly conventional, tightly regulated form as the fourteen-lined little poem; *Poetic Form and British Romanticism* (Oxford: Oxford University Press, 1990), pp. 31–2. Placing Smith's sonnets in their eighteenth-century context, Bethan Roberts has provided a full and thorough assessment of Smith's 'engagement with tradition alongside her innovation' in *Charlotte Smith and the Sonnet: Form, Tradition and Place in the Eighteenth Century* (Liverpool: Liverpool University Press, 2019), p. 3.
80. Meg Tyler, in Paul Muldoon, Meg Tyler and Jeff Hilson, 'Contemporary Poets and the Sonnet: A Trialogue', in *The Cambridge Companion to the Sonnet*, ed. by Anthony D. Cousins and Peter Howarth (Cambridge: Cambridge University Press, 2011), 6–24 (pp. 6, 8).
81. p. 8.
82. Coleridge's pamphlet was first published without a title, but later given the perfunctory heading by which it is now widely known. Three copies of the pamphlet survive and are held in the Cornell University Library, the Huntingdon Library and the Victorian and Albert Museum. The pamphlet has been reprinted by Paul M. Zall in *Coleridge's "Sonnets from Various Authors"* (Glendale, CA: La Siesta Press, 1968), p. 2.
83. Dora Wordsworth, quoted in Juliet Barker, *Wordsworth: A Life* (London: Penguin, 2000), p. 648.
84. Wordsworth's biographer Stephen Gill observes the 'fresh scrutiny' to which the poems were subjected when the poet revised them 'right down to the commas and semi-colons' for publication, an obsessive eye for detail which inevitably became a point of contention between Wordsworth and his publishers; Gill, *William Wordsworth: A Life* (Oxford: Oxford University Press, 1990), pp. 366–7, 388–9.
85. William Wordsworth, *The Sonnets of William Wordsworth, Collected in One Volume, With a Few Additional Ones, Now First Published* (London: Moxon, 1838). The three sonnets I discuss here ('Hark! 'Tis the Thrush, undaunted, undeprest', 'Oh what a wreck! how changed in mien and speech', and ''Tis he who's yester-evening's high disdain') were all published for the first time in

this volume, pp. 445, 113, 446. The two thrush sonnets are included in the final six 'annexed' to this edition; according to the author's note, these were 'composed as this volume was going through the Press, but too late for insertion in the miscellaneous ones, to which they belong', p. 442.
86. Henry Crabb Robinson, quoted in Barker, p. 714.
87. Newlyn, *All in Each Other*, p. 306.
88. NHS England's National Clinical Director for Dementia, Alistair Burns, discusses music's power to trigger memories and benefit those suffering with dementia on the service's webpage: https://bit.ly/3OKgIBf, last accessed 31 August 2021. The extraordinary effects of this therapy may be seen in this short video: www.youtube.com/watch?v=fyZQf0p73QM, last accessed 31 August 2021.
89. The practice is sometimes known as 'singing for the brain'. For further information, see Aniruddh D. Patel, *Music, Language and the Brain* (Oxford: Oxford University Press, 2007), Kay Norton, *Singing and Wellbeing: Ancient Wisdom, Modern Proof* (London: Routledge, 2016) and David Aldridge (ed.), *Music Therapy in Dementia Care: More New Voices* (London: Jessica Kingsley, 2000).
90. William Wordsworth, *The Fenwick Notes of William Wordsworth*, ed. by Jared Curtis (London: Gerald Duckworth, 1993), p. 19.
91. Daniel Robinson, 'The Sonnet', in *William Wordsworth in Context*, ed. by Andrew Bennett (Cambridge: Cambridge University Press, 2015), 136–44 (p. 137).
92. Newlyn, *All in Each Other*, pp. 37, 6.
93. Joseph Phelan, *The Nineteenth-Century Sonnet* (London: Palgrave, 2005), p. 3.

4 'Undersong': John Clare

1. Unsigned review, *New Monthly Magazine* (1820), *John Clare: The Critical Heritage*, ed. by Mark Storey (London: Routledge, 1973), p. 68.
2. John Taylor, quoted in John Clare, *The Letters of John Clare*, ed. by Mark Storey (Oxford: Clarendon, 1985), p. 99, n. 7.
3. John Barrell, *The Idea of Landscape and the Sense of Place, 1730–1840: An Approach to the Poetry of John Clare* (Cambridge: Cambridge University Press, 1972), p. 131.
4. Gorji, *John Clare and the Place of Poetry*, p. 2; although Clare's poems 'stake their truth claims in a maximal assertion of mimetic fidelity', Weiner points out they also, and in doing so, 'foreground the linguistic and formal medium of poetry', p. 2.
5. Hugh Haughton, 'Progress and Rhyme: "The Nightingale's Nest" and Romantic Poetry', in *John Clare in Context*, ed. by Hugh Haughton, Adam Philips and

Geoffrey Summerfield (Cambridge: Cambridge University Press, 1994), 51–86 (pp. 54–5).
6. Noting Clare's use of the word 'russet' and its wider 'sociological significance', Haughton points out that Clare's nightingale is 'dressed like a farm-labourer – or John Clare'; p. 83. Gorji further traces the word's literary associations and 'pedigree in pastoral verse' (notably Milton's description of 'russet Lawns' in one of Clare's 'favourite poems', 'L'Allegro'); since 'the word, like the nightingale herself, is at once commonplace poetical', Gorji argues that Clare's use of it reflects his 'self-consciousness about levels of language and style' and 'sensitivity to the ways in which language could place poet and reader'; *John Clare and the Place of Poetry*, p. 3.
7. John Keats, 'Ode to a Nightingale', in *The Complete Poems*, ed. by John Barnard, 3rd ed. (London: Penguin, 2006), l. 7. Like 'other inhabitants of great citys', Keats, in Clare's view, 'described nature as she ... appeared to his fancys & not as he would have described her had he witnessed the things he describes'; *Letters*, p. 519. Intriguingly, the criticism which Clare levels at Keats here recalls Coleridge's earlier admonishment of 'youths and maidens most poetical' who waste the summer months 'in ballrooms and hot theatres', but nevertheless continue to 'heave their sighs | O'er Philomela's pity-pleading strains'; 'The Nightingale', *Poetical Works*, I, ll. 35–9. Highlighting the authenticity of his own direct and first-hand encounters with the nightingale, Clare deploys an established tenet of Romanticism in order to shore up authority for his own aesthetic and 'right to song'; 'The Progress of Ryhme', *Middle Period*, III, l. 80.
8. Weiner, p. 9; for a full analysis of Clare's 'considerable and extensive Romantic preoccupations', see Adam White, *John Clare's Romanticism* (London: Palgrave, 2017), p. 3.
9. For a general overview of the history and development of Clare's natural history writings, see Margaret Grainger's Introduction to Clare's *Natural History Prose*, esp. pp. 81–2. Robert Heyes has since challenged some of the myths surrounding Clare's attempts in the genre in 'John Clare's Natural History', in *New Essays on John Clare: Poetry, Culture and Community*, ed. by Simon Kövesi and Scott McEathron (Cambridge: Cambridge University Press, 2015), 169–88.
10. William Hazlitt, editions of whose works Hessey and his partner, John Taylor, published in 1818, is likely to have inspired both Clare's and Hessey's interest in Chaucer's lines. Hazlitt identified the description of the 'new abashed nightingale' as 'one of the most beautiful passages' in Chaucer and used it as an example of the Chaucerian 'simile': 'every thing in Chaucer has a downright reality'; see *Characters of Shakespeare's Plays*, 2nd ed. (London: Taylor and Hessey, 1818), p. 92. Also see Hazlitt's subsequent

remarks on the passage in *Lectures on the English Poets* (London: Taylor and Hessey, 1818), pp. 42–3. Undoubtedly, the passage directly influenced Clare's own descriptions of the nightingale and offered an authority for a mode of description firmly rooted in the 'downright reality' of the natural world.
11. Eric Robinson and Richard Fitter, Introduction to *John Clare's Birds* (Oxford: Oxford University Press, 1982), vii–xx (p. xii).
12. Karlin, p. 79.
13. p. 78.
14. Weiner, p. 1.
15. Matthew Arnold, Preface to *Poems of William Wordsworth* (London: Macmillan, 1879), v–xxvi (p. xxi).
16. Weiner, p. 1.
17. Emily Dickinson, Poem 402, in *The Poems of Emily Dickinson*, ed. by Ralph W. Franklin, 3 vols. (Cambridge, MA: Harvard University Press, 1998), I, l. 7; the poem is known by its first line, 'To hear an Oriole sing'.
18. Thomas Hardy, *Far from the Madding Crowd* (1872), ed. by Rosemarie Morgan and Shannon Russell (London: Penguin, 2003), pp. 51–2. It may be noted that nighttime fears and anxieties are similarly seen to work upon the imagination of Coleridge's 'night-wandering Man' as they lead him to interpret the nightingale's song as 'melancholy' in 'The Nightingale'; *Poetical Works*, I, ll. 15–16.
19. Clare, 'An Invite to Eternity', in *The Later Poems of John Clare*, ed. by Eric Robinson and David Powell, 2 vols. (Oxford: Clarendon, 1984), I, l. 12.
20. I am indebted to Jeremy Mynott, who first drew my attention to the unmusical, even slightly hysterical cry of the red kite and the consequent irony of Clare's description here.
21. Robinson and Fitter discuss Clare's 'passion for exactitude' in their Introduction to *John Clare's Birds*, p. xiii.
22. Haughton, p. 59.
23. Charles Lamb is said to have enjoyed poking fun at Clare's vehement outbursts against Murray and his *Grammar*, which he regarded as a 'perplexing construction' and 'conventional gagging-bill'; see Thomas Griffiths Wainewright's article in *The London Magazine* (January, 1823), rpt in Wainewright's *Essays and Criticisms* (London: Reeves and Turner, 1880), 303–23 (p. 312). For a wider discussion of Clare's 'rage against the pronouncements of Lindley Murray', see Alan D. Vardy, *John Clare: Politics and Poetry* (London: Palgrave, 2003), esp. pp. 64–8.
24. Anon., 'Proofs of the Increasing Taste for Natural History', *Blackwood's Magazine*, vol. 2, no. 10 (1818): 380; for a detailed account of this 'taste' for natural history and its influence on Clare, see Grainger, Introduction to *Natural History Prose*, p. xlii, and Marilyn Gaull, 'Clare and "The Dark System"', in *John Clare in Context*, ed. by Hugh Haughton, Adam Philips

and Geoffrey Summerfield (Cambridge: Cambridge University Press, 1994), 279–94.
25. Clare's 'Bird Lists' are cross-referenced to this work; see *Natural History Prose*, p. 121.
26. Anon., *Natural History of Birds*, 2 vols. (Bungay: Brightly and Childs, T. Kinnersly, 1815), pp. xxxii–v. The work is listed in Powell, p. 31; no. 316. The volume is held in the John Clare Collection at Northamptonshire Central Library; I am grateful to the library for allowing me to view this work.
27. Robert Burns, 'To a Mouse', in *Poems and Songs*, ed. by James Kinsley (Oxford: Oxford University Press, 1969), ll. 43–8.
28. See Aaron Garrett, 'Human Nature', in *The Cambridge History of Eighteenth-Century Philosophy*, ed. by Knud Haakonsen, 2 vols. (Cambridge: Cambridge University Press, 2006), I, 160–235 (p. 163).
29. Percy Bysshe Shelley, 'To a Skylark', in *Major Works*, ed. by Zachary Leader and Michael O'Neill (Oxford: Oxford University Press, 2009), ll. 86–90.
30. Haughton, pp. 55–6.
31. Bechstein, p. 94. Bechstein's comments were reiterated word-for-word in magazines such as *The Sportman's Magazine of Life in London and The Country* (1836), *The Mirror of Literature, Amusement and Instruction* (1836), *The Penny Cyclopædia of the Society for the Diffusion of Useful Knowledge* (1836) and *Graham's Magazine* (1849). In the 1970s, Edward A. Armstrong remarked that 'the abandonment or forgetting of sounds' had received far less attention than 'the learning of them', though he noted that the 'bird-fanciers' had long been familiar with the tendency; *A Study of Bird Song*, revised ed. (New York: Dover, 1973), p. 86. The process by which birds form their repertoire, retaining some passages and suppressing or forgetting others, has since become known as 'selective attrition' and is now the subject of scientific investigation; see Don Kroodsma, 'The Diversity and Plasticity of Birdsong', in *Nature's Music: The Science of Birdsong*, ed. by Peter Marler and Hans Slabberkoorn (London: Elsevier, 2004), 108–31 (esp. pp. 121–2).
32. Gorji, *John Clare and the Place of Poetry*, pp. 29–30; the line is from Milton's 'L'Allegro', l. 134.
33. Hannah More, Prefatory Letter to Ann Yearsley, *Poems on Several Occasions* (London: Cadell, 1785), iii–xiii (pp. viii, vii).
34. Edmund Drury, Letter to Clare (9th February, 1821), cited in Gorji, *John Clare and the Place of Poetry*, p. 30.
35. Gorji, *John Clare and the Place of Poetry*, p. 13.
36. In order to define an 'intentional' action, John Farrell uses a 'common example': 'a wink is an action while a blink is not. It is a mere reflex'; although 'all true actions are intentional, no one', he points out, 'can imagine that all true actions are perfectly rational or planned or that the

people who perform them have a complete and infallible sense of what they are doing'; see Farrell, pp. 21, 25. Since philosophers, poets and literary critics have all shared the common experience 'of uttering or writing a sentence, then stopping and realising that it wasn't exactly what we meant to say', the overwhelming feeling that there is 'a "what we meant to say" that is different from what we said' calls attention to the eternal struggle to both realise our own intentions and interpret or divine the intentions of others; see Pinker, p. 55.

37. Jonathan Bate, *John Clare: A Biography* (Kent: Macmillan, 2003), pp. 490–1; Clare's prose essay 'Self Identity' is printed in *The Prose of John Clare*, ed. by John W. Tibble and Anne Tibble (London: Routledge, 1951), 239; the antonym, 'this sad non-identity', appears in 'An Invite to Eternity', in *Later Poems*, I, ll. 14.
38. McKusick, alluding to Milton, in 'John Clare and the Tyranny of Grammar', *Studies in Romanticism*, vol. 2, no. 14 (1994): 255–77 (p. 255); in a more balanced and sympathetic reading, Gorji observes the 'borrowed terms' through which Taylor actively plays to poetic ideals of 'natural genius' and 'artlessness'; *John Clare and the Place of Poetry*, p. 40.
39. McKusick, 'John Clare and the Tyranny of Grammar', p. 255; Clare, quoted in P. M. S. Dawson, 'The Making of Clare's *Poems Descriptive of Rural Life and Scenery* (1820)', *The Review of English Studies*, vol. 56, no. 224 (2005): 276–312 (p. 290).
40. John Taylor, Introduction to Clare, *Poems Descriptive of Rural Life and Scenery* (London: Taylor and Hessey, 1820), vii–xxviii (pp. xiv–xv). Taylor is quoting from Clare's poem 'To an April Daisy', in *Poems Descriptive*, pp. 120–1; rpt. in *The Early Poems of John Clare: 1804–1822*, ed. by Eric Robinson and David Powell, 2 vols. (Oxford: Clarendon, 1989), I, l. 3.
41. Weiner, p. 56.
42. Ibid.
43. John Clare, *John Clare's Autobiographical Writings*, ed. by Eric Robinson (Oxford: Oxford University Press, 1983), p. 31. This edition standardises Clare's use of ampersands to 'and'; I have reverted to '&' in order to be consistent with other editions of Clare's prose quoted in this chapter.
44. Erin Lafford, 'Clare's Muttering, Murmurings, and Ramblings: The Sounds of Health', *The John Clare Society Journal*, no. 33 (2014): 1–18 (p. 1).
45. For a detailed assessment of the highly contradictory character of Clare's 'man of taste', see Paul Chirico, *John Clare and the Imagination of the Reader* (London: Palgrave, 2007), pp. 73–6; also see Adam White, 'John Clare: "The Man of Taste"', *John Clare Society Journal*, no. 28 (2009): 38–55.
46. The *OED* cites Milton's description of Thyris, 'whose artfull strains have oft delayd | The huddling brook to hear his madrigal' in *Comus* (London: Macmillan, 1891), ll. 495–6, and Thomas Campbell's description of his

heroine, who 'oft amid the lonely rocks | She sings sweet madrigals' in 'O'Connor's Child; Or The Flower of Love Lies Bleeding', in *Poems in Two Volumes*, 2 vols. (London: Longman, 1810), I, p. 74.

47. Clare, 'To a City Girl', in *The Village Minstrel* (London: Taylor and Hessey, 1821), pp. 177–9; rpt. *Early Poems*, II, ll. 29, 31.
48. The boy of Winander passage was first published as a fragment in the 1800 edition of *Lyrical Ballads* and later incorporated into the fifth book of *The Prelude*. Clare would have known the poem as a fragment, as it was reprinted in his edition of *The Miscellaneous Poems of William Wordsworth*, 4 vols. (London: Longman et al., 1820); this is edition is listed in Powell, p. 34, no. 407.
49. Weiner, p. 42; also see Karlin, p. 80.
50. Sara Lodge, 'Contested Bounds: John Clare, John Keats, and the Sonnet', *Studies in Romanticism*, vol. 51, no. 4 (2012): 533–54 (esp. p. 535).
51. The poem was published under the title 'The Happy Bird' in *The Rural Muse* (London: Whittaker, 1835), p. 134.
52. Weiner, p. 53; Jonathan Culler, *The Pursuit of Signs: Semiotics, Literature, Deconstruction* (Ithaca, NY: Cornell University Press, 2001), p. 68.
53. Earl R. Wasserman, *The Finer Tone: Keats' Major Poems* (Baltimore, MD: Johns Hopkins University Press, 1967), pp. 49, 61.
54. William D. Brewer, 'John Clare and Lord Byron', *John Clare Society Journal*, no. 11 (1992): 43–57 (pp. 43–4).
55. Lodge, p. 545.
56. Weiner, p. 50; according to Phelan, Clare's late sonnets are so 'lacking' in structure as to seem 'not real sonnets at all, but "only fourteen-line poems"', pp. 41–2.
57. Weiner, pp. 50, 57.
58. Barrell, pp. 158–9.
59. Weiner, p. 65; Seamus Heaney, 'John Clare: A Bicentenary Lecture', in *John Clare in Context*, ed. by Hugh Haughton, Adam Philips and Geoffrey Summerfield (Cambridge: Cambridge University Press, 1994), 130–47 (p. 137); in an article on 'John Clare and the Poetics of Mess', Gorji argues that Clare's sonnets are 'not messy in the sense of being imprecise or rough'; their 'messiness', she asserts, is 'true to life' even if 'it was not true to certain notions of the poetical' in the late eighteenth and early nineteenth centuries; 'John Clare and the Poetics of Mess', *Moveable Type*, vol. 5 (2009): 1–11 (p. 1).
60. Lafford, pp. 6–7.
61. See Eric Robinson, David Powell and P. M. S. Dawson's Introduction to John Clare, *Northborough Sonnets* (Manchester: Carcanet, 1995), vii–xxii (p. xiii).
62. Ted Hughes, 'Poetry in the Making' (1967), in *Winter Pollen: Occasional Prose*, ed. by William Scammell (New York: Picador, 1994), 10–24 (esp. pp. 10–12).

63. Henry David Thoreau, *A Week on the Concord and Merrimack Rivers* (Boston: Houghton and Mifflin, 1891), p. 360.
64. For example, poems like 'Impulses of Spring', *Middle Period*, III, p. 183, and 'Pastoral Poesy', *Middle Period*, III, pp. 581–4, are followed by 'Signs of Winter', *Middle Period*, IV, pp. 336–7, and 'Musings of Melancholly', *Middle Period*, IV, pp. 556–68.
65. Thomas Hardy, Preface to *Wessex Poems and Other Verses*, in *The Complete Poems*, ed. by James Gibson (Basingstoke: Palgrave, 2001), p. 6; page numbers are given as opposed to line numbers, in accordance with this edition's own conventions.
66. Heaney, 'John Clare: A Bicentenary Lecture', p. 136.
67. p. 132; Gorji, *John Clare and the Place of Poetry*, pp. 5–6.
68. Heaney, 'Feeling into Words', in *Preoccupations: Selected Prose, 1968–78* (London: Faber, 1980), 41–60 (p. 47).
69. p. 45.
70. Ibid.
71. p. 44.
72. p. 47.
73. pp. 41, 47.
74. Heaney, 'John Clare: A Bicentenary Lecture', p. 139.
75. pp. 135–6.
76. p. 131.
77. pp. 132, 131.
78. p. 131.

5 'We Teach 'Em Airs That Way': Thomas Hardy

1. Hardy, 'The Profitable Reading of a Fiction' (1888), in *Personal Writings*, ed. by Harold Orel (London: Macmillan, 1967), 110–24 (p. 124).
2. Dennis Taylor, *Hardy's Literary Language and Victorian Philology* (Oxford: Clarendon, 1993), p. 92.
3. Hardy presented himself as 'among the earliest acclaimers of the *Origin of Species*' in *The Early Life of Thomas Hardy, 1840–1891* (Cambridge: Cambridge University Press, 2011), p. 198. As Pamela Gossin's analysis of Hardy's notebooks has shown, the novelist and poet read Darwin 'firsthand', 'recorded extensive notes' to Francis Darwin's *Life and Letters of Charles Darwin* (1888) and 'noted miscellaneous instances of Darwinian thought as they appeared in other writers'; *Thomas Hardy's Novel Universe: Astronomy, Cosmology, and Gender in the Post-Darwinian World* (Aldershot: Ashgate, 2007), p. 54; also see Hardy, *The Literary Notebooks of Thomas Hardy*, ed. by Björk A. Lennart, 2 vols. (London: Macmillan, 1985), I, p. 401. Prominent

critical discussions of Darwin's influence on Hardy's writing include Tess Cosslett, *The 'Scientific Movement' and Victorian Literature* (Brighton: Harvester, 1982) and Gillian Beer's chapter on Hardy in *Darwin's Plots: Evolutionary Narrative in Darwin, George Eliot and Nineteenth-Century Fiction*, 3rd ed. (Cambridge: Cambridge University Press, 2009), pp. 220–41. George Levine discusses Hardy's novels in *Darwin and the Novelists: Patterns of Science in Victorian Fiction* (Chicago, IL: University of Chicago Press, 1988), pp. 227–33. Also see Levine's discussion of Hardy's fiction in 'Hardy and Darwin: An Enchanting Hardy?', in *A Companion to Thomas Hardy*, ed. by Keith Wilson (London: Blackwell, 2009), 36–53.

4. John Hughes, *Ecstatic Sound: Music and Individuality in the Work of Thomas Hardy* (Surrey: Ashgate, 2001), p. 29.
5. Mark Asquith, *Thomas Hardy, Metaphysics and Music* (London: Palgrave, 2005), p. 66; Thomas Hardy, *The Return of the Native*, ed. by Simon Gatrell (Oxford: Oxford University Press, 2008), p. 56. Critics have long recognised the prevalence of musical metaphors and allusions in Hardy's novels. In the twentieth century, Francis B. Pinion compiled a list of the many references to music and song in Hardy's writing in *A Hardy Companion: A Guide to the Works of Thomas Hardy and Their Background* (London: Macmillan, 1968), pp. 187–93. Joan Grundy observes the unique role of music in Hardy's novel as a means of expressing 'the very state and experience of sentience' in *Hardy and the Sister Arts* (London: Macmillan, 1979), p. 137. Thom Gunn discovered structural parallels between Hardy's narratives and traditional ballads in his article on 'Hardy and the Ballads', *Agenda*, vol. 10, nos. 2–3 (1972): 19–46. In his biography of Hardy, Ralph Pite outlines the social and historical context of church-music and other oral traditions, which inform Hardy's representation of, for example, the Mellstock Choir in *Under the Greenwood Tree* (1872); see Pite, *Thomas Hardy: The Guarded Life* (London: Picador, 2006), pp. 28–31. Also see Claire Seymour's engaging reading of music in Hardy's novels and short stories in 'Hardy and Music: Uncanny Sounds', in *A Companion to Thomas Hardy*, 233–38.
6. Anna West, *Thomas Hardy and Animals* (Cambridge: Cambridge University Press, 2017), p. 90.
7. Ibid.
8. Ibid.
9. p. 109.
10. Leslie Stephen, 'Darwinism and Divinity', in *Essays on Freethinking and Plainspeaking* (London: Longmans, 1873), 72–109 (p. 81).
11. Stephen, p. 81; Hardy's biographers have emphasised Stephen's influence on the young author's ideas in the 1870s, particularly regarding religion and

morality. Michael Millgate notes that 'Stephen was, as philosopher, polemicist, and editor, near the centre of the great contemporary controversies of thought and belief' in *Thomas Hardy: A Biography Revisited* (Oxford: Oxford University Press, 2004), p. 159. Pite emphasises the significance of Stephen's 'positivist' ideas to Hardy, particularly following the death of his friend and early mentor, Horace Moule, in 1873; according to Pite, Stephen embodied and appeared to reconcile the conflicting feelings of 'religious doubt and moral resolve' with which Hardy himself was struggling at this time; he showed a willingness to confront 'the clash between Christianity and the modern world' which, Pite suggests, would have appealed to Hardy for its insistence that 'virtue could be separated from religion ... you could renounce one without losing the other'; see Pite, pp. 212–13. For further discussion of Stephen's influence on Hardy's 'agnosticism', see Ilaria Mallozzi, 'Agnosticism and Free-Thinking: The Influence of Leslie Stephen', in *Thomas Hardy, Poet: New Perspectives*, ed. by Adrian Grafe and Laurence Estanove (Jefferson: McFarland, 2015), 100–15.

12. For critical discussions of Hardy's letter to the Secretary of the Humanitarian League, see, for example, Angelique Richardson, 'Hardy and the Place of Culture', in *A Companion to Thomas Hardy*, 54–70 (p. 68), and Elisha Cohn, '"No Insignificant Creature": Thomas Hardy's Ethical Turn', *Nineteenth-Century Literature*, vol. 64, no. 4 (2010): 494–520.

13. Hardy, quoted by William Archer, 'Real Conversations', in *Thomas Hardy Remembered*, ed. by Martin Ray (Aldershot: Ashgate, 2007), 28–37 (p. 35).

14. Asquith, pp. 78–103. Some of the most prominent examples of music and sexuality in Hardy's writing include Manston's organ-playing in Hardy's first published novel, *Desperate Remedies* (1871); as the narrator describes the effect of the music on the heroine, 'the varying strains ... shook and bent her to themselves .... The power of the music did not show itself so much by attracting her attention to the subject of the piece, as by taking up and developing as its libretto the poem of her own life and soul, shifting her deeds and intentions from the hands of her judgment, and holding them in its own'; *Desperate Remedies*, ed. by Patricia Ingham (Oxford: Oxford University Press, 2009), pp. 131–2. Other instances include the makeshift eolian harp which Bob Loveday fixes to a mill-head so that the 'strange mixed music of water, wind, and strings' affects the heroine 'most painfully at night' in *The Trumpet Major* (1880), ed. by Linda M. Shires (London: Penguin, 1997), p. 158. Also see the 'moving effect' which Mop's satanic fiddle-playing has on the 'souls of grown-up persons, especially young women of fragile and responsive organisation' in Hardy's short story *The Fiddler of the Reels* (1893), in *Life's Little Ironies*, ed. by Alan Manford (Oxford: Oxford University Press, 1996), 137–55 (p. 139).

15. Barrell, p. 119; Andrew Lang, 'A Rejoinder [to Hardy's Preface to *Tess of the D'Urbervilles*]' (*Longman's Magazine*, 1892); rpt. in Reginald G. Cox (ed.), *Thomas Hardy: The Critical Heritage* (London: Routledge, 2005), 249–54 (p. 252).
16. William Watson, 'Review of *Tess of the D'Urbervilles*' (*Academy*, 6th Feb. 1892); rpt. in Reginald G. Cox (ed.), *Thomas Hardy: The Critical Heritage* (London: Routledge, 2005), 213–17 (p. 213).
17. p. 214.
18. Peter Widdowson, *On Thomas Hardy: Late Essays and Earlier* (Basingstoke: MacMillan, 1998), p. 72.
19. Taylor, *Hardy's Literary Language*, p. 8.
20. Watson, p. 214.
21. Margaret Oliphant, 'Review of *Tess of the D'Urbervilles*' (*Blackwoods*, March 1892), rpt. in Reginald G. Cox (ed.), *Thomas Hardy: The Critical Heritage* (London: Routledge, 2005), 219–27 (pp. 220–1).
22. pp. 221, 223.
23. p. 223.
24. p. 227.
25. See Asquith, pp. 92–4.
26. Thomas Hardy, *The Hand of Ethelberta*, ed. by Tim Dolin (London: Penguin, 2006), pp. 378–9.
27. Samuel Richardson, *Clarissa; Or, the History of a Young Lady*, ed. by Angus Ros (London: Penguin, 1985), p. 557.
28. Charles Dickens, *David Copperfield*, ed. by Jeremy Tambling (London: Penguin, 2007), p. 223.
29. See Dolin's note to the passage in *Tess*, p. 412, n. 7. Feminist critics have examined in detail how Tess's 'purity' is complicated by revisions to the novel, so that 'the heroine is too often caught in the middle of Hardy's own evolving ideas'; see Laura Claridge, 'Tess: A Less than Pure Woman Ambivalently Represented', *Texas Studies in Literature and Language*, vol. 28, no. 3 (1986): 324–38 (p. 332). Also see Penny Bouhmelha's discussion of this scene in *Thomas Hardy and Women: Sexual Ideology and Narrative Form* (Totowa, NJ: Barnes and Noble, 1982), pp. 117–34, and Mary Jacobus's essay, 'Tess: The Making of a Pure Woman', in *Tearing the Veil: Essays on Femininity*, ed. by Susan Lipshitz (London: Routledge, 1978), 77–92. For an intriguing discussion of the issue of consent in nineteenth-century law, see William A. Davis, *Thomas Hardy and the Law: Legal Presences in Hardy's Life and Fiction* (Newark: University of Delaware Press, 2003), pp. 77–86.
30. Hardy, 'Candour in English Fiction' (1890), in *Personal Writings*, 125–33 (p. 130).
31. Asquith, for example, argues that 'much of the dialogue in Hardy's novels consists of Metternich's "bubbles"', p. 100; Widdowson discusses Arabella's

parodic subversions of patriarchal discourse about women, pp. 181–3, and Joe Fisher comments on the 'pathetically ludicrous' language of Jude and Sue in *Jude the Obscure* (1895); Fisher, *The Hidden Hardy* (London: Macmillan, 1992), pp. 175–6.

32. Among the earliest and most influential studies to explore the tragi-comic elements of Hardy's mature fiction is Jean R. Brooks's study *Thomas Hardy: The Poetic Structure* (Ithaca, NY: Cornell University Press, 1971). I have already mentioned some discussions of Hardy's 'parodic' imitations of intellectual speech, which arguments are supported by reference to Hardy's comments here; see, for example, Asquith, p. 100; Widdowson, pp. 181–3 and Fisher, pp. 175–6.

33. Hardy, quoted in Archer, p. 35.

34. Although David J. de Laura's research brought out the extent and subtlety of Hardy's engagement with 'modern European thought', he lifts the phrase 'the ache of modernism' from its context and uses it as a title for an essay primarily concerned with Hardy's response to Matthew Arnold and others 'grappling *intellectually*' with the implications of Darwinian theory in the late nineteenth century; see David J. de Laura, '"The Ache of Modernism" in Hardy's Later Novels', *ELH*, vol. 34, no. 3 (1967): 380–99 (p. 381). Scott Rode has since suggested that the phrase reflects Hardy's 'dissatisfaction' with other aspects of 'modernity', such as 'the intrusion of powerful technology as well as the unsettled and alienated mood of unhappiness and isolation that accompanied the disruption of traditional community and the destabilization of personal relationships'; Scott Rode, *Reading and Mapping Hardy's Roads* (London: Routledge, 2006), p. 122.

35. Watson, p. 213.

36. Barbara Hardy describes *Tess of the D'Urbervilles* as a 'portrait of the artist as a young countrywoman' in *Thomas Hardy: Imagining Imagination in Hardy's Poetry and Fiction* (London: Athlone, 2000), p. 46.

37. Asquith, p. 76.

38. West, p. 104.

39. Karlin, p. 69. Writing in the 1990s, Ulrich C. Knopflemacher referred to a 'generally accepted sense' among critics that Keats's ode 'somehow lurks behind' Hardy's poem, 'The Darkling Thrush'; Ulrich C. Knopflemacher, 'The Return of a Native Singer: Keats in Hardy's Dorset', in *Influence and Resistance in Nineteenth-Century Poetry*, ed. by Gregory Kim Blank and Margot K. Louis (London: Palgrave, 1993), 112–30 (p. 112). Similarly noting how Hardy's bird-poems 'consciously evoke a Romantic inheritance', Tim Armstrong uses the substantial set of 'almost forty-five poems with significant references to birdsong' as a key example by which to explore 'sequence and series in Hardy's poetry'; Tim Armstrong, 'Sequence and Series in Hardy's

Poetry', in *A Companion to Thomas Hardy*, ed. by Keith Wilson (London: Blackwell, 2009), 378–94 (pp. 391–2). Barbara Hardy discusses how the novelist also appears to resist literary traditions in his treatment of birds and birdsong in his fiction, notably in the description of the nightingale which sings at the end of *Under the Greenwood Tree*; since Fancy Day does not respond 'rapturously' to the bird's note, the heroine's response appears to show that Hardy 'knows the real pastoral world too well to romanticize it'; Barbara Hardy, pp. 20–1; also see Thomas Hardy, *Under the Greenwood Tree*, ed. by Tim Dolin (London: Penguin, 2004), p. 159.

40. Mark Sandy, *Romanticism, Memory and Mourning* (London: Routledge, 2013), p. 150; Michael O'Neill has similarly argued that Hardy's 'aged thrush' is the direct 'antithesis' of Keats's nightingale or Shelley's skylark, and the poem as a whole decisively 'debunks the finest hopes of Romanticism'; see Michael O'Neill, 'The Romantic Bequest: Arnold and Others', in *The Oxford Handbook of Victorian Poetry*, ed. by Matthew Bevis (Oxford: Oxford University Press, 2013), 217–34 (p. 223).

41. Merryn Williams, *A Preface to Hardy* (Essex: Parson Education, 1993), pp. 152–3.

42. Levine, 'An Enchanting Hardy?', p. 37.

43. For further details of the history of blinding and its prohibition in European countries, see Birkhead, p. 223.

44. Quoted in Verstraete, p. 46.

45. p. 49.

46. pp. 49–50.

47. Karlin sites an article in the *New York Times* which reports that 'Blinded veterans from World War I successfully campaigned to ban the practice in 1920'; however, the blinding of birds was banned in the UK in 1905, as part of the Wild Birds Captivity Act (1905), over a decade before Hardy's poem was composed. See Karlin, p. 63, and Dan Bilefsky, 'One-Ounce Belgian Idols Vie for Most Tweets Per Hour', report in *The New York Times* (21 May 2007), www.nytimes.com/2007/05/21/world/europe/21finch.html, last accessed 31 August 2021. The particularities of the case aside, there can be little doubt of the connection that Hardy is making most poignantly in this poem, as throughout his writing more generally, between the cruelty shown towards birds and the cruelty shown towards human beings in the post-war period.

48. The allusion is to St Paul's eulogy of charity in Corinthians (13: 4–7); see Karlin, pp. 63–4.

49. Anon. 'Performing Animals: The Psychology of Pain in Man and Beast', report in *The Times* (17 December 1913): 6.

50. Hardy, 'Performing Animals'.

51. Fulljames, 'Mr. Hardy and Cage Birds'.
52. Edmund Gosse, 'A Plea for Certain Exotic Forms of Verse', *The Cornhill Magazine*, vol. 36 (1877): 53–71 (p. 62).
53. Monboddo emphasised the importance of memory to the development of 'the *comparative* faculty, called by the an[c]ient philosophers, the *rational* or *logical* faculty; by which [man] compares the perceptions of sense, being all the materials with which his mind is stocked'; *Origin and Progress*, I, pp. 179–80. In descriptions of the operations of the human mind, memory, reason and imagination were often placed in consecutive order; as Robert Blakey summarised in his *History of the Philosophy of Mind* (1848), 'if we place Reason before Imagination, it is because this order appears to us conformable to the natural progress of our intellectual operations. The Imagination is a creative faculty; and the mind, before it attempts to create, begins by reasoning on what it sees and knows'; *History of the Philosophy of Mind; Embracing the Opinions of all Writers on Mental Science, from the Earliest Period to the Present Time*, 4 vols. (London: Longman, Brown and Green, 1850), III, p. 175.
54. The poem is often cited as a comparison in critical footnotes; for example, see Francis B. Pinion's note to this scene in *Thomas Hardy: Art and Thought* (London: Macmillan, 1978), pp. 144, 207 (n. 7), and Dolin's notes to the Penguin edition of *Tess of the D'Urbervilles*, p. 447; n. 8.
55. Leonard Lutwack, *Birds in Literature* (Gainesville: University Press of Florida, 1994), p. 12; also see Karlin, p. 77.
56. Mynott, p. 161.
57. Hardy's 'Baby' poems were first collected by Bernard Jones in his edition of *Fifty-Seven Poems by Thomas Hardy* (Gillingham: Meldon, 2002); the collection includes poems which were published in Florence's three books for children: *The Book of Baby Beasts* (1911), *The Book of Baby Birds* (1912) and *The Book of Baby Pets* (1913). For a further discussion of Hardy's probable authorship of the poems, see Michael Irwin, 'Hardy and the "Baby" Poems', *The Thomas Hardy Journal*, vol. 21 (2005): 9–26. Also see Millgate, *Thomas Hardy: A Biography Revisited*, pp. 434–5.
58. Writers such as Sarah Trimmer and Mary Wollstonecraft, for example, commonly sought to educate their young readers as to their role, duties and place within society through their relation to animals and birds. 'You are often troublesome', Wollstonecraft's schoolteacher informs her pupils, 'I am stronger than you—yet I do not kill you'; *Original Stories* (1796), in *The Works of Mary Wollstonecraft*, ed. by Janet Todd and Marilyn Butler, 7 vols. (London: Pickering and Chatto, 1989), IV, 352–451 (p. 368).
59. Florence Emily Dugdale, *The Book of Baby Birds, with Pictures in Colour by E. J. Detmold* (New York: Hodder and Stoughton, 1912), p. 11. All references

to both poetry and prose passages in this volume are to page numbers, in accordance with this edition's own conventions.
60. The phrase 'sad to say' also appears on pp. 23, 42, 60, 72 and 83.
61. Shelley, 'A Defence of Poetry', in *Major Works*, 674–701 (p. 695).

Conclusion

1. Bertram Lloyd (ed.), *The Great Kinship: An Anthology of Humanitarian Poetry* (London: Allen and Unwin, 1921), pp. vi, v.
2. de Waal, 'Anthropomorphism and Anthropodenial', p. 65.
3. Virginia Woolf, *To the Lighthouse*, ed. by Stella McNichol (London: Penguin, 2000), p. 38.

Bibliography

Aarsleff, Hans, *From Locke to Saussure: Essays on the Study of Language and Intellectual History* (London: Athlone, 1982).
— *The Study of Language in England, 1780–1860* (London: Athlone, 1983).
Addison, Joseph, *Spectator* (21 April 1711), vol. 3, no. 45, https://bit.ly/3vTbDhk, last accessed 31 August 2021.
Aldridge, David (ed.), *Music Therapy in Dementia Care: More New Voices* (London: Jessica Kingsley, 2000).
Alexander, John H., *Reading Wordsworth* (London: Routledge, 1987).
Allen, Francis H., 'The Evolution of Birdsong', *Auk*, vol. 36, no. 4 (1919): 528–36.
Angliss, Sarah, 'The Bird Fancer's Delight', www.bbc.co.uk/programmes/b0128pyp, last accessed 31 August 2021.
Anon., *The Britannica Encyclopaedia; Or, a Dictionary of the Arts, Sciences, and Miscellaneous Literature*, 6th ed., 20 vols. (Edinburgh: Constable, 1820–3).
— 'Man In Nursing Home Reacts to Hearing Music from His Era', www.youtube.com/watch?v=fyZQfop73QM, last accessed 31 August 2021.
— *Natural History of Birds*, 2 vols. (Bungay: Brightly and Childs, T. Kinnersly, 1815).
— 'Performing Animals: The Psychology of Pain in Man and Beast', report in *The Times* (17 December 1913): 6.
— 'Proofs of the Increasing Taste for Natural History', *Blackwood's Magazine*, vol. 2, no. 10 (1818): 380.
Archer, William, 'Real Conversations', in *Thomas Hardy Remembered*, ed. by Martin Ray (Aldershot: Ashgate, 2007), 28–37.
Aristotle, *Categories and De Interpretatione*, trans. by John L. Ackrill (Oxford: Oxford University Press, 1963).
— *Historia Animalium*, trans. by A. Peck, 3 vols. (London: William Heinemann, 1965).
— *Politics*, trans. by Lord Carnes, 2nd ed. (Chicago, IL: University of Chicago Press, 2013).
Armstrong, Edward A., *A Study of Bird Song*, revised ed. (New York: Dover, 1973).
Armstrong, Tim, 'Sequence and Series in Hardy's Poetry', in *A Companion to Thomas Hardy*, ed. by Keith Wilson (London: Blackwell, 2009), 378–94.
Arnold, Matthew (ed.), *Poems of William Wordsworth* (London: Macmillan, 1879).
Asquith, Mark, *Thomas Hardy, Metaphysics and Music* (London: Palgrave, 2005).

Averill, James, 'Wordsworth and "Natural Science": The Poetry of 1798', *The Journal of English and Germanic Philology*, vol. 77, no. 2 (1978): 232–46.
  Wordsworth and the Poetry of Human Suffering (Ithaca, NY: Cornell University Press, 1980).
Bailey, Nathan, *An Universal Etymological Dictionary*, 26th ed. (Edinburgh: Neill, 1789).
Barker, Juliet, *Wordsworth: A Life* (London: Penguin, 2000).
Barrell, John, *The Idea of Landscape and the Sense of Place, 1730–1840: An Approach to the Poetry of John Clare* (Cambridge: Cambridge University Press, 1972).
Barrington, Daines, 'Experiments and Observations on the Singing of Birds', *Philosophical Transactions*, vol. 63 (1773–4): 249–91.
  'On the Expiration of the Cornish Language', *Archaeologia*, vol. 3 (1775): 279–84.
Bate, Jonathan, *John Clare: A Biography* (Kent: Macmillan, 2003).
  Romantic Ecology, 2nd ed. (London: Routledge, 2013).
Bechstein, Johann Matthäus, *The Natural History of Cage Birds* (London: Groombridge, 1837).
Beer, Gillian, *Darwin's Plots: Evolutionary Narrative in Darwin, George Eliot and Nineteenth-Century Fiction*, 3rd ed. (Cambridge: Cambridge University Press, 2009).
Bellanca, Mary Ellen, *Daybooks of Discovery: Nature Diaries in Britain, 1770–1870* (Charlottesville: University of Virginia Press, 2007).
Bennett, Andrew, *Wordsworth Writing* (Cambridge: Cambridge University Press, 2007).
  (ed.), *William Wordsworth in Context* (Cambridge: Cambridge University Press, 2015).
Bentley, Richard, *Sermons Preached at Boyle's Lecture; Remarks upon a Discourse of Free Thinking* (London: MacPherson, 1838).
Berwick, Robert C., and Noam Chomsky, 'Foreword', in *Birdsong, Speech and Language: Exploring the Evolution of Mind and Brain*, ed. by Johan J. Bolhuis and Martin Everaert (Cambridge, MA: MIT Press, 2013), ix–xii.
  Why Only Us: Language and Evolution (Cambridge, MA: MIT Press, 2016).
Bilefsky, Dan, 'One-Ounce Belgian Idols Vie for Most Tweets Per Hour', report in the *New York Times* (21 May 2007), www.nytimes.com/2007/05/21/world/europe/21finch.html, last accessed 31 August 2021.
Birkhead, Tim, *The Red Canary: The Story of The First Genetically Engineered Animal* (London: Bloomsbury, 2014).
Blackmore, Richard, *Creation: A Philosophical Poem* (London: Buckley and Tonson, 1712).
Blakey, Robert, *History of the Philosophy of Mind; Embracing the Opinions of All Writers on Mental Science, from the Earliest Period to the Present Time*, 4 vols. (London: Longman, Brown and Green, 1850).
Bolhuis, Johan J., and Martin Everaert (eds.), *Birdsong, Speech and Language: Exploring the Evolution of Mind and Brain* (Cambridge, MA: MIT Press, 2013).

Boswell, James, *The Life of Samuel Johnson; Together with the Journal of a Tour to the Hebrides*, 10 vols. (London: Murray, 1835).
Bouhmelha, Penny, *Thomas Hardy and Women: Sexual Ideology and Narrative Form* (Totowa, NJ: Barnes and Noble, 1982).
Brewer, William D., 'John Clare and Lord Byron', *John Clare Society Journal*, no. 11 (1992): 43–57.
Bright, Michael, *Animal Language* (London: British Broadcasting Corporation, 1984).
Brooks, Jean R., *Thomas Hardy: The Poetic Structure* (Ithaca, NY: Cornell University Press, 1971).
Budge, Gavin, *Romanticism, Medicine and the Natural Supernatural* (London: Palgrave, 2012).
Buffon, George Louis Leclerc, Comte de, *Natural History of Birds*, trans. by William Smellie, 9 vols. (London: Strahan, Cadell, Murray, 1793).
Burns, Alistair, 'Music and Dementia: A Powerful Connector', in *NHS England* (blog), https://bit.ly/3OKgIBf, last accessed 31 August 2021.
Burns, Robert, *Poems and Songs*, ed. by James Kinsley (Oxford: Oxford University Press, 1969).
Campbell, Thomas, *Poems in Two Volumes*, 2 vols. (London: Longman, 1810).
Chaucer, Geoffrey, *The Canterbury Tales*, ed. by Arthur C. Cawley (London: Everyman, 1992).
Chirico, Paul, *John Clare and the Imagination of the Reader* (London: Palgrave, 2007).
Cicero, *De inventione; De optimo genere oratorum; Topica*, trans. by Harry Mortimer Hubbell (Cambridge, MA: Harvard University Press, 2014).
Clare, John, *The Early Poems of John Clare: 1804–1822*, ed. by Eric Robinson and David Powell, 2 vols. (Oxford: Clarendon, 1989).
 John Clare's Autobiographical Writings, ed. by Eric Robinson (Oxford: Oxford University Press, 1983).
 John Clare's Birds, ed. by Eric Robinson and Richard Fitter (Oxford: Oxford University Press, 1982).
 The Later Poems of John Clare, ed. by Eric Robinson and David Powell, 2 vols. (Oxford: Clarendon, 1984).
 The Letters of John Clare, ed. by Mark Storey (Oxford: Clarendon, 1985).
 The Natural History Prose Writings of John Clare, ed. by Margaret Grainger (Oxford: Oxford University Press, 1983).
 Northborough Sonnets, ed. by Eric Robinson, David Powell and P. M. S. Dawson (Manchester: Carcanet, 1995).
 Poems Descriptive of Rural Life and Scenery (London: Taylor and Hessey, 1820).
 Poems of the Middle Period, 1822–37, ed. by Eric Robinson, David Powell and P. M. S. Dawson, 5 vols. (Oxford: Clarendon, 1996–2003).
 The Prose of John Clare, ed. by John W. Tibble and Anne Tibble (London: Routledge, 1951).
 The Rural Muse (London: Whittaker, 1835).
 The Village Minstrel (London: Taylor and Hessey, 1821).

Claridge, Laura, 'Tess: A Less than Pure Woman Ambivalently Represented', *Texas Studies in Literature and Language*, vol. 28, no. 3 (1986): 324–38.
Cobbett, William, *A Grammar of the English Language, in a Series of Letters; Intended for the Use of Schools and of Young Persons in General; But, More Especially, for the Use of Soldiers, Sailors, Apprentices and Plough-Boys* (Cambridge: Cambridge University Press, 2014).
Cohn, Elisha, '"No Insignificant Creature": Thomas Hardy's Ethical Turn', *Nineteenth-Century Literature*, vol. 64, no. 4 (2010): 494–520.
Coleridge, Samuel Taylor, *Biographia Literaria*, ed. by James Engell and Walter Jackson Bate, 2 vols. (Princeton, NJ: Princeton University Press, 1983).
  Coleridge's Miscellaneous Criticism, ed. by Thomas Middleton Raysor (Cambridge, MA: Harvard University Press, 1936).
  Coleridge's 'Sonnets from Various Authors', ed. by Paul M. Zall (Glendale, CA: La Siesta Press, 1968).
  Coleridge's Writings; On Language, ed. by Alfred C. Goodson (London: Palgrave, 1998).
  The Collected Letters of Samuel Taylor Coleridge, ed. by Earl Leslie Griggs, 6 vols. (Oxford: Clarendon, 1956–71).
  Poetical Works, ed. by James C. C. Mays, 2 vols. [Reading Text] (Princeton, NJ: Princeton University Press, 2001).
  Shorter Works and Fragments, ed. by H. J. Jackson and James Robert de Jager Jackson, 2 vols. (London: Routledge, 1995).
Colwell, Mary, *John Muir: The Scotsman who Saved America's Wild Places* (Oxford: Lion Hudson, 2014).
Cosslett, Tess, *The 'Scientific Movement' and Victorian Literature* (Brighton: Harvester, 1982).
Cousins, Anthony D., and Peter Howarth (eds.), *The Cambridge Companion to the Sonnet* (Cambridge: Cambridge University Press, 2011).
Cowper, William, *The Poems of William Cowper*, ed. by John D. Baird and Charles Ryskamp, 3 vols. (Oxford: Clarendon, 1980–95).
Cox, Reginald G. (ed.), *Thomas Hardy: The Critical Heritage* (London: Routledge, 2005).
Crowley, Tony, *Standard English and the Politics of Language* (Urbana: University of Illinois Press, 1989).
Culler, Jonathan, *The Pursuit of Signs: Semiotics, Literature, Deconstruction* (Ithaca, NY: Cornell University Press, 2001).
Curran, Stuart, *Poetic Form and British Romanticism* (Oxford: Oxford University Press, 1990).
Darwin, Charles, *The Correspondence of Charles Darwin*, ed. by Frederick H. Burkhardt et al., 30 vols. (Cambridge: Cambridge University Press, 1985–2006).
  The Descent of Man, and Selection in Relation to Sex, ed. by James Moore and Adrian Desmond (London: Penguin, 2004).
  The Expression of the Emotions in Man and Animals, ed. by Joe Cain and Sharon Messenger (London: Penguin, 2009).

On the Origin of Species, ed. by Gillian Beer (Oxford: Oxford University Press, 2008).
Darwin, Erasmus, *The Temple of Nature; Or, The Origin of Society* (London: Johnson, 1803).
Zoonomia; Or, the Laws of Organic Life, 2 vols. (London: Johnson, 1794–6).
Davis, William A., *Thomas Hardy and the Law: Legal Presences in Hardy's Life and Fiction* (Newark: University of Delaware Press, 2003).
Dawson, P. M. S., 'The Making of Clare's *Poems Descriptive of Rural Life and Scenery* (1820)', *The Review of English Studies*, vol. 56, no. 224 (2005): 276–312.
Dickens, Charles, *David Copperfield*, ed. by Jeremy Tambling (London: Penguin, 2007).
Little Dorrit, ed. by Stephen Wall and Helen Small (London: Penguin, 2003).
Dickinson, Emily, *The Poems of Emily Dickinson*, ed. by Ralph W. Franklin, 3 vols. (Cambridge, MA: Harvard University Press, 1998).
Donald, Diana, *Picturing Animals in Britain (1750–1850)* (New Haven, CT: Yale University Press, 2007).
Dugdale, Florence Emily, *The Book of Baby Birds, with Pictures in Colour by E. J. Detmold* (New York: Hodder and Stoughton, 1912).
Eitner, Lorenz, 'Cages, Prisons, and Captives in Eighteenth-Century Art', in *Images of Romanticism*, ed. by Karl Kroeber and William Walling (New Haven, CT: Yale University Press, 1978), 13–38.
Esterhammer, Angela, 'Spontaneity, Immediacy and Improvisation in Romantic Poetry', in *A Companion to Romantic Poetry*, ed. by Charles Mahoney (London: Wiley, 2010), 321–36.
Farrell, John, *Varieties of Authorial Intention* (London: Palgrave, 2017).
Feldman, Paula A., and Daniel Robinson, Introduction to *A Century of Sonnets: The Romantic-Era Revival, 1750–1850*, ed. by 'Paula A. Feldman and Daniel Robinson (Oxford: Oxford University Press, 1999), 3–19.
Ferguson, Moira, *Animal Advocacy and English Women, 1770–1900* (Michigan: University of Michigan Press, 1998).
Finch, Stanley, *Wordsworth's Birds* (Carnforth: Lunesdale, 1986).
Fisher, Joe, *The Hidden Hardy* (London: Macmillan, 1992).
Fitch, W. Tecumseh, *The Evolution of Language* (Cambridge: Cambridge University Press, 2012).
'Musical Protolanguage: Darwin's Theory of Language Evolution Revisited', in *Birdsong, Speech and Language: Exploring the Evolution of Mind and Brain*, ed. by Johan J. Bolhuis and Martin Everaert (Cambridge, MA: MIT Press, 2013), 489–504.
Frith, Clifford B., *Charles Darwin's Life with Birds: His Complete Ornithology* (Oxford: Oxford University Press, 2016).
Fudge, Erica, 'A Left-Handed Blow: Writing the History of Animals', in *Representing Animals*, ed. by Nigel Rothfels (Bloomington: Indiana University Press, 2002), 3–18.
Fulljames, Henry J., 'Mr. Hardy and Cage Birds', letter to the editor, *The Times* (23 December 1913): 10.

Galef, Bennet G., Jr., 'The Making of a Science', in *Foundations of Animal Behaviour: Classic Papers with Commentaries*, ed. by Lynne D. Houck and Lee C. Drickamer (Chicago, IL: University of Chicago Press, 1996), 5–12.

Garrett, Aaron, 'Human Nature', in *The Cambridge History of Eighteenth-Century Philosophy*, ed. by Knud Haakonsen, 2 vols. (Cambridge: Cambridge University Press, 2006), I, 160–235.

Gaull, Marilyn, 'Clare and "The Dark System"', in *John Clare in Context*, ed. by Hugh Haughton, Adam Philips and Geoffrey Summerfield (Cambridge: Cambridge University Press, 1994), 279–94.

Gerard, Alexander, *An Essay on Taste* (London: Millar, 1759).

Gill, Stephen, *William Wordsworth: A Life* (Oxford: Oxford University Press, 1990).

Gilpin, William, *Observations, Relative Chiefly to Picturesque Beauty, Made in the Year 1772, on Several Parts of England, Particularly the Mountains and Lakes of Cumberland, and Westmoreland*, 2 vols. (London: Blamire, 1788).

Goldsmith, Oliver, *A History of the Earth and Animated Nature*, 8 vols. (London: Nourse, 1774).

Goodridge, John (ed.), *The Independent Spirit: John Clare and the Self-Taught Tradition* (Helpston: John Clare Society and Margaret Grainger Memorial Trust, 1994).

Goodson, Alfred C., Introduction to *Coleridge's Writings; On Language*, ed. by Alfred C. Goodson (London: Palgrave, 1998), 10–11.

Gorji, Mina, *John Clare and the Place of Poetry* (Liverpool: Liverpool University Press, 2008).

   'John Clare and the Poetics of Mess', *Moveable Type*, vol. 5 (2009): 1–11.

Gosse, Edmund, 'A Plea for Certain Exotic Forms of Verse', *The Cornhill Magazine*, vol. 36 (1877): 53–71.

Gossin, Pamela, *Thomas Hardy's Novel Universe: Astronomy, Cosmology, and Gender in the Post-Darwinian World* (Aldershot: Ashgate, 2007).

Gower, John, *The Complete Works of John Gower*, ed. by George C. Macaulay, 4 vols. (Oxford: Clarendon, 1899–1902).

Grew, Sydney and Eva Mary Grew, 'William Cowper: His Acceptance and Rejection of Music', *Music & Letters*, vol. 13, no. 1 (1932): 31–41.

Grundy, Joan, *Hardy and the Sister Arts* (London: Macmillan, 1979).

Gunn, Thom, 'Hardy and the Ballads', *Agenda*, vol. 10, nos. 2–3 (1972): 19–46.

Hadamard, Jacques, *The Mathematician's Mind: The Psychology of Invention in the Mathematical Field* (Princeton, NJ: Princeton University Press, 1945).

Hall, Dewey W., 'Naturalists' Interpretations: Daffodils, Swallows and a Floating Island', in *Romantic Ecocriticism: Origins and Legacies*, ed. by Dewey W. Hall (London: Lexington, 2016), 43–60.

   (ed.), *Romantic Ecocriticism: Origins and Legacies* (London: Lexington, 2016).

Hardy, Barbara, *Thomas Hardy: Imagining Imagination in Hardy's Poetry and Fiction* (London: Athlone, 2000).

Hardy, Thomas, *The Collected Letters of Thomas Hardy*, ed. by Richard Little Purdy, Michael Millgate and Keith Wilson, 8 vols. (Oxford: Clarendon, 1978–2012).

The Complete Poems, ed. by James Gibson (Basingstoke: Palgrave, 2001).
The Early Life of Thomas Hardy, 1840–1891 (Cambridge: Cambridge University Press, 2011).
Desperate Remedies, ed. by Patricia Ingham (Oxford: Oxford University Press, 2009).
Far from the Madding Crowd, ed. by Rosemarie Morgan and Shannon Russell (London: Penguin, 2003).
Fifty-Seven Poems by Thomas Hardy, ed. by Bernard Jones (Gillingham: Meldon House, 2002).
The Hand of Ethelberta, ed. by Tim Dolin (London: Penguin, 2006).
The Later Years of Thomas Hardy, 1892–1928 (Cambridge: Cambridge University Press, 2011),
Life's Little Ironies, ed. by Alan Manford (Oxford: Oxford University Press, 1996).
The Literary Notebooks of Thomas Hardy, ed. by Björk A. Lennart, 2 vols. (London: Macmillan, 1985).
The Major of Casterbridge, ed. by Keith Wilson (London: Penguin, 2003).
'Performing Animals: Mr Hardy's Protest', letter to the editor, *The Times* (19 December 1913): 9.
Personal Writings, ed. by Harold Orel (London: Macmillan, 1967).
The Return of the Native, ed. by Simon Gatrell (Oxford: Oxford University Press, 2008).
Tess of the D'Urbervilles, ed. by Tim Dolin (London: Penguin, 2003).
The Trumpet Major, ed. by Linda M. Shires (London: Penguin, 1997).
Under the Greenwood Tree, ed. by Tim Dolin (London: Penguin, 2004).
Harley, Alexis, 'Darwin's Ants: Evolutionary Theory and the Anthropomorphic Fallacy', in *Representing the Modern Animal in Culture*, ed. by Jeanne Dubino, Ziba Rashidian and Andrew Smyth (London: Palgrave, 2014), 103–18.
Harris, James, *Hermes; Or, a Philosophical Inquiry concerning Universal Grammar* (London: Woodfall, 1751).
Haughton, Hugh, 'Progress and Rhyme: "The Nightingale's Nest" and Romantic Poetry', in *John Clare in Context*, ed. by Hugh Haughton, Adam Philips and Geoffrey Summerfield (Cambridge: Cambridge University Press, 1994), 51–86.
Haughton, Hugh, Adam Philips and Geoffrey Summerfield (eds.), *John Clare in Context* (Cambridge: Cambridge University Press, 1994).
Haupt, Lyanda Lynn, *Mozart's Starling* (London: Corsair, 2017).
Hazlitt, William, *Characters of Shakespeare's Plays*, 2nd ed. (London: Taylor and Hessey, 1818).
Lectures on the English Poets (London: Taylor and Hessey, 1818).
Selected Writings, ed. by Jon Cook (Oxford: Oxford University Press, 2009).
Heaney, Seamus, 'John Clare: A Bicentenary Lecture', in *John Clare in Context*, ed. by Hugh Haughton, Adam Philips and Geoffrey Summerfield (Cambridge: Cambridge University Press, 1994), 130–47.

Preoccupations: Selected Prose, 1968–78 (London: Faber, 1980).
Hinchliffe, Keith, 'Wordsworth and the Kinds of Metaphor', *Studies in Romanticism*, vol. 23, no. 1 (1984): 81–100.
Holmes, John, *Darwin's Bards: British and American Poetry in the Age of Evolution* (Edinburgh: Edinburgh University Press, 2009).
Heffernan, James A. W., 'Wordsworth and Landscape', in *The Oxford Handbook of William Wordsworth*, ed. by Richard Gravil and Daniel Robinson (Oxford: Oxford University Press, 2015), 614–28.
Herder, Johann Gottfried, *Philosophical Writings*, trans. and ed. by Michael N. Forster (Cambridge: Cambridge University Press, 2002).
Heyes, Robert, 'John Clare's Natural History', in *New Essays on John Clare: Poetry, Culture and Community*, ed. by Simon Kövesi and Scott McEathron (Cambridge: Cambridge University Press, 2015), 169–88.
Hudson, William H., *Birds in London* (London: Longmans, 1898).
Hughes, John, *Ecstatic Sound: Music and Individuality in the Work of Thomas Hardy* (Surrey: Ashgate, 2001).
Hughes, Ted, *Winter Pollen: Occasional Prose*, ed. by William Scammell (New York: Picador, 1994).
Irwin, Michael, 'Hardy and the "Baby" Poems', *The Thomas Hardy Journal*, vol. 21 (2005): 9–26.
Jackson, Wallace, and Paul Yoder, 'Wordsworth Reimagines Thomas Gray: Notations on Begetting a Kindred Spirit', *Criticism*, vol. 31, no. 3 (1989): 287–300.
Jacobus, Mary, 'Tess: The Making of a Pure Woman', in *Tearing the Veil: Essays on Femininity*, ed. by Susan Lipshitz (London: Routledge, 1978), 77–92.
Jarvis, Simon, *Wordsworth's Philosophic Song* (Cambridge: Cambridge University Press, 2006).
Jefferies, Richard, *Nature Near London* (London: Chatto and Windus, 1913).
Round About a Great Estate (London: Smith, Elder, 1880).
Jones, Bernard, *Fifty-Seven Poems by Thomas Hardy* (Gillingham: Meldon, 2002).
Jones, John, *The Egotistical Sublime: A History of Wordsworth's Imagination* (Westport, CT: Greenwood Press, 1978).
Johnson, Robert Sherlaw, *Messiaen* (London: Omnibus, 2008).
Johnson, Samuel, *A Dictionary of the English Language*, 2 vols. (London: Offor, Allason, et al., 1824).
Karlin, Daniel, *The Figure of the Singer* (Oxford: Oxford University Press, 2013).
Keats, John, *The Complete Poems*, ed. by John Barnard, 3rd ed. (London: Penguin, 2006).
Kennedy, John S., *The New Anthropomorphism* (Cambridge: Cambridge University Press, 1992).
Kenyon-Jones, Christine, *Kindred Brutes: Animals in Romantic-Period Writing* (London: Ashgate, 2001).
King, Joshua, 'Broken Promises and Blind Pleasures in Wordsworth's "The Idiot Boy"', *CEA Critic*, vol. 73, no. 3 (2011): 48–68.
Kircher, Athanasius, *Musurgia Universalis* (Rome: Corbelletti, 1650).

Kittler, Friedrich A., *Discourse Networks: 1800–1900*, trans. by Michael Metteer, with Chris Cullins (Stanford, CA: Stanford University Press, 1990).
Kneale, J. Douglas, *Romantic Aversions: Aftermaths of Classicism in Wordsworth and Coleridge* (Quebec: McGill-Queen's University Press, 1999).
Knight, William Angus, *Lord Monboddo and Some of His Contemporaries* (London: Murray, 1900).
Knopflemacher, Ulrich C., 'The Return of a Native Singer: Keats in Hardy's Dorset', in *Influence and Resistance in Nineteenth-Century Poetry*, ed. by Gregory Kim Blank and Margot K. Louis (London: Palgrave, 1993), 112–30.
Kövesi, Simon, and Scott McEathron, *New Essays on John Clare: Poetry, Culture and Community* (Cambridge: Cambridge University Press, 2015).
Kroodsma, Don, 'The Diversity and Plasticity of Birdsong', in *Nature's Music: The Science of Birdsong*, ed. by Peter Marler and Hans Slabberkoorn (London: Elsevier, 2004), 108–31.
Lafford, Erin, 'Clare's Muttering, Murmurings, and Ramblings: The Sounds of Health', *The John Clare Society Journal*, no. 33 (2014): 1–18.
Lamb, Charles and Mary Anne Lamb, *The Letters of Charles and Mary Anne Lamb*, ed. by Edwin W. Marrs, Jr., 3 vols. (Ithaca, NY: Cornell University Press, 1975–8).
Land, Stephen K., 'The Silent Poet: An Aspect of Wordsworth's Semantic Theory', *University of Toronto Quarterly*, vol. 42, no. 2 (1973): 157–69.
Lang, Andrew, 'A Rejoinder [to Hardy's Preface to Tess of the D'Urbervilles]', in Reginald G. Cox (ed.), *Thomas Hardy: The Critical Heritage* (London: Routledge, 2005), 249–54.
de Laura, David J., '"The Ache of Modernism" in Hardy's Later Novels', *ELH*, vol. 34, no. 3 (1967): 380–99.
Leader, Zachary, *Revision and Romantic Authorship* (Oxford: Clarendon, 1996).
Levine, George, *Darwin and the Novelists: Patterns of Science in Victorian Fiction* (Chicago, IL: University of Chicago Press, 1988).
  'Hardy and Darwin: An Enchanting Hardy?', in *A Companion to Thomas Hardy*, ed. by Keith Wilson (London: Blackwell, 2009), 36–53.
Lévi-Strauss, Claude, *Totemism*, trans. by Rodney Needham (Boston, MA: Beacon Press, 1963).
Lewes, George Henry, *Sea-Side Studies at Ilfracombe, Tenby, the Scilly Isles, and Jersey*, 2nd ed. (Edinburgh: Blackwood, 1860).
Lloyd, Bertram (ed.), *The Great Kinship: An Anthology of Humanitarian Poetry* (London: Allen and Unwin, 1921).
Locke, John, *An Essay Concerning Human Understanding*, ed. by Roger Woolhouse (London: Penguin, 1997).
Lodge, Sara, 'Contested Bounds: John Clare, John Keats, and the Sonnet', *Studies in Romanticism*, vol. 51, no. 4 (2012): 533–54.
Lowes, John Livingston, *The Road to Xanadu: A Study in the Ways of the Imagination* (Boston, MA: Houghton Mifflin, 1955).
Lucretius, *Titus Lucretius Carus. The Epicurean Philosopher; His Six Books 'De Rerum Natura'; Done into English Verse, With Notes*, trans. by Thomas Creech (Oxford: Lichfield, 1682).

Lutwack, Leonard, *Birds in Literature* (Gainesville: University Press of Florida, 1994).
Macloc, J., *A Natural History of the Most Remarkable Quadrupeds, Birds, Fishes, Serpents, Reptiles, and Insects in the Known World*, 3rd ed. (London: Dean and Munday, 1820).
Magnuson, Paul, 'The "Conversation" Poems', in *The Cambridge Companion to Coleridge*, ed. by Lucy Newlyn (Cambridge: Cambridge University Press, 2002), 32–44.
Mahoney, Charles (ed.), *A Companion to Romantic Poetry* (London: Wiley, 2010).
Mallozzi, Ilaria, 'Agnosticism and Free-Thinking: The Influence of Leslie Stephen', in *Thomas Hardy, Poet: New Perspectives*, ed. by Adrian Grafe and Laurence Estanove (Jefferson: McFarland, 2015), 100–15.
de Man, Paul, 'Time and History in Wordsworth', *Diacritics*, vol. 17, no. 4 (1987): 4–17.
Marler, Peter, 'Animal Communication and Human Language', in *The Origin and Diversification of Language*, ed. by Nina G. Jablonski, Leslie C. Aiello and Nancy Gee (San Francisco: California Academy of Sciences, 1998), 1–20.
Marler, Peter, and Hans Slabberkoorn (eds.), *Nature's Music: The Science of Birdsong* (London: Elsevier, 2004).
Matlak, Richard, 'Wordsworth's Reading of *Zoonomia* in Early Spring', *The Wordsworth Circle*, vol. 21, no. 2 (1990): 76–81.
Mayhew, Henry, *London Labour and the London Poor: The Condition and Earnings of Those that Will Work, Cannot Work, and Will Not Work*, 4 vols. (London: Griffin, Bohn, 1861–2).
McEathron, Scott, 'Wordsworth and Coleridge, *Lyrical Ballads*', in *A Companion to Romanticism*, ed. by Duncan Wu (Oxford: Blackwell, 1999), 144–54.
McKusick, James C., *Coleridge's Philosophy of Language* (New Haven, CT: Yale University Press, 1956).
  'John Clare and the Tyranny of Grammar', *Studies in Romanticism*, vol. 2, no. 14 (1994): 255–77.
Messiaen, Olivier, 'Messiaen on Birds', www.youtube.com/watch?v=XRRhsX4j1Oc&t=2s, last accessed 31 August 2021.
Midgley, Mary, *Animals and Why They Matter* (Athens: Georgia University Press, 1983).
Millgate, Michael, *Thomas Hardy: A Biography Revisited* (Oxford: Oxford University Press, 2004).
Milton, John, *The Complete Poems*, ed. by John Leonard (London: Penguin, 1998).
  Comus (London: Macmillan, 1891).
Modiano, Raimonda, 'Words and "Languageless" Meanings: Limits of Expression in *The Rime of the Ancient Mariner*', *Modern Language Quarterly*, vol. 38, no. 1 (1977): 40–61.
Monboddo, James Burnett Lord, *Of the Origin and Progress of Language*, 6 vols., 2nd ed. (Edinburgh: Balfour, 1774–92).
  Preface to *An Account of a Savage Girl, Caught Wild in the Woods of Champagne*, translated from the French of Madame Hecquet (Edinburgh: Kincaid and Bell, 1768), iii–xviii.

Morgan, Conwy Lloyd, *An Introduction to Comparative Psychology* (London: Walter Scott, 1894).
Muldoon, Paul, Meg Tyler and Jeff Hilson, 'Contemporary Poets and the Sonnet: A Trialogue', in *The Cambridge Companion to the Sonnet*, ed. by Anthony D. Cousins and Peter Howarth (Cambridge: Cambridge University Press, 2011), 6–24.
Müller, Max, 'Lectures on Mr Darwin's Philosophy of Language, Lect. 1', *Fraser's Magazine*, vol. 7, no. 41 (1873): 525–41.
  'Lectures on Mr Darwin's Philosophy of Language, Lect. 2', *Fraser's Magazine*, vol. 7, no. 42 (1873): 659–78.
  'Lectures on Mr Darwin's Philosophy of Language, Lect. 3', *Fraser's Magazine*, vol. 8, no. 43 (1873): 1–24.
  Lectures on the Science of Language; Delivered at the Royal Institution of Great Britain in April, May and June 1861, 2 vols. (London: Longman, 1861).
Mundy, Rachel, *Animal Musicalities: Birds, Beasts and Evolutionary Listening* (Middletown, CT: Wesleyan University Press, 2018).
Murray, Lindley, *An English Grammar; Comprehending the Principles and Rules of Language; Illustrated by Appropriate Exercises*, new ed., 2 vols. (York: Wilson et al., 1808).
Mynott, Jeremy, *Birdscapes: Birds in Our Imagination and Experience* (Princeton, NJ: Princeton University Press, 2009).
Nagel, Thomas, 'What Is It Like to Be a Bat?', *The Philosophical Review*, vol. 83, no. 4 (1974): 435–50.
Nattrass, Leonora, 'John Clare and William Cobbett: The Personal and the Political', in *The Independent Spirit: John Clare and the Self-Taught Tradition*, ed. by John Goodridge (Helpston: John Clare Society and Margaret Grainger Memorial Trust, 1994), 44–54.
Newey, Vincent, 'Cowper Prospects: Self, Nature and Society', in *Romanticism and Religion from Cowper to Wallace Stevens*, ed. by Gavin Hopps and Jane Stabler (London: Routledge, 2006), 41–56.
Newlyn, Lucy (ed.), *The Cambridge Companion to Coleridge* (Cambridge: Cambridge University Press, 2002).
  Reading, Writing and Romanticism: The Anxiety of Reception (Oxford: Oxford University Press, 2000).
  William and Dorothy Wordsworth: All in Each Other (Oxford: Oxford University Press, 2013).
Newsome, J. (ed.), *Pliny's Natural History: A Selection from Philemon Holland's Translation* (Oxford: Clarendon, 1964).
Noiré, Ludwig, *The Origin and Philosophy of Language*, 2nd revised ed. (Chicago, IL: Open Court, 1917).
Norton, Kay, *Singing and Wellbeing: Ancient Wisdom, Modern Proof* (London: Routledge, 2016).
Oliphant, Margaret, 'Review of Tess of the D'Urbervilles', in Reginald G. Cox (ed.), *Thomas Hardy: The Critical Heritage* (London: Routledge, 2005), 219–27.

O'Neill, Michael, '"Even Now While I Write": Leigh Hunt and Romantic Spontaneity', in *Leigh Hunt: Life, Poetics, Politics*, ed. by Nicholas Roe (London: Routledge, 2003), 135–55
  'The Romantic Bequest: Arnold and Others', in *The Oxford Handbook of Victorian Poetry*, ed. by Matthew Bevis (Oxford: Oxford University Press, 2013), 217–34.
Packham, Catherine, *Eighteenth-Century Vitalism: Bodies, Culture, Politics* (London: Palgrave, 2012).
Patel, Aniruddh D., *Music, Language and the Brain* (Oxford: Oxford University Press, 2007).
Pater, Walter, 'Wordsworth', in *Appreciations, with an Essay on Style* (London: Macmillan, 1889).
Pepperberg, Irene, *The Alex Studies: Cognitive and Communicative Abilities of Grey Parrots* (Cambridge, MA: Harvard University Press, 1999).
Perkins, David, *Romanticism and Animal Rights* (Cambridge: Cambridge University Press, 2003).
Perry, Seamus, *Coleridge and the Uses of Division* (Oxford: Oxford University Press, 1999).
Phelan, Joseph, *The Nineteenth-Century Sonnet* (London: Palgrave, 2005).
Pinion, Francis B., *A Hardy Companion: A Guide to the Works of Thomas Hardy and Their Background* (London: Macmillan, 1968).
  Thomas Hardy: Art and Thought (London: Macmillan, 1978).
Pinker, Stephen, *The Language Instinct: The New Science of Language and Mind* (London: Penguin, 2015).
Pite, Ralph, *Thomas Hardy: The Guarded Life* (London: Picador, 2006).
Pliny, the Elder, *The Historie of the World, Commonly called, The Naturall Historie of C. Plinius Secundus*, trans. by Philemon Holland, 2 vols. (London: Adam Islip, 1601).
Potkay, Adam, 'Ear and Eye: Counteracting Senses in Loco-Descriptive Poetry', in *A Companion to Romantic Poetry*, ed. by Charles Mahoney (London: Wiley, 2010), 176–94.
  Wordsworth's Ethics (Baltimore, MD: Johns Hopkins University Press, 2012).
Powell, David, *Catalogue of the John Clare Collection in the Northampton Public Library* (Northampton: County Borough of Northampton Public Libraries, Museum and Art Galleries Committee, 1964).
Radick, Gregory, *The Simian Tongue: The Long Debate about Animal Language* (Chicago, IL: University of Chicago Press, 2007).
Randel, Fred V., 'Coleridge and the Contentiousness of Romantic Nightingales', *Studies in Romanticism*, vol. 21, no. 1 (1982): 33–55.
Rawnsley, Hardwicke D., *Reminiscences of Wordsworth among the Peasantry of Westmoreland* (London: Dillon's University Bookshop, 1969).
Ray, Martin (ed.), *Thomas Hardy Remembered* (Aldershot: Ashgate, 2007).
Rehder, Robert, *Wordsworth and the Beginnings of Modern Poetry* (London: Routledge, 1981).

Reiman, Donald, *The Romantics Reviewed: Part A – The Lake Poets*, 2 vols. (New York: Garland, 1972).
Richardson, Alan, *British Romanticism and the Science of the Mind* (Cambridge: Cambridge University Press, 2001).
Richardson, Angelique, 'Hardy and the Place of Culture', in *A Companion to Thomas Hardy*, ed. by Keith Wilson (London: Blackwell, 2009), 54–70.
Richardson, Samuel, *Clarissa; Or, the History of a Young Lady*, ed. by Angus Ros (London: Penguin, 1985).
Ritvo, Harriet, *The Animal Estate: The English and Other Creatures in Victorian England* (Cambridge, MA: Harvard University Press, 1987).
Roberts, Bethan, *Charlotte Smith and the Sonnet: Form, Tradition and Place in the Eighteenth Century* (Liverpool: Liverpool University Press, 2019).
Robinson, Daniel, 'The Sonnet', in *William Wordsworth in Context*, ed. by Andrew Bennett (Cambridge: Cambridge University Press, 2015), 136–44.
Roe, Nicholas, *Wordsworth and Coleridge: The Radical Years*, 2nd ed. (Oxford: Oxford University Press, 2018),
Rode, Scott, *Reading and Mapping Hardy's Roads* (London: Routledge, 2006).
Rothenberg, David, *Why Birds Sing: One Man's Quest to Solve an Everyday Mystery* (London: Penguin, 2005).
Rousseau, Jean-Jacques, *A Discourse on Inequality*, trans. by Maurice Cranston (London: Penguin, 1984).
Rousseau, Jean-Jacques and Johann Gottfried Herder, *On the Origin of Language*, trans. by John H. Moran and Alexander Gode (Chicago, IL: University of Chicago Press, 1966).
Rowe, Richard, *Life in the London Streets; Or, Struggles for Daily Bread* (London: Nimmo and Bain, 1881).
Rowland, Ann Wierda, *Romanticism and Childhood: The Infantilization of British Literary Culture* (Cambridge: Cambridge University Press, 2012).
Russel, Bertrand, *The Basic Writings of Bertrand Russel*, ed. by Robert E. Egner and Lester E. Dennon (London: Routledge, 1961).
Ryan, Robert M., *Charles Darwin and the Church of Wordsworth* (Oxford: Oxford University Press, 2016).
Sandy, Mark, *Romanticism, Memory and Mourning* (London: Routledge, 2013).
Serjeantson, Richard W., 'The Passions and Animal Language, 1540–1700', *Journal of the History of Ideas*, vol. 62, no. 3 (2001): 425–44.
Seymour, Claire, 'Hardy and Music: Uncanny Sounds', in *A Companion to Thomas Hardy*, ed. by Keith Wilson (London: Blackwell, 2009), 233–38.
Shakespeare, William, *The Riverside Shakespeare*, ed. by Gwynne Blakemore Evans et al., 2nd ed. (Boston, MA: Houghton Mifflin, 1997).
Shelley, Percy Bysshe, *Major Works*, ed. by Zachary Leader and Michael O'Neill (Oxford: Oxford University Press, 2009).
Smith, Adam, *Essays on Philosophical Subjects: The Glasgow Edition of the Works and Correspondence of Adam Smith* (Oxford: Oxford University Press, 1967–1983).

Smith, Charlotte, *The Poems of Charlotte Smith*, ed. by Stuart Curran (Oxford: Oxford University Press, 1993).
Smith, Olivia, *The Politics of Language: 1791–1819* (Oxford: Clarendon, 1984).
Spencer, Herbert, *Essays: Scientific, Political and Speculative*, 3 vols. (London: Williams and Norgate, 1891).
Stafford, Fiona, 'Inhabited Solitudes: Wordsworth in Scotland, 1803', in *Scotland, Ireland and the Romantic Aesthetic*, ed. by David Duff and Catherine Jones (Lewisberg, PA: Buckness University Press, 2007), 93–113.
Stap, Don, *Birdsong: A Natural History* (Oxford: Oxford University Press, 2005).
Stark, Robert, *Ezra Pound's Early Verse and Lyric Tradition: A Jargoner's Apprenticeship* (Edinburgh: Edinburgh University Press, 2012).
Starobinski, Jean, *Blessings in Disguise; Or, the Morality of Evil* (Cambridge, MA: Harvard University Press, 1993).
Stephen, Leslie, *Essays on Freethinking and Plainspeaking* (London: Longmans, 1873).
Storey, Mark, *John Clare: The Critical Heritage* (London: Routledge, 1973).
Taylor, Dennis, *Hardy's Literary Language and Victorian Philology* (Oxford: Clarendon, 1993).
  Hardy's Metres and Victorian Prosody (Oxford: Clarendon, 1988).
Thoreau, Henry David, *A Week on the Concord and Merrimack Rivers* (Boston, MA: Houghton and Mifflin, 1891).
Thorpe, William, 'Comments on *The Bird-Fancyer's Delight*, Together with Notes on Imitation in the Sub-song of the Chaffinch', *Ibis*, vol. 97, no. 2 (1955): 247–51.
  'The Process of Song-Learning in the Chaffinch as Studied by Means of the Sound Spectrograph', *Nature*, vol. 173, no. 4402 (1954): 465–9.
Turley, Richard Marggraff, *The Politics of Language in Romantic Literature* (London: Palgrave, 2002).
Turner, Paul (ed.), *Selections from the History of the World, Commonly Called the Natural History of C. Plinius Secundus* (Carbondale: Southern Illinois University Press, 1962).
Vardy, Alan D., *John Clare: Politics and Poetry* (London: Palgrave, 2003).
Verstraete, Pieter, 'The Blind Finch: Expanding the Role of Disability in Heritage Studies', *Revista Pasages*, no. 1 (2015): 37–54.
de Waal, Frans, 'Anthropomorphism and Anthropodenial', in *Primates and Philosophers: How Morality Evolved*, ed. by Stephen Macedo and Josiah Ober (Princeton, NJ: Princeton University Press, 2009), 59–68.
  Are We Smart Enough to Know How Smart Animals Are? (London: Norton, 2016).
Wainewright, Thomas Griffiths, *Essays and Criticisms* (London: Reeves and Turner, 1880).
Warton, Joseph, *The Works of Virgil, in Latin and English*, 4 vols. (London: Dodsley, 1753).
Wasserman, Earl R., *The Finer Tone: Keats' Major Poems* (Baltimore, MD: Johns Hopkins University Press, 1967).

Watson, William, 'Review of Tess of the D'Urbervilles', in Reginald G. Cox (ed.), *Thomas Hardy: The Critical Heritage* (London: Routledge, 2005), 213–17.
Weiner, Stephanie Kuduk, *Clare's Lyric: John Clare and Three Modern Poets* (Oxford: Oxford University Press, 2014).
Weinfield, Henry, *The Blank-Verse Tradition from Shakespeare to Milton* (Cambridge: Cambridge University Press, 2012).
  The Poet without a Name: Gray's Elegy and the Problem of History (Carbondale: Southern Illinois University Press, 1991).
West, Anna, *Thomas Hardy and Animals* (Cambridge: Cambridge University Press, 2017).
White, Adam, 'John Clare: "The Man of Taste"', *John Clare Society Journal*, no. 28 (2009): 38–55.
  John Clare's Romanticism (London: Palgrave, 2017).
White, Gilbert, *A Natural History of Selborne*, ed. by Anne Secord (Oxford: Oxford University Press, 2013).
Whitney, William Dwight, *Oriental and Linguistic Studies: The Veda; The Avesta; The Science of Language* (New York: Scribner, 1873).
Widdowson, Peter, *On Thomas Hardy: Late Essays and Earlier* (Basingstoke: MacMillan, 1998).
Williams, Merryn, *A Preface to Hardy* (Essex: Parson Education, 1993).
Wilson, Keith (ed.), *A Companion to Thomas Hardy* (London: Blackwell, 2009).
Wimsatt, William K., and Monroe C. Beardsley, 'The Intentional Fallacy', *The Sewanee Review*, vol. 54, no. 3 (1946): 468–88.
Wittgenstein, Ludwig, *Philosophical Investigations*, trans. by Gertrude Elizabeth Margaret Anscombe, 2nd ed. (Oxford: Blackwell, 1958).
Wollstonecraft, Mary, *The Works of Mary Wollstonecraft*, ed. by Janet Todd and Marilyn Butler, 7 vols. (London: Pickering and Chatto, 1989).
Woof, Pamela, *Dorothy Wordsworth, Writer* (Grasmere: The Wordsworth Trust, 1988).
Woolf, Virginia, *To the Lighthouse*, ed. by Stella McNichol (London: Penguin, 2000).
Wordsworth, Dorothy, *Dorothy Wordsworth*, ed. by Susan M. Levin (London: Longman, 2009).
  The Grasmere and Alfoxden Journals, ed. by Pamela Woof (Oxford: Oxford University Press, 2002).
Wordsworth, Jonathan, *Ancestral Voices: Fifty Books from the Romantic Period*, new ed. (Poole: Woodstock Books, 1996).
Wordsworth, William, *Descriptive Sketches*, ed. by Eric Birdsall (Ithaca, NY: Cornell University Press, 1984).
  An Evening Walk, ed. by James Averill (Ithaca, NY: Cornell University Press, 1984).
  The Excursion, ed. by Sally Bushell, James Butler and Michael C. Jaye (Ithaca, NY: Cornell University Press, 2007).
  The Fenwick Notes of William Wordsworth, ed. by Jared Curtis (London: Gerald Duckworth, 1993).

Last Poems, 1821–1850, ed. by Jared R. Curtis, Apryl Lea Denny-Ferris and Jillian Heydt-Stevenson (Ithaca, NY: Cornell University Press, 1999).
'Lyrical Ballads', and Other Poems, 1797–1800, ed. by James Butler and Karen Green (Ithaca, NY: Cornell University Press, 1992).
The Miscellaneous Poems of William Wordsworth, 4 vols. (London: Longman et al., 1820).
Poems in Two Volumes, and Other Poems, 1800–1807 (Ithaca, NY: Cornell University Press, 1983).
The Poems of William Wordsworth, new ed. (London: Moxon, 1849).
The Poems of William Wordsworth: Collected Reading Texts from the Cornell Wordsworth, ed. by Jared Curtis, 3 vols. (Penrith: Humanities Ebooks, 2011).
The Prose Works of William Wordsworth, ed. by Warwick J. B. Owen and Jane Worthington Smyser, 3 vols. (Oxford: Oxford University Press, 1974).
Sonnet Series and Itinerary Poems, 1820–1845, ed. by Geoffrey Jackson (Ithaca, NY: Cornell University Press, 2004).
The Sonnets of William Wordsworth, Collected in One Volume, with a Few Additional Ones, Now First Published (London: Moxon, 1838).
The Thirteen-Book Prelude, ed. by Mark L. Reed, 2 vols. (Ithaca, NY: Cornell University Press, 1991).
Wordsworth's Literary Criticism, ed. by W. J. B. Owen (London: Routledge, 1974).
Wordsworth, William, and Dorothy Wordsworth, *The Letters of William and Dorothy Wordsworth: The Early Years*, ed. by Ernest de Sélincourt and Chester L. Shaver, 2nd rev. ed. (Oxford: Oxford University Press, 1967).
Letters of William and Dorothy Wordsworth: The Later Years, ed. by Ernest de Sélincourt and Alan G. Hill, 2nd rev. ed., 4 vols. (Oxford: Clarendon, 1978–88).
Letters of William and Dorothy Wordsworth: The Middle Years, 1787–1805, ed. by Ernest de Sélincourt, Mary Moorman and Alan G. Hill, 2 vols. (Oxford: Oxford University Press, 1969–70).
Wright, John (ed.), *Buffon's Natural History; Of the Globe, and of Man*, 4 vols. (London: Tegg, 1831).
Yearsley, Ann, *Poems on Several Occasions* (London: Cadell, 1785).
Yerkes, Robert, *Almost Human* (New York: Century, 1925).

Index

Aarsleff, Hans, 50
anthropodenial, 10, 30, 176, 181
anthropomorphism, 1, 4, 8–12, 30, 53, 55, 70, 73, 113, 153, 154, 176, 181
Aristotle, 20, 35, 44, 110, 188 n. 41
Arnold, Matthew, 105
   'Poor Matthias', 181–3
Asquith, Mark, 139, 144, 147, 160–1

Bailey, Nathan, 12
Barrell, John, 129, 203 n. 3
Barrington, Daines
   'Experiments and Observations on the Singing of Birds', 2, 20–1, 29–32
   influence on Clare, 110
   influence on Darwin, 32, 35–6
Bate, Jonathan, 116
Bechstein, J. M., 23, 32, 168
Bennett, Andrew, 58, 81
Bewick, Thomas, 110
bird-catchers, 20–7, 31, 114, 166–8, 172
birds
   bullfinch, 19, 23, 49, 115, 146, 151, 168
   chaffinch, 6, 23, 26, 31
   corncrake (or 'land rail'), 5, 106, 107
   cuckoo, 28, 115, 119, 183
   goldfinch, 31, 137, 181
   lapwing (or 'peewit'), 107, 129
   magpie, 113, 114, 131, 133, 177–8
   nighthawk, 107
   nightingale, 1, 3, 6, 16, 18, 20, 23, 25–6, 27–8, 30, 31, 52, 58, 63, 65–6, 69, 93–4, 98–9, 101–6, 107, 108, 109, 112, 113–14, 115–16, 123, 124–6, 133–4, 136, 163
   owl, 27–8, 74–6, 86, 107
   parrot, 14, 34, 35, 45, 46, 49, 55, 95, 139
   raven, 78
   red kite (or 'puddock'), 108, 119
   redbreast, 11, 84–5, 88, 90–2, 129, 130
   skylark (or 'lavrock'), 66–7, 112, 131, 163, 170, 171, 181
   swallow, 69, 72–3, 99
   thrush, 69, 96–7, 99–100, 113–14, 162–6
   turtle dove, 71–2
   whitethroat, 127, 128, 176–7
   wren, 89–90, 95
   yellowhammer, 4, 129, 130
birdsong, science of, 2, 6, 16–17, 18, 20–37, 109–10, *See also* sexual selection
   forgetting motifs, 115, 183
   instinct to learn, 36
   song variations or 'dialects', 21, 31, 36
   sonogram, 6
   subsong (juvenile 'babbling' or 'recording' phase), 2, 3, 30, 36, 54–5, 94, 103–4, 112, 114, 125–6, 136
   subsong (winter singing), 11, 69, 84–5, 88
Buffon, Comte de, 32, 72, 110
Burnett, James. *See* Monboddo, James Burnett Lord
Burns, Robert, 91
   'To a Mouse', 111–12

Chaucer, Geoffrey, 65, 103, 112, 126
Chomsky, Noam, 12, 62, 188 n. 47
Cicero, 12, 75
Clare, John, 18, 101–36
   compositional habits, 3, 115–21, 134–6
   Hardy, contrast with, 132–3, 145, 154, 162
   illness, 108, 116–17
   language and thought, 115, 118, 119–21, 122–5, 134–6
   mimesis, 104–8
   natural history, engagement with, 103, 109–15
   peasant poet, 47, 101, 102, 107, 115–16, 123, 136
   Romanticism, relation to, 101–2, 108, 119, 123, 134
   sonnets, 125–34
Clare, John, works of
   'Birds & St Valentine, The', 114
   'Birds Nesting', 106–7, 115
   'Flitting, The', 108

Clare, John, works of (cont.)
  'Going to the Fair', 107
  'Invite to Eternity, An', 108, 116–17
  'Land Rail, The', 106
  Midsummer Cushion, The, 131–2
  'Nightingales Nest, The', 101–3
  Poems Descriptive, 117
  'Progress of Ryhme, The', 118, 121–5, 131
  Rural Muse, The, 127, 132–3
  'Shadows of Taste', 128, 136
  Shepherd's Calendar, The, 126
  'The fire tail tells the boys when nests are nigh', 129–30
  'The happy white throat on the sweeing bough', 127–8
  'The wild duck startles like a sudden thought', 130–1
  'There is a cruelty in all', 133–4
  'When first we hear the shy come nightingales', 3, 30, 112, 125–6, 136
Cobbett, William, 48–9
Coleridge, Samuel Taylor, 17, 60–9
  language, theories of, 62–4
  metrical complexity, 67–9
  primitivism, responses to, 15, 60, 63
  rustic speech, 62–4, 119
  Wordsworth, Dorothy, contrast with, 69, 71
  Wordsworth, William, literary relationship with, 17–18, 60–1, 62–4, 73–4, 77, 83, 94, 96, 119
Coleridge, Samuel Taylor, works of
  Biographia Literaria, 62–4, 77, 119
  'Eolian Harp, The', 17, 60–1, 67, 69, 123, 167
  'Foster Mother's Tale, The', 15
  'Nightingale, The: A Conversation Poem', 16, 63, 69, 105, 108, 112, 126, 134, 167
  'Rime of the Ancyent Marinere, The', 61, 65–9, 164, 165
Cowper, William
  'On a Goldfinch Starved to Death in its Cage', 181
  Task, The, 84–8, 89, 90
Culler, Jonathan, 128
Cuvier, Georges, 9

Darwin, Charles. *See also* sexual selection
  anthropomorphism, accusations of, 9, 10–11, 53
  birdsong, science of, 3, 21, 32–7
  Hardy, influence on, 18–19, 138–41, 147, 159, 175
  language, science of, 34–7, 50–4, 140–1
  mental powers of animals, 19, 32–4, 54
  Müller, Max, conflict with, 9, 10, 19, 32, 35, 50, 53–4, 139, 140–1

Darwin, Charles, works of
  Descent of Man, 2, 11, 12, 17, 19, 20–1, 32–7, 51–2, 53–4, 140–1
  Expression of the Emotions in Man and Animals, 50, 54, 157
  Origin of Species, 9, 12, 18, 27, 53, 159
Darwin, Erasmus, 32, 71
Dickens, Charles, 44, 148
Dickinson, Emily, 106, 174
Dugdale, Florence Emily, 138, 175–6

Flourens, Marie-Jean Pierre, 9
Frith, Clifford B., 11

Gilpin, William, 76
Goldsmith, Oliver, 23, 110, 136
Gorji, Mina, 58, 101, 115–16, 135
Gower, John, 65–6
Gray, Thomas, 79, 136

Hardy, Florence Emily. *See* Dugdale, Florence Emily
Hardy, Thomas, 18–19, 137–79, 180
  censorship, 149–50
  Clare, contrast with, 132–3, 145, 154, 162
  Darwinian theory, responses to, 18–19, 138–41, 147, 159, 175
  humanitarianism, 26–7, 38, 137, 142–3, 168–72, 179, 180
  metrical complexity, 161, 165–6
  music, 139, 144, 147, 160–1
  philology, engagement with, 18–19, 42, 51, 137–41, 149
  poetry, return to, 19, 138, 161–2
  Romanticism, response to, 162–8
  rustic speech, 138, 143–6, 153–4, 159–60, 175
Hardy, Thomas, works of
  'August Midnight, An', 164
  'Bird-Catcher's Boy, The', 166–8
  'Blinded Bird, The', 138, 168–73, 180
  Book of Baby Birds, The, 138, 175–9
  'Caged Goldfinch, The', 137
  'Candour in English Fiction', 149–50
  'Christmas 1924', 179
  'Darkling Thrush, The', 138, 162–6, 178
  Far From the Madding Crowd, 107
  Hand of Ethelberta, The, 147, 150
  Poems of the Past and Present, 132–3
  'Profitable Reading of a Fiction, The', 143–5, 158, 159–60
  'Puzzled Game-Birds, The', 138, 173–4, 180
  Return of the Native, The, 139
  'Selfsame Song, The', 162, 166
  'Shelley's Skylark', 162, 166
  'Spring Call, The', 138, 174–5, 177

Tess of the D'Urbervilles, 19, 51, 137–8, 139, 141, 144–61, 163, 166, 170, 174, 175, 177
Wessex Poems, 132
Harley, Alexis, 9
Haughton, Hugh, 101, 113
Hazlitt, William, 67, 68, 92
Heaney, Seamus, 130, 135–6
Herder, Johann Gottfried, 13, 38, 50
   'Essay on the Origin of Language', 45–7
   Coleridge, comparison with, 63
   poetry, theory of, 40
   Rousseau, criticism of, 39, 42
   Wordsworth, William, comparison with, 76, 92
Hessey, James, 25, 102, 103, 109, 126
Holmes, John, 9
Hudson, W. H.
   Birds in London, 21, 26
Hughes, John, 139
Hughes, Ted, 131
Humboldt, Alexander von, 37

interdisciplinarity, 3–8, 12

Jarvis, Simon, 83
Jefferies, Richard
   Nature Near London, 26
   Round About a Great Estate, 4
Johnson, Samuel, 42, 75, 103

Karlin, Daniel, 1, 6, 8, 105, 125, 169–70
Keats, John, 101
   'Ode to a Nightingale', 102, 104, 112, 163
Kircher, Athanasius, 4
Kneale, J. Douglas, 75–6

Lafford, Erin, 119, 130
language, science of, 12–15, 17, 32, 38–59
   animal origins, 13, 15, 37, 38, 39, 43–4, 46–7, 54–6, 62, 76, 175
   language and thought, 17, 44–9, 52–9, *See also under* individual authors' names
   New Philology, 17, 50, 52–4, 137, 138, 140–1
   ongoing debates, 12, 14, 55–7
   rustic and vulgar speech, 15, 17, 44, 47, 48, 49, 118, *See also under* individual authors' names
   'savage' languages, 11, 15, 17, 37, 38, 39, 43, 44, 46–7, 48, 51, 52, 63, 138
   Universal Grammar, 44, 47, 118
de Laura, David J., 159
Leader, Zachary, 58
Levine, George, 163
Lewes, George Henry, 9–10
Lloyd, Bertram
   Great Kinship, The, 180–4

Locke, John, 54–5, 84
Lodge, Sara, 128
Lucretius, 38, 43, 61, 74, 75

Mayhew, Henry, 21, 23–6
McKusick, James C., 117
Messiaen, Olivier, 5
Midgely, Mary, 8
Milton, John, 134, 169
   'L'Allegro', 115–16
   Paradise Lost, 75, 103, 163
   sonnets, 94, 98–9, 128, 129
Monboddo, James Burnett Lord, 38, 42–4, 47–8, 50
Morgan, Conwy Lloyd, 10
Mozart, Wolfgang Amadeus, 4–5, 21
Müller, Max
   Darwin, Charles, conflict with, 9, 10, 19, 32, 35, 50, 53–4, 139, 140–1
   'Lectures on Mr Darwin's Philosophy of Language', 53, 140
   Lectures on the Science of Language, 10, 12, 32, 52–3, 137
Mundy, Rachel, 14
Murray, Lindley, 13–14, 109
music. *See also under* individual authors' names
   animal musicality, 14
   memory, 84, 87–8, 90, 98
   musical proto-language, 38, 39–40, 41–2, 43–4, 47, 50–1, 52
   musical renderings of birdsong, 4–5
   sexuality, 41–2, *See also* sexual selection
Mynott, Jeremy, 8

Nagel, Thomas, 9
Newlyn, Lucy, 72, 88, 98, 99

Oliphant, Margaret, 145–6

Paine, Thomas, 48, 87
Pater, Walter, 82
Pepperberg, Irene, 14, 35, 56
Perry, Seamus, 65
Phelan, Joseph, 100
philology. *See* language, science of
Pinker, Stephen, 56–7, 59
Pliny, the Elder, 1–2, 11, 20, 110
Potkay, Adam, 85

Radick, Gregory, 9, 54
Rawnsley, H. D., 58
Richardson, Samuel
   Clarissa, 147–8, 149
Ritvo, Harriet, 8
Robinson, Henry Crabb, 98

Roe, Nicholas, 89
Rothenberg, David, 3, 6
Rousseau, Jean-Jacques, 39–42, 47
  responses to, 42–3, 45, 46, 50, 51, 87, 88, 91
Rousseau, Jean-Jacques, works of
  Confessions, 41–2
  Discourse on Inequality, 39, 42, 45
  Essay on the Origin of Languages, 39–41
  Narcisse, 41
Rowe, Richard
  Life in London Streets, 26
Rowland, Ann Wierda, 13, 45–6, 76

sexual selection, 37, 42, 52, 147, 175
Shakespeare, William, 77, 90, 99, 115–16, 117, 133
Shelley, Percy Bysshe
  Defence of Poetry, 179
  'To a Skylark', 112, 131, 163, 181
Smith, Adam, 42
Smith, Charlotte, 93–4, 98, 126
Smith, Olivia, 43, 47, 48
Spencer, Herbert, 38, 50–1, 139
Stark, Robert, 65, 68
Starobinski, Jean, 41–2
Stephen, Leslie, 140–1

Taylor, Dennis, 83, 138, 145
Taylor, John, 101, 122
  Introduction to *Poems Descriptive*, 117–18
Thoreau, Henry David, 131
Thorpe, William, 6

de Waal, Frans
  Are We Smart Enough to Know How Smart Animals Are?, 14, 55–6
  'Anthropomorphism and Anthropodenial', 10, 181
Watson, William, 145, 159
Weiner, Stephanie Kuduk, 6–7, 101, 105–6, 118, 125, 127
West, Anna, 139–40, 161
White, Gilbert, 2, 21, 27–9, 32, 34, 70, 110
Whitney, William Dwight, 54
Widdowson, Peter, 145
Williams, Merryn, 163
Wittgenstein, Ludwig, 10
women
  as hunted birds, 155–6
  music, responsiveness to, 41–2
  speech and intellectual capacity, 17, 39, 52, 138, 170–1
  trained to sing, 147–8
Woof, Pamela, 70, 71
Woolf, Virginia
  To the Lighthouse, 183–4
Wordsworth, Dorothy, 69–73
  Clare, comparison with, 113
  Coleridge, contrast with, 69, 71
  illness, 62, 97–8
  journals, 60–1, 69–73, 84, 88
  poetry, 80–1
  Wordsworth, William, literary relationship with, 73, 80–1, 84, 88, 95, 96–9
Wordsworth, Jonathan, 77
Wordsworth, William, 73–100
  Coleridge, literary relationship with, 17–18, 60–1, 62–4, 73–4, 77, 83, 94, 96, 119
  compositional habits, 57–9, 94–5, 100
  language and thought, 17–18, 39, 59, 61–2, 76–7, 79–80, 81–2, 95–6
  metrical complexity, 78–9, 83–4, 89–90, 92–3
  music, 61–2, 84, 85–8, 90–3, 98
  rustic speech, 62, 64, 79–80, 119
  sonnets, 93–100
  Wordsworth, Dorothy, literary relationship with, 73, 80–1, 84, 88, 95, 96–9
Wordsworth, William, works of
  'Contrast, The', 95
  'Essay on Morals', 86
  Evening Walk, An, 73, 91, 99
  Excursion, The, 92
  'Hark! 'tis the Thrush, undaunted, undeprest', 96–7, 99
  Memorials of a Tour on the Continent, 92
  'Oh what a Wreck! how changed in mien and speech!', 93, 97–8
  'Old Man Travelling', 167
  'On Approaching the Staub-Bach, Laterbrunne', 92
  Poems in Two Volumes, 69
  Poems, 1815 Preface to, 77, 78–9
  Prelude, The, 26, 64, 74–84, 86, 87, 89–92, 95–6, 106, 164, 166
  Recluse, The, 94
  Sonnets of William Wordsworth, 97
  'Sparrow's Nest, The', 69
  'Tintern Abbey', 79, 96
  ''Tis He whose yester-evening's high disdain', 99–100

Yearsley, Ann, 116

CAMBRIDGE STUDIES IN NINETEENTH-CENTURY
LITERATURE AND CULTURE

GENERAL EDITORS
Kate Flint, *University of Southern California*
Clare Pettitt, *King's College London*

Titles published

1. *The Sickroom in Victorian Fiction: The Art of Being Ill*
   MIRIAM BAILIN, *Washington University*
2. *Muscular Christianity: Embodying the Victorian Age*
   edited by DONALD E. HALL, *California State University, Northridge*
3. *Victorian Masculinities: Manhood and Masculine Poetics in Early Victorian Literature and Art*
   HERBERT SUSSMAN, *Northeastern University, Boston*
4. *Byron and the Victorians*
   ANDREW ELFENBEIN, *University of Minnesota*
5. *Literature in the Marketplace: Nineteenth-Century British Publishing and the Circulation of Books*
   edited by JOHN O. JORDAN, *University of California, Santa Cruz* and ROBERT L. PATTEN, *Rice University, Houston*
6. *Victorian Photography, Painting and Poetry*
   LINDSAY SMITH, *University of Sussex*
7. *Charlotte Brontë and Victorian Psychology*
   SALLY SHUTTLEWORTH, *University of Sheffield*
8. *The Gothic Body: Sexuality, Materialism and Degeneration at the* Fin de Siècle KELLY HURLEY, *University of Colorado at Boulder*
9. *Rereading Walter Pater*
   WILLIAM F. SHUTER, *Eastern Michigan University*
10. *Remaking Queen Victoria*
    edited by MARGARET HOMANS, *Yale University* and ADRIENNE MUNICH, *State University of New York, Stony Brook*
11. *Disease, Desire, and the Body in Victorian Women's Popular Novels*
    PAMELA K. GILBERT, *University of Florida*
12. *Realism, Representation, and the Arts in Nineteenth-Century Literature*
    ALISON BYERLY, *Middlebury College, Vermont*
13. *Literary Culture and the Pacific*
    VANESSA SMITH, *University of Sydney*
14. *Professional Domesticity in the Victorian Novel*
    WOMEN, WORK AND HOME MONICA F. COHEN
15. *Victorian Renovations of the Novel: Narrative Annexes and the Boundaries of Representation*
    SUZANNE KEEN, *Washington and Lee University, Virginia*

16. *Actresses on the Victorian Stage: Feminine Performance and the Galatea Myth*
    GAIL MARSHALL, *University of Leeds*
17. *Death and the Mother from Dickens to Freud: Victorian Fiction and the Anxiety of Origin*
    CAROLYN DEVER, *Vanderbilt University, Tennessee*
18. *Ancestry and Narrative in Nineteenth-Century British Literature: Blood Relations from Edgeworth to Hardy*
    SOPHIE GILMARTIN, *Royal Holloway, University of London*
19. *Dickens, Novel Reading, and the Victorian Popular Theatre*
    DEBORAH VLOCK
20. *After Dickens: Reading, Adaptation and Performance*
    JOHN GLAVIN, *Georgetown University, Washington DC*
21. *Victorian Women Writers and the Woman Question*
    edited by NICOLA DIANE THOMPSON, *Kingston University, London*
22. *Rhythm and Will in Victorian Poetry*
    MATTHEW CAMPBELL, *University of Sheffield*
23. *Gender, Race, and the Writing of Empire: Public Discourse and the Boer War*
    PAULA M. KREBS, *Wheaton College, Massachusetts*
24. *Ruskin's God*
    MICHAEL WHEELER, *University of Southampton*
25. *Dickens and the Daughter of the House*
    HILARY M. SCHOR, *University of Southern California*
26. *Detective Fiction and the Rise of Forensic Science*
    RONALD R. THOMAS, *Trinity College, Hartford, Connecticut*
27. *Testimony and Advocacy in Victorian Law, Literature, and Theology*
    JAN-MELISSA SCHRAMM, *Trinity Hall, Cambridge*
28. *Victorian Writing about Risk: Imagining a Safe England in a Dangerous World*
    ELAINE FREEDGOOD, *University of Pennsylvania*
29. *Physiognomy and the Meaning of Expression in Nineteenth-Century Culture*
    LUCY HARTLEY, *University of Southampton*
30. *The Victorian Parlour: A Cultural Study*
    THAD LOGAN, *Rice University, Houston*
31. *Aestheticism and Sexual Parody 1840–1940*
    DENNIS DENISOFF, *Ryerson University, Toronto*
32. *Literature, Technology and Magical Thinking, 1880–1920*
    PAMELA THURSCHWELL, *University College London*
33. *Fairies in Nineteenth-Century Art and Literature*
    NICOLA BOWN, *Birkbeck, University of London*
34. *George Eliot and the British Empire*
    NANCY HENRY *The State University of New York, Binghamton*
35. *Women's Poetry and Religion in Victorian England: Jewish Identity and Christian Culture*
    CYNTHIA SCHEINBERG, *Mills College, California*
36. *Victorian Literature and the Anorexic Body*
    ANNA KRUGOVOY SILVER, *Mercer University, Georgia*

37. *Eavesdropping in the Novel from Austen to Proust*
    ANN GAYLIN, *Yale University*
38. *Missionary Writing and Empire, 1800–1860*
    ANNA JOHNSTON, *University of Tasmania*
39. *London and the Culture of Homosexuality, 1885–1914*
    MATT COOK, *Keele University*
40. *Fiction, Famine, and the Rise of Economics in Victorian Britain and Ireland*
    GORDON BIGELOW, *Rhodes College, Tennessee*
41. *Gender and the Victorian Periodical*
    HILARY FRASER, *Birkbeck, University of London* JUDITH JOHNSTON and STEPHANIE GREEN, *University of Western Australia*
42. *The Victorian Supernatural*
    edited by NICOLA BOWN, *Birkbeck College, London* CAROLYN BURDETT, *London Metropolitan University* and PAMELA THURSCHWELL, *University College London*
43. *The Indian Mutiny and the British Imagination*
    GAUTAM CHAKRAVARTY, *University of Delhi*
44. *The Revolution in Popular Literature: Print, Politics and the People*
    IAN HAYWOOD, *Roehampton University of Surrey*
45. *Science in the Nineteenth-Century Periodical: Reading the Magazine of Nature*
    GEOFFREY CANTOR, *University of Leeds* GOWAN DAWSON, *University of Leicester* GRAEME GOODAY, *University of Leeds* RICHARD NOAKES, *University of Cambridge* SALLY SHUTTLEWORTH, *University of Sheffield* and JONATHAN R. TOPHAM, *University of Leeds*
46. *Literature and Medicine in Nineteenth-Century Britain from Mary Shelley to George Eliot*
    JANIS MCLARREN CALDWELL, *Wake Forest University*
47. *The Child Writer from Austen to Woolf*
    edited by CHRISTINE ALEXANDER, *University of New South Wales* and JULIET MCMASTER, *University of Alberta*
48. *From Dickens to Dracula: Gothic, Economics, and Victorian Fiction*
    GAIL TURLEY HOUSTON, *University of New Mexico*
49. *Voice and the Victorian Storyteller*
    IVAN KREILKAMP, *University of Indiana*
50. *Charles Darwin and Victorian Visual Culture*
    JONATHAN SMITH, *University of Michigan-Dearborn*
51. *Catholicism, Sexual Deviance, and Victorian Gothic Culture*
    PATRICK R. O'MALLEY, *Georgetown University*
52. *Epic and Empire in Nineteenth-Century Britain*
    SIMON DENTITH, *University of Gloucestershire*
53. *Victorian Honeymoons: Journeys to the Conjugal*
    HELENA MICHIE, *Rice University*
54. *The Jewess in Nineteenth-Century British Literary Culture*
    NADIA VALMAN, *University of Southampton*

55. *Ireland, India and Nationalism in Nineteenth-Century Literature*
    JULIA WRIGHT, *Dalhousie University*
56. *Dickens and the Popular Radical Imagination*
    SALLY LEDGER, *Birkbeck, University of London*
57. *Darwin, Literature and Victorian Respectability*
    GOWAN DAWSON, *University of Leicester*
58. *'Michael Field': Poetry, Aestheticism and the Fin de Siècle*
    MARION THAIN, *University of Birmingham*
59. *Colonies, Cults and Evolution: Literature, Science and Culture in Nineteenth-Century Writing*
    DAVID AMIGONI, *Keele University*
60. *Realism, Photography and Nineteenth-Century Fiction*
    DANIEL A. NOVAK, *Lousiana State University*
61. *Caribbean Culture and British Fiction in the Atlantic World, 1780–1870*
    TIM WATSON, *University of Miami*
62. *The Poetry of Chartism: Aesthetics, Politics, History*
    MICHAEL SANDERS, *University of Manchester*
63. *Literature and Dance in Nineteenth-Century Britain: Jane Austen to the New Woman*
    CHERYL WILSON, *Indiana University*
64. *Shakespeare and Victorian Women*
    GAIL MARSHALL, *Oxford Brookes University*
65. *The Tragi-Comedy of Victorian Fatherhood*
    VALERIE SANDERS, *University of Hull*
66. *Darwin and the Memory of the Human: Evolution, Savages, and South America*
    CANNON SCHMITT, *University of Toronto*
67. *From Sketch to Novel: The Development of Victorian Fiction*
    AMANPAL GARCHA, *Ohio State University*
68. *The Crimean War and the British Imagination*
    STEFANIE MARKOVITS, *Yale University*
69. *Shock, Memory and the Unconscious in Victorian Fiction*
    JILL L. MATUS, *University of Toronto*
70. *Sensation and Modernity in the 1860s*
    NICHOLAS DALY, *University College Dublin*
71. *Ghost-Seers, Detectives, and Spiritualists: Theories of Vision in Victorian Literature and Science*
    SRDJAN SMAJIĆ, *Furman University*
72. *Satire in an Age of Realism*
    AARON MATZ, *Scripps College, California*
73. *Thinking About Other People in Nineteenth-Century British Writing*
    ADELA PINCH, *University of Michigan*
74. *Tuberculosis and the Victorian Literary Imagination*
    KATHERINE BYRNE, *University of Ulster, Coleraine*

75. *Urban Realism and the Cosmopolitan Imagination in the Nineteenth Century: Visible City, Invisible World*
    TANYA AGATHOCLEOUS, *Hunter College, City University of New York*
76. *Women, Literature, and the Domesticated Landscape: England's Disciples of Flora, 1780–1870*
    JUDITH W. PAGE, *University of Florida* ELISE L. SMITH, *Millsaps College, Mississippi*
77. *Time and the Moment in Victorian Literature and Society*
    SUE ZEMKA, *University of Colorado*
78. *Popular Fiction and Brain Science in the Late Nineteenth Century*
    ANNE STILES, *Washington State University*
79. *Picturing Reform in Victorian Britain*
    JANICE CARLISLE, *Yale University*
80. *Atonement and Self-Sacrifice in Nineteenth-Century Narrative*
    JAN-MELISSA SCHRAMM, *University of Cambridge*
81. *The Silver Fork Novel: Fashionable Fiction in the Age of Reform*
    EDWARD COPELAND, *Pomona College, California*
82. *Oscar Wilde and Ancient Greece*
    IAIN ROSS, *Colchester Royal Grammar School*
83. *The Poetry of Victorian Scientists: Style, Science and Nonsense*
    DANIEL BROWN, *University of Southampton*
84. *Moral Authority, Men of Science, and the Victorian Novel*
    ANNE DEWITT, *Princeton Writing Program*
85. *China and the Victorian Imagination: Empires Entwined*
    ROSS G. FORMAN, *University of Warwick*
86. *Dickens's Style*
    edited by DANIEL TYLER, *University of Oxford*
87. *The Formation of the Victorian Literary Profession*
    RICHARD SALMON, *University of Leeds*
88. *Before George Eliot: Marian Evans and the Periodical Press*
    FIONNUALA DILLANE, *University College Dublin*
89. *The Victorian Novel and the Space of Art: Fictional Form on Display*
    DEHN GILMORE, *California Institute of Technology*
90. *George Eliot and Money: Economics, Ethics and Literature*
    DERMOT COLEMAN, *Independent Scholar*
91. *Masculinity and the New Imperialism: Rewriting Manhood in British Popular Literature, 1870–1914*
    BRADLEY DEANE, *University of Minnesota*
92. *Evolution and Victorian Culture*
    edited by BERNARD LIGHTMAN, *York University, Toronto* and BENNETT ZON, *University of Durham*
93. *Victorian Literature, Energy, and the Ecological Imagination*
    ALLEN MACDUFFIE, *University of Texas, Austin*
94. *Popular Literature, Authorship and the Occult in Late Victorian Britain*
    ANDREW MCCANN, *Dartmouth College, New Hampshire*

95. *Women Writing Art History in the Nineteenth Century: Looking Like a Woman*
    HILARY FRASER *Birkbeck, University of London*
96. *Relics of Death in Victorian Literature and Culture*
    DEBORAH LUTZ, *Long Island University, C. W. Post Campus*
97. *The Demographic Imagination and the Nineteenth-Century City: Paris, London, New York*
    NICHOLAS DALY, *University College Dublin*
98. *Dickens and the Business of Death*
    CLAIRE WOOD, *University of York*
99. *Translation as Transformation in Victorian Poetry*
    ANNMARIE DRURY, *Queens College, City University of New York*
100. *The Bigamy Plot: Sensation and Convention in the Victorian Novel*
     MAIA MCALEAVEY, *Boston College, Massachusetts*
101. *English Fiction and the Evolution of Language, 1850–1914*
     WILL ABBERLEY, *University of Oxford*
102. *The Racial Hand in the Victorian Imagination*
     AVIVA BRIEFEL, *Bowdoin College, Maine*
103. *Evolution and Imagination in Victorian Children's Literature*
     JESSICA STRALEY, *University of Utah*
104. *Writing Arctic Disaster: Authorship and Exploration*
     ADRIANA CRACIUN, *University of California, Riverside*
105. *Science, Fiction, and the Fin-de-Siècle Periodical Press* WILL TATTERSDILL, *University of Birmingham*
106. *Democratising Beauty in Nineteenth-Century Britain: Art and the Politics of Public Life*
     LUCY HARTLEY, *University of Michigan*
107. *Everyday Words and the Character of Prose in Nineteenth-Century Britain*
     JONATHAN FARINA, *Seton Hall University, New Jersey*
108. *Gerard Manley Hopkins and the Poetry of Religious Experience*
     MARTIN DUBOIS, *Newcastle University*
109. *Blindness and Writing: From Wordsworth to Gissing*
     HEATHER TILLEY, *Birkbeck College, University of London*
110. *An Underground History of Early Victorian Fiction: Chartism, Radical Print Culture, and the Social Problem Novel*
     GREGORY VARGO, *New York University*
111. *Automatism and Creative Acts in the Age of New Psychology*
     LINDA M. AUSTIN, *Oklahoma State University*
112. *Idleness and Aesthetic Consciousness, 1815–1900*
     RICHARD ADELMAN, *University of Sussex*
113. *Poetry, Media, and the Material Body: Autopoetics in Nineteenth-Century Britain*
     ASHLEY MILLER, *Albion College, Michigan*
114. *Malaria and Victorian Fictions of Empire*
     JESSICA HOWELL, *Texas A&M University*

115. *The Brontës and the Idea of the Human: Science, Ethics, and the Victorian Imagination*
    edited by ALEXANDRA LEWIS, *University of Aberdeen*
116. *The Political Lives of Victorian Animals: Liberal Creatures in Literature and Culture*
    ANNA FEUERSTEIN, *University of Hawai'i-Manoa*
117. *The Divine in the Commonplace: Recent Natural Histories and the Novel in Britain*
    AMY KING, *St John's University, New York*
118. *Plagiarizing the Victorian Novel: Imitation, Parody, Aftertext*
    ADAM ABRAHAM, *Virginia Commonwealth University*
119. *Literature, Print Culture, and Media Technologies, 1880–1900: Many Inventions*
    RICHARD MENKE, *University of Georgia*
120. *Aging, Duration, and the English Novel: Growing Old from Dickens to Woolf*
    JACOB JEWUSIAK, *Newcastle University*
121. *Autobiography, Sensation, and the Commodification of Identity in Victorian Narrative: Life upon the Exchange*
    SEAN GRASS, *Rochester Institute of Technology*
122. *Settler Colonialism in Victorian Literature: Economics and Political Identity in the Networks of Empire*
    PHILLIP STEER, *Massey University, Auckland*
123. *Mimicry and Display in Victorian Literary Culture: Nature, Science and the Nineteenth-Century Imagination*
    WILL ABBERLEY, *University of Sussex*
124. *Victorian Women and Wayward Reading: Crises of Identification*
    MARISA PALACIOS KNOX, *University of Texas Rio Grande Valley*
125. *The Victorian Cult of Shakespeare: Bardology in the Nineteenth Century*
    CHARLES LAPORTE, *University of Washington*
126. *Children's Literature and the Rise of 'Mind Cure': Positive Thinking and Pseudo-Science at the Fin de Siècle*
    ANNE STILES, *Saint Louis University, Missouri*
127. *Virtual Play and the Victorian Novel: The Ethics and Aesthetics of Fictional Experience*
    TIMOTHY GAO, *Nanyang Technological University*
128. *Colonial Law in India and the Victorian Imagination*
    LEILA NETI, *Occidental College, Los Angeles*
129. *Convalescence in the Nineteenth-Century Novel: The Afterlife of Victorian Illness*
    HOSANNA KRIENKE, *University of Wyoming*
130. *Stylistic Virtue and Victorian Fiction: Form, Ethics and the Novel*
    MATTHEW SUSSMAN, *The University of Sydney*
131. *Scottish Women's Writing in the Long Nineteenth Century: The Romance of Everyday Life*
    JULIET SHIELDS, *University of Washington*
132. *Reimagining Dinosaurs in Late Victorian and Edwardian Literature: How the 'Terrible Lizard' Became a Transatlantic Cultural Icon*
    RICHARD FALLON, *The University of Birmingham*

133. *Decadent Ecology in British Literature and Art, 1860–1910: Decay, Desire, and the Pagan Revival*
    DENNIS DENISOFF, *University of Tulsa*
134. *Vagrancy in the Victorian Age: Representing the Wandering Poor in Nineteenth-Century Literature and Culture*
    ALISTAIR ROBINSON, *New College of the Humanities*
135. *Collaborative Writing in the Long Nineteenth Century: Sympathetic Partnerships and Artistic Creation*
    HEATHER BOZANT WITCHER, *Auburn University, Montgomery*
136. *Visual Culture and Arctic Voyages: Personal and Public Art and Literature of the Franklin Search Expeditions*
    EAVAN O'DOCHARTAIGH, *Umeå Universitet, Sweden*
137. *Music and the Queer Body in English Literature at the Fin de Siècle*
    FRASER RIDDELL, *University of Durham*
138. *Victorian Women Writers and the Other Germany: Cross-Cultural Freedoms and Female Opportunity*
    LINDA K. HUGHES, *Texas Christian University*
139. *Conversing in Verse: Conversation in Nineteenth-Century English Poetry*
    ELIZABETH HELSINGER, *University of Chicago*
140. *Birdsong, Speech and Poetry: The Art of Composition in the Long Nineteenth Century*
    FRANCESCA MACKENNEY, *University of Leeds*

For EU product safety concerns, contact us at Calle de José Abascal, 56–1°,
28003 Madrid, Spain or eugpsr@cambridge.org.

www.ingramcontent.com/pod-product-compliance
Lightning Source LLC
LaVergne TN
LVHW020343260326
834688LV00045B/1509